The Sensory Processing Handbook for Parents

Practical Strategies for
Supporting Children with Autism,
ADHD, and Sensory Processing Disorder
at Home, School, and Beyond

Richard Bass

Table of Contents

Introduction

Beneath every behavior is a feeling. And beneath every feeling is a need.
And when we meet that need rather than focus on the behavior, we begin to
deal with the cause and not the symptom.
–Ashleigh Warner

A Dad's Search for Answers

I was raised to believe that children who don't wear the clothes laid out
for them, refuse to eat certain foods on their plate, or cling to you in
public spaces are acting out. As a result, when my second-born son,
Jeremy, displayed these behaviors, my initial thoughts were to change
how I disciplined him.

Fortunately, around the time I noticed these patterns, I stumbled upon a daytime show for parents and homemakers. On one particular episode, the topic was sensory processing issues, and the host spoke at length with a child psychologist who explained what they were and how to recognize them.

As I listened to the psychologist, I kept whispering to myself: This sounds like Jeremy. The mixture of relief for finally having a name to call his behavior and guilt for how I handled his triggers overwhelmed me. I spent the next few weeks researching the condition, then consulted my GP, who referred me to a nearby children's hospital where we later conducted assessments and got a diagnosis. It turned out that Jeremy was on the autism spectrum, and sensory difficulties and poor social skills were among the recurring symptoms he struggled with.

– Patrick

Introduction to Sensory Processing

Our five basic senses were designed to help us process information around us so we could recognize and respond to danger and pleasure. For this to happen, our brains need to work together with our bodies to exchange information and interpret stimuli correctly. For example, it's instinctual for our heart rates to accelerate when we hear loud bangs from nearby. The intensity of the sound might cause our brains to believe that we are unsafe and need to get ourselves out of there quickly.

Children with sensory processing challenges have the same senses as we do; however, their brain-to-body connection may not work in the same way. Sensory information tends to be misinterpreted and therefore elicits inappropriate responses. Some children may feel hyperaroused by stimuli, which means everything around them is experienced more intensely, creating extreme bouts of energy or anxiety.

Other children may be hypoaroused by stimuli, meaning they are often underwhelmed and unfeeling toward what they see, hear, taste, touch, and smell. They may come across as bored, aloof, or emotionally numb when presented with activities that cause their peers to respond with excitement and curiosity.

Essentially, there isn't a *right* or *wrong* way of experiencing the world, so children with sensory processing challenges do not need to be "fixed." In most cases, however, understanding these difficulties and how they impact children's development can help parents identify other co-occurring neurological or behavioral conditions like attention-deficit hyperactivity disorder (ADHD) or autism spectrum disorder (ASD).

Moreover, learning about the unique ways that children, and yours in particular, interpret everyday routines and responsibilities can transform your parenting approach, encouraging more empathy than expectations. What might look to others as bad behavior could be disguising a real problem your child is facing. By addressing the underlying sensory need, you can create a safe and nurturing space for your child to grow and develop confidence.

Why This Book Is Different

The internet isn't short of sensory processing disorder books; however, few explore the topic from the perspective of the child, helping parents build a stronger and more compassionate bond with their children. You've heard what doctors and therapists have had to say about your child's behaviors, but how often have you heard it from them?

Every chapter of this book seeks to help you better understand your child's sensory needs to empower your parenting. You'll learn how they see the world, what excites them, and what makes them afraid. Additionally, you will be taught effective strategies for addressing triggers, meltdowns, and other forms of resistance in a proactive and positive way. Forget about power struggles to get your child to follow your lead; this book teaches you how to influence your little one without taking away their sense of control.

What to Expect

Continuing with the benefits of this book, parents will learn how to enforce sensory-friendly habits inside and outside of the home. With our DIY assessment tool, you can identify your child's sensory profile and draw up personalized home routines for mealtimes, playtime, and getting ready for school.

Furthermore, with your child's sensory profile on hand, you can keep track of their day-to-day behaviors and identify the early warning signs of co-occurring conditions like ADHD and ASD. This means that you can receive quality medical care and school support for your child, which can significantly reduce and manage their sensory challenges.

What's great about this book is its focus on changing the environment to accommodate your child instead of changing your child to fit into an overstimulating environment. Get ready to learn how to adapt each room in your home to create a sensory sanctuary, how to advocate for your child's education needs at school, and how to plan social events and vacations to ensure that your whole family enjoys the outings.

After reading this book, you'll have a toolbox of sensory skills, activities, and interventions to support your child's emotional regulation, create safe sensory zones at home, and support their long-term development.

The truth is, you don't need to walk on eggshells around your sensitive child to keep them happy. You simply need to make an effort to understand their world. This book is designed to teach you how to do this and ultimately strengthen your parent-child bond!

Note to Readers:

Throughout this book, you'll find that each chapter includes two main sections. The first part provides essential, practical information that every parent needs to support a child with sensory processing challenges. Following this foundation, you'll find "Advanced Concepts" sections that dive deeper into the science, research, and specialized approaches for those seeking more comprehensive understanding.

These advanced sections are designed to be explored when you're ready for more depth, after you've become comfortable with the foundational concepts. Feel free to return to them as your journey with your child evolves and your questions become more specific.

Whether you're just beginning to understand sensory processing or looking to expand your knowledge, this book is designed to grow with you and support your family's unique needs.

Chapter 1:

Defining Sensory Processing

There is no such thing as a "bad kid"—just angry, hurt, tired, scared, confused, impulsive ones expressing their feelings and needs the only way they know how. We owe it to every single one of them to always remember that.

—Jessica Stephens

What Does the World Feel Like to You?

The world feels like a giant puzzle that no one gave me the pieces for. It's like I was dropped into a big, loud, colorful place where everyone else just knows what to do, but I'm still trying to figure out the rules. The lights in stores are so bright that they make my eyes feel tired, but no one else seems to mind. People's voices mix together like a storm, and even though I know they're talking to me, sometimes I can't grab the words fast enough before they're gone.

And then there are the days when everything feels too much—when my shirt is too itchy, my socks have that one annoying bump, and even the air around me seems to be pushing on my skin. I don't want to be difficult, I just want to feel safe in my own body. But I don't always know how to tell people that without them getting frustrated with me.

—Daniel, 7 years old

What Is Sensory Processing?

Sensory processing refers to the methods the brain uses to understand and interpret information collected from the sensory organs, such as the eyes, ears, nose, skin, and mouth (Kong & Moreno, 2018). Thereafter, it provides instructions to the body to respond accordingly.

For example, you might step outside and feel a cold breeze brushing against your skin, so you decide to go back inside the house to fetch a jacket. Or maybe you walk into the office and see coworkers near your workstation. Your brain nudges your body to make eye contact and greet or flash a smile instead of proceeding to sit at your desk and ignore them.

Sensory processing challenges occur whenever the brain is overresponsive or under responsive when interpreting stimuli (Kong & Moreno, 2018). Outwardly, this causes irrational, exaggerated, dramatic, or inappropriate behavioral responses. Adults may be capable of displaying self-control and managing uncomfortable sensations. However, children don't have the same kind of patience, emotional intelligence, or self-regulation. In most cases, they react to what they are thinking or feeling and need guidance to manage their triggers.

When your child encounters triggering stimuli, they go through two states: the first is an internal state, and the second is seen externally. Let's explore both of them together.

Fight-or-Flight Mode

Before you notice a sudden change in your child's behavior, they will experience an internal shift. Their brain processes the sensory input as "dangerous" or "uncomfortable," which induces stress, and gives the body two options: fight or flee. The choice your child makes depends on the level of threat and their unique personality. Some children naturally have over-the-top responses to stress and might seek your attention to remove the trigger from their space. Other children might retreat to their "safe place," appear withdrawn, and be quieter than usual. Same stress-evoking stimuli. Two different responses.

Tantrums and Mood Swings

The stress response puts your child in survival mode. For as long as this state is active, they cannot think and function with logic and reasoning. Science backs this by revealing our prefrontal cortex, which is the region of the brain responsible for cognitive and emotional processing, is temporarily disabled whenever we are stressed (Woo et al., 2021).

Thus, when your child is exposed to sensory triggers (things that make them overresponsive or under responsive), you'll likely notice the following behaviors that are a result of a weakened prefrontal cortex (Seladi-Schulman, 2020):

- poor planning or organization skills
- weakened impulse control
- decreased motivation

- inattention and memory problems

- apathy, moodiness, or irritability

- inappropriate social behaviors

- difficulty solving problems or judging situations accurately

- insisting on one way of thinking

- performing the same set of behaviors or following specific rules

As a parent, it's normal to overlook these signs and instead rule them off as disruptive or difficult behavior. This is especially true if you were raised to see behaviors that are out of the norm as a lack of obedience. However, the reality—which is often a struggle for your child to communicate—is they are stressed and having a hard time thinking and behaving rationally.

Sensory difficulties can cause chaos in your home and at school, particularly when they haven't been identified. For instance, your child may be grouchy when woken up to loud noises coming from different areas of the house, or eating crunchy cereal that feels like it's cutting their gums. At school, they might become irritable when exposed to bright LED classroom lights or encounter pungent smells, from a classmate's sandwich to the superglue on their desk.

Children who are underresponsive to sensory stimuli behave differently. Instead of verbalizing or acting out their discomfort, they usually show little to no response to physical touch, verbal instructions, or activities happening in front of them. For example, they may not indicate whether they are hungry or tired, or respond when someone calls their name. Their brains process sensory information slowly, which can impact their response times.

For instance, a typical child would cry immediately after falling and scraping a knee, but a child who is underresponsive to physical pain might get up and continue running without noticing the bloody open cut. Falling over things and general clumsiness are common among these children due to a lack of body awareness and coordination.

The Eight Sensory Systems

What makes identifying sensory processing issues particularly interesting is that not every sensory input will be a problem for your child. We often speak about the five basic senses, but there are eight in total. Out of the eight, you may find that your hyperaroused child is triggered by one or two, and the rest are processed normally.

Below is a breakdown of the eight senses and how your child might have trouble processing them.

Visual System (Sight)

The primary brain area controlling sight is known as the occipital lobe. It receives information from the retina through the thalamus, where different visual inputs, such as shapes, colors, and motions, are processed and interpreted (*Your 8 Senses*, n.d.).

Children who have challenges with visual processing tend to experience(*Understanding SPD: The Visual System*, 2024):

- extreme sensitivity to light (e.g., not being able to fully open their eyes under direct sunlight).

- easily distracted by people or objects in motion (e.g., finds it difficult to focus on completing class assignments when peers stand up or move about).

- squinting or rubbing eyes or completing a task demanding visual focus (e.g., feeling eye strain after watching TV or reading).

- discomfort maintaining eye contact during conversations.

Auditory System (Hearing)

Hearing is regulated in a brain region known as the auditory cortex, which can be found in the superior temporal gyrus (Your 8 Senses, n.d.). Here, different ranges and frequencies of sounds are encoded so that the brain understands what is happening in the external environment (e.g., is the loud bang a signal of celebration or danger?) Other areas of the brain are responsible for interpreting combinations of sounds, such as tone and language.

A few things happen when your child experiences difficulties with auditory processing, like:

- trouble understanding speech in noisy environments (e.g., asking the speaker to repeat what they said too frequently).

- delayed literacy skills (e.g., finds it difficult to read or spell certain words).

- sensitive to high volumes and uncommon sounds (e.g., puts hands over ears in public spaces where multiple sounds submerge).

- trouble following and remembering instructions or directions (e.g., frequently misses steps when completing homework assignments).

Olfactory System (Smell)

The olfactory bulb is the part of the brain that processes information coming through the nose, providing (Your 8 Senses, n.d.). It has a filtering function that works to complete four tasks; namely, differentiating scents, accurately detecting distinct scents, picking up on subtle scents, and working with other parts of the brain responsible for attention and arousal to identify particularly pleasing or threatening smells.

Whenever your child has challenges with olfactory processing, you'll notice (*Understanding SPD: The Olfactory System*, 2024):

- extreme reaction to smells that others may not pick up or be sensitive to (e.g., refusing to eat broccoli because of its perceived smell).

- preference for fragrance-free products (e.g., refusal to wear fragrances, scented fabrics, or bathe with scented soaps).

- impulsive need to smell products that may or may not carry a pungent odor (e.g., smelling food before deciding to eat it or not).

- how they feel about people based on their scents (e.g., disliking an English teacher who wears an off-putting floral fragrance).

Tactile System (Touch)

A structure known as the somatosensory cortex regulates the sensation of touch in the region of the brain called the postcentral gyrus. The information is then fed to the spinal cord, thalamus, and brain stem (*Your 8 Senses*, n.d.). Beyond processing touch, the postcentral gyrus helps the nervous system process the sensations of pain, pressure, and temperature.

Children with tactile processing issues may experience touch sensitivity or underresponsiveness. Common signs might include (*Understanding Sensory Processing Disorder: Tactile System*, 2024):

- being particular about the type of touch they prefer or dislike (e.g., being opposed to handshakes but open to closed fist pumps).

- becoming upset when they are touched by others, especially if it's unexpected (e.g., crying when embraced by someone they are unfamiliar with).

- showing frustration when their body is exposed to certain textures or fabrics (e.g., becoming irritated by clothing tags).

- showing little to no response to extreme temperatures (e.g., not feeling cold or hot).

Gustatory System (Taste)

The gustatory cortex, responsible for the sense of taste, is located within the lateral sulcus, a part of the brain found between the frontal and temporal lobes (Your 8 Senses, n.d.). This little but powerful structure helps us identify safe and unsafe foods and beverages. It works with our taste buds to pick up on sweet, sour, salty, and bitter edibles. Generally, we are inclined to sweet and salty foods and tend to avoid sour and bitter foods due to how they resemble danger. Our brains could believe that sour foods are spoiled or unripened and bitter foods are poisonous (*Not Everything That Tastes Bitter Is Potentially Harmful*, 2024).

Nevertheless, children with gustatory processing issues tend to have a unique relationship with food, marked by a vast number of intolerances, sensitivities, and preferences. They might experience (*Understanding SPD: The Gustatory System*, 2024):

- picky eating or refusal to eat certain foods (e.g., anxiety when trying out new foods or gagging when presented with specific foods).

- specific rules regarding the texture, temperature, and taste of food (e.g., only eating foods at room temperature or preferring dry foods without sauce).

- chews or licks inedible objects such as clothing, toys, or pencils.

- disliking brushing teeth or using certain toothpaste.

Vestibular System (Balance and Orientation)

The vestibular system is responsible for helping us move our bodies and maintain balance. It operates through the semicircular canals, which monitor the way we rotate our bodies or how we move forward and backward (Your 8 Senses, n.d.). In addition to this, the semicircular canals influence other parts of the brain that assist with functions like eye or head movements, staring at specific objects without breaking focus, adjusting breathing when changing to a new body position, and allowing quick body reflexes to prevent things like falls or bumping into objects.

When your child experiences vestibular processing challenges, you might notice (*Sensory Processing Disorder: The Vestibular System*, 2024):

- a fear of activities that require feet to lift from the ground (e.g., being afraid or suspicious of swings, riding bicycles, or climbing).

- frequently falling or tripping over objects.

- preference for running instead of walking in tight spaces (e.g., seemingly unaware of the risks of bumping into people or stationary objects.

- difficulty finding objects; appearing "lost" or "confused" in their environment.

Proprioceptive System (Muscle and Joint Movement)

The proprioceptive system gives us the ability to move different parts of our body to achieve specific movements. Sensory information is collected from the inner ear and stretch receptors in different joints and muscle groups to instruct the body on the best response (Your 8 Senses, n.d.).

You may seldom be aware of your child's proprioceptive reflexes because they often become habitual or instinctual. However, when this aspect of their senses hasn't been developed, you might see distinct signs such as (Proprioception Explained, n.d.):

- poor coordination or posture (e.g., clumsiness, inability to stand on one foot, or the need to rest the head on one hand while working).

- lack of body awareness and motor planning (e.g., frequently bumping into people or objects, difficulty climbing or going down stairs, difficulty holding a pencil or writing with ease).

- frequently using force or pressure when using muscles (e.g., pressing a pen too hard on paper, squeezing tightly when giving hugs, preferring rough play).

Interoception System (Physiological Condition of the Body)

Interceptors are sensors in our bodies that help us recognize what our internal organs are feeling (Your 8 Senses, n.d.). Think of the ability to feel your heart rate increasing or hunger pains when you have skipped a meal. These internal sensors work together with other body functions, such as the respiratory system, digestive system, and nervous system.

Researchers believe that our interception system is vital for emotional regulation and self-awareness (*Your 8 Senses*, n.d.). Some of the struggles your child may encounter if they are experiencing interoceptive processing difficulties include (Morin, 2019):

- not recognizing sensations of hunger, thirst, or satiation.

- not being able to feel pain or tell when their bladder is full.

- difficulty connecting internal cues (e.g., accelerating heartbeat) with emotional states (e.g., feeling afraid).

- not being able to feel oncoming triggers or discomfort, thus leading to frequent meltdowns.

Sensory Processing and Child Development

You have learned how sensory processing issues impact how some children interpret information received from their senses. It's not that they do not experience the same sensations as we do, but that their brains generate different meanings, which influence their reactions.

Recognizing sensory processing challenges in young children becomes tricky for parents since each child's developmental stages occur at different times. For instance, if you are a parent to multiple children, you'll agree that some of your children learned how to walk, talk, or write sooner than others. This is normal and not something to see a doctor about. However, it also makes it that much harder to identify sensory triggers. They may go unnoticed and undiagnosed until later in life when children start school or spend more time in social settings outside of the home.

Fortunately, there are common developmental signs that you can look out for to identify sensory processing problems in young children. We can group these signs into two categories: sensory modulation dysfunction and dyspraxia.

Sensory Modulation Dysfunction

One of the milestones that children reach early in their development is the ability to recognize sensory information, such as recognizing the sound of their name. This allows them to take the necessary course of action, like turning their head to look at the speaker seeking their attention. The more diverse sensory stimuli children can process, the more tasks and reactions they can adequately perform. Sensory modulation dysfunction occurs when children cannot interpret the correct reaction upon receiving sensory input or when they struggle to ignore sensory input that isn't relevant to the task at hand (Ayres, 2023).

There are two subtypes that fall under sensory modulation dysfunction, each manifesting different challenges. The first subtype is called *over-responsivity*, and this occurs when children have a heightened reaction to stimuli, causing them to display the following behaviors (Ayres, 2023):

- picky eating and several food intolerances
- discomfort with loud noises or unexpected sounds
- sensitivity to touch and certain textures like coarse fabric
- finding brushing teeth, nail cutting, or messy play off-putting
- feeling overwhelmed by large playground equipment like swings and slides

The second subtype is called *under-responsivity*, and shows up as a downplayed reaction to stimuli, leading to the following behaviors (Ayres, 2023):

- frequently rock themselves, fidget, or chew on inedible objects
- appearing numb to pain, pressure, and extreme temperatures
- inability to express the appropriate emotions when they are happy or sad
- need for intense activities like rough play or constantly being on the move
- inability to pay attention or focus on objects or people for long amounts of time

Dyspraxia

The second sign you may notice in your developing child is a condition known as dyspraxia, which is the difficulty with body awareness and coordinated movements (Ayres, 2023). Similar to sensory modulation dysfunction, this condition also has two subtypes that children may experience. The first is called Vestibular Bilateral Integration and Sequencing (VBIS). This subtype affects vestibular and proprioceptive sensory processing, meaning your child may display:

- clumsiness and frequently bumping into objects.

- difficulty with movements that require engaging multiple muscle groups and spatial awareness (e.g., kicking a ball or riding a bicycle).

- trouble completing physical exercises that involve memorizing a process (e.g., writing, making the bed, or tying shoelaces).

- difficulty performing activities that require eye-to-body coordination (e.g., spilling food when feeding themselves, playing catch, cutting paper with scissors).

The second subtype, *somatodyspraxia*, occurs when children struggle to carry out new (rather than habitual) motor tasks. The sensory systems impacted include the tactile, proprioceptive, and vestibular systems. Behaviors common with this subtype are (Ayres, 2023):

- frequently bumps into objects that are obstructing their path.

- difficulty executing new routines (e.g., may struggle to use a knife and fork if they are accustomed to eating with a spoon).

- taking longer to learn skills such as brushing teeth or reading.

- poor control over their body when running, climbing, or going up and down stairs.

- delayed response to transitions from one task to another.

If you struggle to identify these developmental signs of sensory processing issues, seek the guidance of a therapist trained in sensory integration. They can run tests and perform assessments to identify your child's unique sensory challenges and then develop tailored exercises to improve how they respond to sensory information.

The Relationship Between Sensory Processing Disorder, Attention-Deficit Hyperactivity Disorder, and Autism Spectrum Disorder

Doctors diagnose sensory processing difficulties under the medical term sensory processing disorder (SPD); this condition can be defined as challenges in identifying, regulating, interpreting, and responding to sensory information (Passarello et al., 2022).

It's worth mentioning that not every child with sensory issues will be diagnosed with SPD. For some, sensory triggers could be related to learned habits from watching other family members. Other children may be living with neurological disorders like ADHD or ASD, where sensory processing dysfunction is a symptom (we'll explore these co-morbidities in a short while).

With that said, research indicates that approximately 5–13% of children between the ages of 4–6 years old are impacted by SPD and subsequently experience a range of developmental delays and challenges, such as poor social skills, emotional dysregulation, sensory impairments, learning disabilities, and much more (Passarello et al., 2022).

SPD is linked to significant differences in brain structure and processing, impacting various functions related to attention, learning, spatial awareness, body awareness, balance and coordination, language processing, and emotional regulation (to name a few). This is why SPD is often accompanied by other neurological and behavioral disorders (Schwartz, 2014):

- reading and learning disorders (i.e., dyslexia)

- movement and coordination problems (i.e., dyspraxia)

- handwriting difficulties (i.e., dysgraphia)

- speech and language delays

- attention-deficit and hyperactivity disorder

- autism spectrum disorder

- anxiety disorders

- childhood trauma and attachment issues

Finding the correct medical professional to assess your child's symptoms is critical. For instance, if you notice they struggle to recognize their name, follow instructions, or form speech, you can consult with a speech and language pathologist. If your child has frequent meltdowns whenever they have difficulty processing sensory information, a child therapist or psychologist qualified in sensory integration therapy could help them improve their tolerance of sensory inputs.

Sensory Processing Disorder and Attention-Deficit Hyperactivity Disorder

It's common for children with SPD to be misdiagnosed with ADHD, and vice versa. This happens because of the overlap and similarities between these two conditions. The Centers for Disease Control and Prevention (CDC) found that 11% of children between 3 and 17 years old are diagnosed with ADHD in the US (2024). The number of those diagnosed with SPD is higher; however, it's still not talked about as much as ADHD. This means that often what appears to be ADHD on the surface could be SPD underneath.

Both SPD and ADHD are brain-related disorders that have no known cure. In most cases, they are hereditary and evident from birth. Environmental factors like exposure to toxins, pollution, early childhood trauma, or emotional neglect can aggravate these conditions and sometimes cause irreparable neurological damage.

However, here is where the two conditions diverge. ADHD is caused by structural abnormalities in the prefrontal cortex and an underproduction of neurotransmitters like dopamine and norepinephrine (Ochsenbein, n.d.). As a result, children experience learning, regulation, and behavioral issues. For instance, your child may struggle to pay attention, manage time, interpret social cues, solve problems logically, and follow instructions.

In contrast, SPD is caused by abnormal white matter structure in the rear part of the brain, where sensory integration occurs. White matter assists with passing electrical impulses to different brain regions; thus, the lack of white matter impacts the ability for sensory information to be carried and communicated from one part of the brain to another (Ochsenbein, n.d.). Information coming from the environment is often misinterpreted, leading to inappropriate behaviors.

Due to how differently ADHD and SPD impact the brain, treating them requires tailored interventions. Generally, psychotherapy and medication are effective for managing ADHD symptoms, whereas SPD treatment typically involves physiotherapy, speech exercises, and sensory integration activities, presented through gradual exposure in a supportive environment (Ochsenbein, n.d.).

It's possible for your child to be diagnosed with SPD and ADHD. In fact, research shows that 40% of children who live with ADHD also live with SPD (Ochsenbein, n.d.). They may display symptoms of both conditions, such as demonstrating signs of inattention, impulsivity, and sensory sensitivities. The treatment plan would involve a combination of medication, behavioral management, and physiotherapy.

Sensory Processing Disorder and Autism Spectrum Disorder

ASD, also known as autism, is another neurological and developmental disorder that impacts 1 in 36 children, affecting how they learn, behave, and communicate (Centers for Disease Control and Prevention, 2024). Similar to ADHD, it is normally diagnosed in early childhood and has no known cure.

The two distinct signs that doctors look for in children exhibiting symptoms of ASD. The first is social and communication deficits, such as the lack of social-emotional reciprocity, nonverbal communicative behaviors, and the ability to build and nurture relationships. Secondly, they look for recurring restrictive and repetitive behaviors, such as repetitive motor movements, fixating on special interests, insisting on carrying out ritualistic behaviors, and sensory processing issues (Fletcher, 2024).

Since autism occurs on a spectrum, the type and severity of symptoms will range (Fletcher, 2024). This also applies to how children with ASD experience sensory processing issues; they may be hyperresponsive or underresponsive to sensory information. You might notice that your child avoids being touched by others, eating certain foods, or visiting noisy places like malls. Alternatively, they may need constant physical movement, obsessively touch or taste objects, and prefer bright lights and busy areas.

Moreover, children with autism can frequently become overstimulated by sensory information and experience what is known as sensory overload. Picture what happens when a bottle of soda is shaken aggressively and the cap is opened. The liquid explodes out of the bottle rather than gently pouring out. The same occurs when a child with autism has processed one too many sensory inputs. To soothe themselves, they may hyperfocus on a special interest, cover their eye or ears, have sudden and unexplained meltdowns, or perform self-stimulating behaviors (or "stimming") by humming, rocking back and forth, chewing on an object, or making repetitive sounds (*Sensory Processing Disorder (SPD)*, 2024).

A combination of treatments is used to manage ASD, such as medication, behavioral therapy, learning aids, and educational support. If your child is diagnosed with SPD and ASD, a multifaceted treatment approach is required for long-term health benefits.

Advanced Concepts in Sensory Processing

The Neurological Basis of Sensory Processing

While we've explored the basics of sensory processing and how it affects children's behavior, understanding the neurological mechanisms provides deeper insight into why interventions work and how improvements happen over time.

Neural Pathways and Sensory Integration

Sensory processing relies on a complex network of neural pathways that transmit information from sensory receptors to the brain. The process involves several key steps:

1. **Reception**: Sensory receptors in the body detect stimuli from the environment. For example, mechanoreceptors in the skin detect touch, while photoreceptors in the eyes detect light.

2. **Transmission**: Sensory information travels along afferent neural pathways to the central nervous system. Each sensory system uses dedicated neural pathways with varying transmission speeds.

3. **Processing**: Primary processing occurs in specific regions of the brain. For example, visual information is processed in the occipital lobe, while auditory information is processed in the temporal lobe.

4. **Integration**: The thalamus and cerebral cortex

integrate information from multiple sensory systems. The association areas of the brain combine these inputs to create coherent perceptions.

5. **Response**: Based on integrated sensory information, the brain generates appropriate responses through efferent neural pathways to muscles and glands.

For children with sensory processing disorders, disruptions can occur at any of these stages. Research by Marco et al. (2011) demonstrated that children with SPD show differences in white matter microstructure, particularly in posterior cerebral tracts that connect sensory processing regions with higher-order cognitive areas.

Neuroplasticity and Sensory Processing

The brain's remarkable ability to reorganize itself by forming new neural connections—neuroplasticity—offers hope for improving sensory processing difficulties. This adaptive capacity explains why therapeutic interventions can lead to lasting changes in a child's sensory responses over time.

Neuroplasticity operates through several mechanisms:

- **Synaptic strengthening**: Repeated sensory experiences strengthen neural connections through a process called long-term potentiation.

- **Neural pruning**: Unused neural pathways may be eliminated while frequently used pathways are preserved and strengthened.

- **Cortical reorganization**: Brain regions can adapt to perform new functions or compensate for difficulties in other areas.

A groundbreaking study by Owen et al. (2013) used diffusion tensor imaging to identify specific white matter tracts affected in children with SPD. The researchers found that targeted sensory integration therapy led to measurable changes in the structural connectivity of these tracts, correlating with improved function.

This neurological understanding explains why consistent sensory diet activities and therapeutic interventions often require time to show results—they are literally reshaping neural pathways to process sensory information more efficiently.

Biomedical Factors Affecting Sensory Processing

Sensory processing difficulties don't exist in isolation from other bodily systems. A growing body of research points to important connections between sensory processing and biomedical factors that may exacerbate or even underlie sensory challenges.

Inflammation and Sensory Sensitivity

Emerging research suggests a connection between neuroinflammation and sensory processing issues. Inflammatory markers like cytokines can affect neural transmission and sensitivity, potentially leading to sensory over-responsivity.

A study by Ashwood et al. (2011) found that children with both autism and sensory processing difficulties had higher levels of pro-inflammatory cytokines compared to typically developing peers. This suggests that systemic inflammation may play a role in heightened sensory responsiveness.

For some children, addressing inflammation through diet, lifestyle changes, or medical interventions may help reduce sensory sensitivities. Common anti-inflammatory approaches include:

- Omega-3 fatty acid supplementation

- Reduction of inflammatory foods

- Adequate sleep and stress management

- Treatment of underlying allergies or autoimmune conditions

The Gut-Brain Connection

The enteric nervous system—sometimes called our "second brain"—contains more than 500 million neurons and communicates bidirectionally with the central nervous system through the vagus nerve. This gut-brain axis plays a crucial role in sensory processing.

Research by Hsiao et al. (2013) demonstrated that alterations in gut microbiota can influence sensory processing and behavior. In their study, restoration of beneficial gut bacteria reduced sensory abnormalities in animal models with symptoms similar to autism.

Signs that gut health may be affecting your child's sensory processing include:

- Gastrointestinal symptoms coinciding with sensory reactions

- Increased sensory sensitivity after consuming certain foods

- Improvement in sensory regulation when digestive issues are addressed

- Cyclical patterns of sensory difficulties corresponding with digestive cycles

Supporting gut health through probiotics, prebiotics, and a nutrient-dense diet may complement traditional sensory integration approaches for some children.

Sleep Quality and Sensory Regulation

Sleep and sensory processing have a reciprocal relationship—poor sensory regulation can disrupt sleep, while inadequate sleep worsens sensory processing.

Research by Reynolds et al. (2012) found that children with sensory processing disorders experienced significantly more sleep disturbances than typically developing peers. Moreover, improving sleep quality led to better daytime sensory regulation.

Key considerations for supporting sleep in sensory-sensitive children include:

- Creating a sensory-appropriate sleep environment

- Establishing consistent bedtime routines

- Monitoring sensory input in the hours before sleep

- Addressing sleep disorders through medical consultation if necessary

- Using appropriate bedding (weighted blankets, specific textures) based on sensory needs

Food Chemicals That Trigger Sensory Reactions

Certain food ingredients can dramatically affect neurological function and sensory processing in susceptible children. Understanding these chemical triggers can help parents identify and manage dietary factors that may exacerbate sensory issues.

Artificial Food Dyes

Synthetic food colorings have been linked to behavioral and sensory issues in numerous studies. A comprehensive review by Nigg et al. (2012) found that approximately 8% of children with ADHD show significant sensitivity to artificial food dyes, with sensory regulation often affected alongside attention.

Common problematic dyes include:

- **Red 40 (Allura Red)**: Found in fruit-flavored snacks, cereals, candies, and beverages

- **Yellow 5 (Tartrazine)**: Present in pickles, certain chips, cereal, and some medications

- **Yellow 6 (Sunset Yellow)**: Used in orange-flavored

beverages, baked goods, and candy

- **Blue 1 (Brilliant Blue)**: Found in beverages, candy, and baked goods

Many parents report that eliminating artificial food dyes leads to notable improvements in sensory regulation and behavior. A controlled trial by Stevenson et al. (2014) found that children showed increased irritability, restlessness, and sleep disturbance when consuming artificial colors, with improvements when these substances were removed from their diet.

Preservatives and Flavor Enhancers

Several common food additives can affect neurological function and trigger sensory reactions:

- **Monosodium Glutamate (MSG)**: This flavor enhancer can cause heightened sensitivity and irritability in susceptible children. MSG activates glutamate receptors in the brain, which may lead to neurological excitation and sensory overwhelm. It's found in many processed foods, restaurant meals, and savory snacks.

- **BHA and BHT**: These preservatives have been shown to affect neurological function in animal studies. They're commonly found in cereals, chewing gum, potato chips, and vegetable oils.

- **Sodium Benzoate**: Often used as a preservative in acidic foods and beverages, sodium benzoate has been linked to increased hyperactivity, especially when combined with artificial food colors (McCann et al., 2007).

- **Aspartame and Artificial Sweeteners**: Some children experience heightened sensory sensitivity and irritability after consuming artificial sweeteners. Research by

Humphries et al. (2008) suggests that aspartame can alter brain neurotransmitter levels in sensitive individuals.

Naturally Occurring Food Chemicals

Even natural foods contain chemicals that can affect sensory processing in sensitive individuals:

- **Salicylates**: These natural compounds are found in many fruits, vegetables, spices, and herbs. They're chemically similar to aspirin and can trigger sensory reactions in susceptible children. High-salicylate foods include berries, citrus fruits, tomatoes, and cucumbers.

- **Amines**: Foods containing biogenic amines like histamine, tyramine, and phenylethylamine can affect nervous system function. Aged cheeses, fermented foods, chocolate, and some fruits contain high levels of amines that may trigger sensory sensitivities.

- **Glutamates**: Natural glutamates in foods like tomatoes, cheese, and mushrooms can have similar effects to MSG in sensitive children.

Case Study: Sam's Sensory Transformation

Six-year-old Sam experienced extreme tactile defensiveness, auditory sensitivities, and frequent emotional meltdowns. Despite occupational therapy, his progress was minimal. After implementing a comprehensive elimination diet that removed artificial food dyes, preservatives, and high-salicylate foods, his parents noticed dramatic improvements within three weeks.

Sam's occupational therapist reported that his tactile tolerance increased significantly, and he became more responsive to sensory integration activities. His ability to filter auditory input improved, and his emotional regulation during transitions became more consistent.

Blood tests revealed that Sam had elevated inflammatory markers before the dietary changes, which normalized after the elimination diet. This case illustrates how addressing biomedical factors can enhance the effectiveness of traditional sensory integration approaches.

Implementing a Food Detective Approach

If you suspect food chemicals may be affecting your child's sensory processing, consider these steps:

1. **Keep a detailed food and behavior journal**: Track what your child eats and note changes in sensory sensitivities, behavior, and sleep over at least two weeks.

2. **Consider an elimination diet**: Under professional guidance, temporarily remove common trigger foods and additives, then reintroduce them systematically while monitoring responses.

3. **Prioritize whole foods**: Focus on unprocessed foods without artificial additives as the foundation of your child's diet.

4. **Read labels carefully**: Become familiar with the various names and forms of problematic additives.

5. **Work with professionals**: Consult with a registered dietitian or nutritionist who specializes in neurodevelopmental conditions to ensure nutritional adequacy while investigating food sensitivities.

Remember that dietary approaches should complement, not replace, therapeutic interventions for sensory processing challenges. The most effective approach typically combines sensory integration therapy with appropriate biomedical support.

Evolving Research in Sensory Processing

Our understanding of sensory processing continues to evolve as research methodologies advance. Recent developments have enhanced our knowledge of assessment, intervention, and long-term outcomes for children with sensory challenges.

Advanced Assessment Technologies

Traditional assessments for sensory processing difficulties rely heavily on parent questionnaires and clinical observations. However, newer technologies are providing more objective measurements:

- **Electroencephalography (EEG)**: Studies by Gavin et al. (2019) have used EEG to identify distinct patterns of cortical activity in children with sensory processing disorders, showing differences in how their brains respond to sensory stimuli compared to typically developing children.

- **Functional Magnetic Resonance Imaging (fMRI)**: Research using fMRI has identified differences in brain activation patterns during sensory processing tasks, particularly in the somatosensory cortex and insular regions (Tavassoli et al., 2019).

- **Sensory Processing Measure - Integrated Assessment**: This comprehensive assessment system combines standardized testing with physiological measures like heart rate variability and electrodermal activity to capture both behavioral and autonomic nervous system responses to sensory stimuli.

These advanced assessment tools are helping researchers and clinicians better understand the neurological basis of sensory processing difficulties and develop more targeted interventions.

Promising Intervention Approaches

Research continues to identify effective approaches for supporting children with sensory processing challenges:

- DIR/Floortime with Sensory Integration: Integrating the Developmental, Individual-differences, Relationship-based (DIR) model with sensory integration therapy has shown particular promise for children with both sensory and social challenges (Greenspan & Wieder, 2005).

- **Sound-Based Interventions**: Therapeutic listening programs that provide specific auditory input have demonstrated positive effects on sensory processing and regulation in some children (Hall & Case-Smith, 2007).

- **Mindfulness-Based Approaches**: Teaching age-appropriate mindfulness techniques has shown benefits for sensory awareness and self-regulation in children with sensory processing difficulties (Greenland, 2010).

- **Sensory-Cognitive-Motor Integration**: Programs that integrate sensory processing with cognitive strategies and motor planning have shown promising results for children with complex sensory challenges (Miller et al., 2007).

As research continues to advance, we gain a clearer picture of which interventions work best for specific sensory processing profiles, moving toward more personalized approaches

Key Takeaways

- Sensory processing can be described as the ability to recognize and correctly interpret sensory information from the environment. As such, sensory processing difficulties are abnormalities in the way that the brain processes and responds to sensory inputs.

- It's common for children with sensory processing difficulties to have sensory impairments, such as overreacting or underreacting to sights, odors, textures, sounds, and flavors. They may also struggle with body awareness, gross motor skills, and responding to physiological needs.

- Sensory processing issues can cause developmental delays, which become more evident when children start school or spend more time outside of the home. Working with a therapist trained in sensory integration can improve how children process and respond to sensory information.

- SPD, ADHD, and ASD are neurological disorders that can co-exist and are often misdiagnosed and confused with one another due to the common thread of sensory processing dysfunction. Since the causes of these conditions are different, it's important to seek the correct diagnosis so the proper treatment plan can be provided.

- Sensory processing difficulties have identifiable neurological underpinnings, with differences in brain structure and function that can be measured with advanced imaging techniques.

- Neuroplasticity offers hope for improvement through well-designed interventions that strengthen neural pathways for more efficient sensory processing.

- Biomedical factors including inflammation, gut health, sleep quality, and dietary chemicals can significantly impact sensory processing and should be considered alongside traditional sensory integration approaches.

- Specific food chemicals, both artificial and natural, can trigger or exacerbate sensory sensitivities in susceptible children.

- Emerging assessment technologies and intervention approaches continue to enhance our understanding and treatment of sensory processing challenges.

Now that you have learned the foundation of sensory processing, it's time to explore the unique and intricate ways it can manifest for children. The next chapter will help you identify sensory-seeking, sensory-avoiding, and sensory-sensitive behaviors, so you can help your child navigate the world with more success and less frustration.

Chapter 2:

Sensory Seeking and Avoidance

Discipline is helping a child solve a problem. Punishment is making a child suffer for having a problem. To raise problem solvers, focus on solutions, not retribution.
—L.R. Knost

What Makes You Feel Happy or Upset and Why?

I feel really happy when I can run, jump, and move my body. When I swing high up in the air, I feel like I can breathe better, like all the extra noise in my head disappears for a little while. I like the feeling of wind rushing past me because it makes my body feel light instead of heavy and stuck. But when people tell me to stop moving so much, it feels like my body is a soda can being shaken up, and I have no choice but to explode.

—Isla, 5 years old

Sensory-Seeking Behaviors

Not every child with sensory processing difficulties has the same sensory needs and experiences. As a parent, you are responsible for figuring out what environmental stimuli make your child calm, happy, or frustrated. In this chapter, we're exploring two common behaviors your child may display: sensory-seeking and sensory avoidance.

Sensory seekers are children who desire constant, and often intense, stimulation to feel fulfilled. This happens because their sensory receptors aren't as powerful as others, which means they need three or four times more stimuli to experience a normal reaction. Here's an example: When a typical child is given coloring pencils and paper and asked to draw, they will pick up a few colors and make doodles on the page. A sensory-seeking child might lick the pencil to discover the taste, break another pencil in half to break through the resistance of the object, use force when pressing the pencil on the paper, causing tears, and eventually scrunch the artwork into a ball and kick it around.

Unsatisfiable curiosity is common among sensory seekers. It's not enough for them to look at an object to understand what it is; they need to touch it, smell it, and put it in their mouths. Fortunately, this abundant curiosity can be leveraged to help them pay attention and complete tasks. For example, to motivate your sensory-seeking child to pick up their toys after play time, you can gamify the process to increase their adrenaline and make the task competitive. This transforms a seemingly boring activity into one that feels rewarding.

Due to decreased sensory awareness, sensory seekers may struggle to perceive the weight, height, strength, and capabilities of their bodies. As a result, they can trip over their feet, try to squeeze into small spaces, ask to be carried like a toddler, or apply too much force or pressure when embracing others. Children who watch a lot of cartoons may attempt to recreate some of the movements they see on their screens, not realizing that their human bodies have limits and that some moves can be dangerous.

Sensory-seeking behaviors can resemble some ADHD behaviors, so it's important to seek a second or third perspective to receive the correct diagnosis. For instance, a sensory-seeking child can also display the following habits:

- difficulty sitting still
- easily distracted by objects in motion
- fidgeting with objects nearby
- need to run, jump, or climb
- risk-taking behaviors on the playground
- fascination with specific objects or people

Parenting Tips for Regulating Sensory-Seeking Behaviors

Your sensory-seeking child may have a preference for the type of sensory inputs they seek out. For example, a tactile sensory seeker might enjoy touching different textures, being hugged tightly, or playing games that involve physical contact. A vestibular sensory seeker might enjoy activities that involve twisting and turning their bodies, such as spinning around in circles, hanging face down on the edge of their bed, or playing on obstacle courses.

Safety becomes increasingly important as your child gets older and starts exploring their environment. Even though you desire to grant them as much freedom to play as possible, establishing boundaries (and communicating them) helps your child satisfy their curiosity within clearly defined parameters. Let's look at some of the ways you can positively regulate your child's sensory-seeking behaviors to keep them safe.

Create Structured Sensory Stimulation

When left to figure out how they are going to entertain themselves, your child might seek activities that are fun but dangerous, such as jumping off high ledges. By providing opportunities for structured sensory play, you can curate the tasks your child engages with. For example, by flipping half of your basement into a superactive sensory room, filled with a built-in obstacle course, climbing wall, large ball pit, bean bag chairs, and a projector for watching movies, you can give them plenty of things to do that are safe and stimulating. Take into consideration their preferred sensory inputs (e.g., sounds, colors, textures, scents) when designing this space to enhance their experience.

Carry Travel-Sized Sensory Stimulating Toys

It's either to regulate the kind of sensory-seeking activities your child engages in at home. However, as soon as you step outside, you compete with hundreds of stimuli that pique your child's interest but may not be appropriate to explore. Having travel-sized sensory toys or products that you carry with you can be a great way to distract your child and keep them busy while you run errands or socialize. You might pack a cuddly stuffed animal, a chewing toy, a musical instrument, headphones to listen to stories or music, and DIY crafts.

Turn Daily Routines Into Sensory Adventures

One of the best ways to keep your child engaged and prevent boredom or power struggles when completing their daily routine is to transform them into mini sensory adventures. With a little thought and effort, every mundane task can be turned into an enjoyable experience.

For example, it's common for sensory-seeking children to either dislike the texture of toothbrush bristles and toothpaste or use excessive force when brushing their teeth, which can hurt their gums. To encourage teeth brushing, you can allow them to choose their "magic toothpaste" that offers a flavor they prefer (you can also help them assign a special meaning to the toothpaste, like having superpowers, to motivate daily usage). If your child tends to brush their teeth using too much force, create a two-hand challenge where they brush their teeth with one hand and squeeze a stress ball with the other hand to release pressure.

Provide Goal-Directed Activities

Sensory-seeking children love to expend energy, but after a while, resorting to the same activities like kicking a ball, swimming, or riding a bike can get boring. To motivate curiosity and engagement, incorporate goal-directed play into your child's routine. You can do this by creating challenges or competitions that have a main objective and several steps to complete to gain a reward.

Here's an example of how a simple task like running outside

can turn into a goal-directed activity:

1. Set up an outdoor treasure hunt in which your child must race to find specific items, such as a red leaf or a round stone.

2. Create a checklist for your child to mark off each item they find, turning the run into an exciting challenge (this also encourages independence).

3. To enhance engagement, time the runs and reward your child with small treats or stickers for completing the checklist.

4. If you have other children of similar ages (or your child has friends over), introduce a team-based competition for greater collaboration and excitement.

Sensory-Avoiding Behaviors

Sensory-seeking children crave an abundance of certain sensory stimuli, but sensory-avoidant children run away from certain stimuli. They are hyperaware of sensations that are upsetting and react with extreme emotion when presented with them. For example, being pickled by a clothing tag might be irritating for you and me, but a sensory-avoidant child may cry and struggle to continue with their routine until the tag is removed.

Being sensory-avoidant carries social implications. For instance, to limit exposure to certain sounds, objects, odors, or lights, some children may prefer to stay close to their parents or caregivers whom they trust. In group settings, they might pull away from their peers or be emotionally withdrawn. They may have trouble following instructions at school due to avoiding certain triggering tasks. Take a student who is overstimulated by the noise in the classroom; they may put their hands over their ears, appear distracted or disengaged, and have difficulty completing assignments within a given timeframe.

Many children with sensory-avoidant behaviors have difficulty managing daily routines, particularly everyday tasks that other children would easily complete. Look at it from their viewpoint: How would you feel if you had an irrational fear of flushing the toilet and got frightened by the roaring sound of the water that sounded like an explosion? Chances are, you would conveniently "forget" to flush whenever you go to avoid the anxiety that would follow.

The example above may sound similar to experiences you have had with your sensory-avoidant child. They may whine or get upset whenever they need to carry out tasks that trigger stimuli they are attempting to avoid, such as brushing their teeth, washing hands, walking on grass, or sitting in heavily lit places (i.e., a classroom with fluorescent lights). It can be easy to label their behavior as defiant or difficult and push them toward the stimuli they desire to avoid. However, doing this robs your child of the opportunity to learn self-regulation skills.

Parenting Tips for Regulating Sensory-Avoidant Behaviors

Raising a sensory-avoidant child requires adapting your home environment to accommodate their needs. Of course, this doesn't mean eliminating triggers, as that would be counterproductive for teaching them how to self-regulate. Instead, your job is to help them discover coping mechanisms that enable them to interact with different sensory inputs while being aware of their limits.

Below are different ways to help your child engage with their sensory triggers without feeling overwhelmed.

Vestibular

A child with vestibular sensory avoidance tends to dislike activities that would cause physical imbalance and could lead to falling. They may refuse to run, jump, climb, do cartwheels, play catch, or play on swing sets. For them, the safest condition is to have both feet planted on the ground. To help them overcome this fear, you can engage in activities that promote controlled movement, such as:

- Play games that encourage ground movement, like crawling through a tunnel.

- Give your child a sturdy object (e.g., chair) to push while walking.

- Hold your child's hands when walking up and down stairs.

- Hold your child on your lap and bounce on an exercise ball.

- Allow your child to guide the movement so they can feel a greater sense of control (e.g., asking "Do you want me to push you very slowly" when your child is sitting on a rocking chair).

Visual

Visual sensory avoidance can cause your child to avoid places with bright lights, high-contrast colors, and a lot of people or fast-moving objects (think of crossing a busy street). These experiences can make them feel stressed and overwhelmed, impacting their mood, comfort levels, and social interactions. To soothe themselves, they might squint their eyes, avoid eye contact, or refuse to visit certain public spaces. Some of the ways you can help your child regulate their behaviors include:

- Dimmable lights and lamps at home that are easy on your child's eyesight for dimming.

- Use neutral colors around your home and avoid clutter to prevent overstimulation.

- Install blackout curtains in your child's room to avoid sleep interruptions.

- Encourage your child to wear hats and sunglasses when spending time outdoors.

- Schedule outings and vacations during the week or off-peak periods when there are fewer crowds of people in public spaces.

Auditory

If your child is auditory sensory avoidant, you'll frequently see them blocking their ears when family members are talking or when watching TV. They may even get startled by certain sounds, like hearing a siren, fireworks, or a dog barking. Public spaces with loud echoing sounds, like the shopping mall or playground, could also be unbearable for them. Here are some of the ways you can help them regulate their sensitivity to sounds:

- Provide your child with noise-canceling headphones at parties, restaurants, or during class time (with permission from the teacher).

- Create quiet zones around your home where electronics are prohibited and silent activities like reading are encouraged.

- Provide a visual schedule to help your child anticipate when noisy activities will occur (e.g., meal preparation, family bonding time, etc.).

- Place a white noise machine in your child's room to block out noises that might keep them up at night.

- Allow your child to listen to soothing music or watch their favorite animated videos to self-soothe in public spaces.

Tactile

Tactile sensory avoidance causes your child to feel overwhelmed by certain textures or physical sensations. A common example is feeling discomfort wearing clothing made with coarse fabrics, or disliking clothing tags or loose seams. They may also have an obsession with hygiene and cleanliness, often getting upset when they have spilled substances on their clothes, dirtied their hands, or missed their bath time. Other physical sensations that could be triggering include being touched without consent, nail trimming, or having their hair styled. Here are strategies to help your child regulate their tactile avoidance:

- Take your child with you when shopping for clothing and let them choose items that feel comfortable on their bodies.

- Remove clothing tags from your child's clothing and undergarments before they wear them.

- Provide gloves, aprons, hair nets, and other protective gear for your child to wear when performing messy activities.

- Teach your child how to express physical boundaries, like saying no to handshakes and hugs from strangers.

Gustatory

Most picky eaters likely have gustatory sensory avoidance, which is the dislike of the flavor, texture, or temperature of certain foods and beverages. For instance, your child might complain about the food being too spicy, too hot (temperature-wise), too crunchy, or smelling bad. When presented with these foods, they might gag or refuse to eat them. Having specific food preferences is also a sign of gustatory sensory avoidance. Think of a child who only eats egg whites or crustless sandwiches. To help your child manage their food intolerances, you can do the following:

- Separate food groups on your child's plate so they have options for what to eat and how much of each to eat.

- Introduce new foods gradually (e.g., serve familiar favorites alongside new foods).

- Allow your child to lick, smell, and touch their food before putting it in their mouth.

- Identify "safe foods" that your child loves and can eat regularly without fussing.

- Present food in a fun and creative way (cutting sandwiches using molds) to make meal times enjoyable.

Olfactory

Olfactory sensory avoidance occurs when your child is sensitive to certain scents and odors. For instance, they may feel nauseous when they smell cleaning products, rotting food, or strong perfumes. As a result, they may avoid eating specific foods, hugging specific people, or entering places like congested stores or musky bathrooms. It's worth mentioning that not all scents and odors will be repelling for your child. On the other end, they may be obsessed with specific spices, odors, and fragrances (e.g., your child may love the smell of rain or leather). Here's how you can help them regulate smells they dislike while incorporating those they enjoy:

- Opt for fragrance-free soaps, lotions, and laundry detergents.

- Purchase candles and air fresheners with scents your child loves.

- Keep the air circulating throughout your home by opening windows or using air conditioning.

- Encourage your child to wear a mask in public spaces such as busy streets or malls, where they may be exposed to diverse odors.

- Allow your child to chew a mint when they need to freshen their breath.

Proprioception

A child with proprioceptive sensory avoidance may struggle with body awareness, such as understanding the strength, weight, size, and position of their body as it relates to the world around them. As such, they may avoid being picked up (toddlers), carrying objects (which they consider heavy), performing sports or physical exercise, and other movements that may be considered unsafe. Some of the ways that you can help your child manage their avoidance behaviors include:

- Show respect for your child's preferred physical activities and avoid forcing them to engage in rough play, extreme sports, or intense chores.

- Offer alternative physical movements that are gentle and can be controlled at their own pace (e.g., stretching, swimming, or walking).

- Allow your child to choose their house chores and control how they perform tasks (e.g., if your child has specific food preparation methods, avoid correcting them unless it's for their safety).

Interoception

If your child has interoceptive sensory avoidance, they may have trouble recognizing internal body signals such as hunger, thirst, and bowel movements. As a result, they may frequently wet their bed at night, appear dehydrated or fatigued, get anxious when their body temperature increases or decreases, and avoid high-intensity activities that raise their heart rate or make them sweat. To help your child regulate their interoceptive avoidance behaviors, you can do the following:

- Use visual or auditory reminders for mealtimes, drinking water, and bathroom breaks.

- Create a daily routine that ensures all of your child's basic physical needs are met.

- Teach your child mindfulness techniques, such as body scan meditation, to recognize physical pain, tension, and discomfort.

- Guide them through breathing exercises.

How to Identify Sensory Behaviors in Your Child

So far, we have explored two types of behaviors that are signs of sensory processing difficulties. However, despite simplifying the symptoms, recognizing them in your child may not be straightforward. It's important to do your research, but spend more time studying your child's behaviors to learn about their sensory challenges. The following sections will provide you with tools to identify sensory processing issues your child may have.

What Are Your Child's Sensory Sensitivities?

Sensory sensitivity refers to having a heightened awareness of the world around you. In most cases, it can lead to extreme reactions to everyday sensory stimuli (Berry, 2024). The first clear sign that your child could be living with a sensory processing problem is being sensitive to ordinary tasks or experiences that other people may not have a big response to.

One way to discover your child's unique sensory sensitivities is to figure out what tends to upset, stress, or overwhelm them in their day-to-day routine. Nobody's perfect, and we all have bad days once in a while, but those with sensory sensitivities are often triggered by seemingly minor inconveniences, which can impact their moods, energy, engagement, and openness to experiences.

For the next week, carry a notebook and document every incident that triggers your child's stress response. Don't think too hard about whether the event is a sign of a sensory processing challenge or not. Simply write them down. At the end of the week, you might come up with a list similar to the one below:

- loud noises (e.g., vacuum cleaner, children playing)

- crowded places (e.g., grocery stores, playgrounds)

- changes in routine (e.g., a different drop-off time at school)

- unexpected touch (e.g., being hugged or bumped into)

- waiting in line (e.g., at a store or event)

- transitions between activities (e.g., moving from playtime to snack time)

Create a separate list of abnormal activities or behaviors that your child displays. Here, the aim is to identify signs of hypersensitivity (having little to no response to sensory stimuli). However, your list may help you uncover unhealthy habits and other co-occurring medical conditions that need your attention. At the end of the week, your list may turn out like this:

- Having a lack of response to loud noises or sudden sounds.

- Engaging in rough play or risk-taking behavior without caution.

- Seeking out intense sensory experiences, such as jumping from heights or spinning.

- Excessive screen time or lack of interest in physical activities.

- Frequent illness or fatigue, suggesting a weakened immune system.

- Insomnia or restless sleep patterns.

It's not possible to identify all of your child's sensory sensitivities alone. There could be behaviors that tend to appear in specific environments, like daycare, preschool, during extracurricular activities, or on playdates. Ask close friends, family, teachers, coaches, and school counselors for their feedback on your child's behaviors. If possible, have them create their lists of observations too. Together, you could pull more insights that can reveal specific sensory issues your child has, and possibly undiagnosed medical conditions.

What Does Sensory Overload Look Like for Your Child?

Another valuable observation to make is recognizing what sensory overload looks like for your child. Sensory overload is the state reached when your child exceeds the maximum threshold of stimulation they can process at any given time. When this occurs, their body naturally shuts down to recuperate. However, how this "shutdown" manifests is different for every child.

Recognizing what your child does whenever they reach sensory overload is important because it helps you understand what triggers them and when they need additional support. Older children may be capable of communicating their thoughts and feelings and making requests, such as turning down the volume on the TV or dimming the lights. However, smaller children who are still learning to express themselves tend to react to stress by practicing the following behaviors:

Avoidance

When some children are overstimulated, they tend to remove themselves from the triggering situation or environment. For example, a child who hides in their bedroom when guests visit or who leaves certain foods on their plate is exhibiting signs of avoidance. Other signs might include blocking eyes and ears, running out of the room, or choosing to play alone in the playground.

> *When the cafeteria gets too loud, I feel like my head is going to explode. I have to get out of there, so I run to the bathroom and lock the door until it feels safe again.*

> *–Ethan, 8*

Defensiveness

Other children prefer to get their parents' attention whenever they are overstimulated. In most cases, they may "act out" or respond aggressively to express their discomfort and refusal. For example, a child who tends to cry uncontrollably at parties or switches off the TV while everyone is watching, or who hits, bites, or kicks people when they get too close, could be showing signs of defensiveness. Even though this behavior is considered socially unacceptable, think of it as your child's attempt to communicate their boundaries. Being respectful and reassuring can help them calm down and cooperate.

When my shirt feels scratchy, I get really mad. I tell Mom I don't want to wear it, but she makes me. Then I scream and pull at it until she finally lets me change!

–Lily, 6

Overwhelm

When overstimulated, some children appear overwhelmed, although they are unable to communicate it. They might stare blankly into space or at the speaker, struggle to read or write, appear extremely quiet, or appear exhausted. During these moments of unresponsiveness, it can be helpful to remove possible sensory triggers from their environment and allow a few minutes for them to recover. When reengaging with your child, use short, direct prompts to gauge what they need (e.g., Should we take a break from doing homework?)

When the fire alarm went off, everything felt too big and loud. I couldn't move or think. My teacher kept asking if I was okay, but I couldn't say anything. I just sat there, frozen.

–James, 9

Masking or People-Pleasing

Not every child will be comfortable displaying signs of overstimulation due to fear of embarrassment, punishment, or rejection. Some children turn to people-pleasing and mask their discomfort under safe and acceptable social behaviors, like smiling, agreeing to things they don't want to avoid making a scene, and copying the behaviors of others to fit in. Later on, in private or when they are in a perceived safe environment (e.g., at home or in their bedroom), they could have meltdowns. Other children who struggle to release pent-up emotions tend to experience physical symptoms like migraines, stomach cramps, heart palpitations, or insomnia.

When my class went to the arcade, the lights and sounds were too much, but I didn't want my friends to think I was weird. I acted like I was having fun, but when I got home, I cried and stayed in my room all night.

–Sophia, 11

Creating a Sensory Profile for Your Child

The questions above about sensory sensitivities and sensory overload will help you understand your child's sensory world and learn how to respond to their needs. In addition to documenting behaviors and studying their coping mechanisms, you can complete the questionnaire below to identify your child's sensory profile (the specific challenges they are having and how they tend to respond when triggered).

Questionnaire to Identify Your Child's Sensory Profile

Tactile System

1. How does your child react to different textures (e.g., clothing, food, surfaces)?

_____

_____

_____

_____

2. Does your child seek out tactile experiences (e.g., touching, squeezing, or fidgeting with objects)? If so, please describe.

_____

_____

_____

3. How does your child respond to being touched by others (e.g., hugs, gentle touches, and rough play)?

_____

_____

_____

4. Are there specific textures or environments that cause your child distress (e.g., tags in clothes, certain fabrics)?

_____

_____

_____

_____

5. How does your child react to temperature changes (e.g., hot, cold, or wet conditions)?

_____

_____

_____

_____

Auditory System

1. How does your child respond to loud sounds (e.g., sirens, vacuum cleaners, or yelling)?

_____

_____

_____

_____

2. Does your child often cover their ears or become agitated in noisy environments? Please provide examples.

_____

_____

_____

_____

3. How does your child react to conversations or background noise while focused on a task?

_____

_____

_____

_____

4. Are there specific sounds that your child enjoys or seeks out?

_____

_____

_____

_____

5. How does your child manage situations with sudden or unexpected loud noises?

_____

_____

_____

_____

Visual System

1. How does your child respond to bright lights, flashing lights, or strobe effects?

_____

_____

_____

_____

2. Does your child prefer certain colors or visually stimulating environments? Describe their preferences.

_____

_____

_____

_____

3. How does your child react to visual clutter or busy environments?

_____

_____

4. Are there specific visual details your child focuses on or ignores?

_____

_____

_____

_____

5. How does your child respond to screens (e.g., TV, tablets, or phones) in terms of engagement or overstimulation?

_____

_____

_____

_____

Vestibular System (Movement)

1. How does your child respond to spinning, swinging, or jumping activities?

_____

_____

_____

2. Does your child seek out movement opportunities (e.g., climbing or running) or avoid them?

_____

_____

_____

_____

3. How does your child react to changes in balance or quick movements?

_____

_____

_____

_____

4. Are there environments that make your child feel dizzy or unsteady?

_____

_____

_____

_____

5. How does your child respond to riding in vehicles (e.g., cars, buses, or trains)?

_____

_____

_____

_____

Proprioceptive System

1. How aware is your child of their body in space (e.g., bumping into things or needing to be reminded of personal space)?

_____

_____

_____

_____

2. Does your child often seek out deep pressure activities (e.g., squeezing, pushing, or jumping)?

_____

_____

_____

_____

3. How does your child respond to physical challenges (e.g., sports or climbing)?

_____

_____

_____

_____

4. Are there specific movements that your child avoids or seeks out?

_____

_____

_____

_____

5. How does your child react when their body is restricted or confined (e.g., tight clothing, heavy blankets)?

_____

_____

_____

_____

Olfactory System

1. How does your child respond to different smells (e.g., food, perfumes, or cleaning products)?

_____

_____

_____

_____

2. Are there specific scents that your child enjoys or dislikes intensely?

_____

_____

_____

3. How does your child react in environments with strong or unfamiliar odors?

_____

_____

_____

_____

4. Does your child often comment on smells that others may not notice?

_____

_____

_____

_____

5. How does your child respond to smells related to food preparation or other daily activities?

_____

_____

_____

_____

Gustatory System

1. How does your child respond to different flavors (e.g., sweet, sour, bitter, or spicy)?

_____

_____

_____

_____

2. Are there certain foods your child avoids altogether or craves frequently?

_____

_____

_____

_____

3. How does your child react to trying new foods or experiences?

_____

_____

_____

_____

4. Does your child have strong preferences for texture in food (e.g., crunchy vs. smooth)?

_____

_____

_____

_____

5. How does your child cope when faced with unfamiliar or overly strong flavors?

_____

_____

_____

_____

Interoceptive System

1. How does your child communicate their needs (e.g., hunger, thirst, or tiredness)?

_____

_____

_____

_____

2. Does your child struggle to identify when they are feeling uncomfortable or unwell?

_____

_____

_____

_____

3. How well can your child recognize and respond to their emotions?

_____

_____

_____

_____

4. Are there situations where your child seems unaware of bodily signals (e.g., needing to use the restroom)?

_____

_____

_____

_____

5. How does your child respond when experiencing anxiety or discomfort?

_____

_____

_____

_____

After completing the questionnaire, look for patterns indicating hypersensitivity (overreacting to stimuli) or hyposensitivity (underreacting to stimuli). Note specific sensory triggers or experiences that may lead to overstimulation or distress, and consider how these observations align with behaviors you have witnessed.

Use this completed questionnaire, along with your reflections and observations, when discussing your child's sensory profile with their healthcare provider to help them understand their unique sensory needs and challenges.

Advanced Understanding of Sensory Seeking and Avoidance

Differential Diagnosis of Sensory Processing Behaviors

When observing behavioral patterns in children, it can be challenging to determine whether they stem from sensory processing issues or other conditions. Many behaviors associated with sensory seeking or avoidance can resemble symptoms of other disorders, leading to potential misdiagnosis or missed opportunities for appropriate intervention.

Distinguishing Between Sensory and Anxiety-Based Behaviors

Children with anxiety disorders may exhibit behaviors that appear similar to sensory avoidance. For example, a child who refuses to enter crowded spaces might be experiencing sensory overload or social anxiety. The key differences often lie in:

- **Context specificity**: Sensory avoidance typically occurs consistently in the presence of specific stimuli (like loud environments), whereas anxiety may be more variable and situation-dependent.

- **Physical reactions**: Sensory-sensitive children often show immediate physiological responses to stimuli (covering ears, wincing at bright lights) before emotional distress begins, while anxiety reactions may begin with worry and escalate to physical symptoms.

- **Response to sensory modifications**: Children with primary sensory issues often calm quickly when the triggering stimulus is removed, while anxiety may persist even after environmental accommodations.

- **Language used**: When able to communicate, children with sensory sensitivities often describe specific physical discomfort ("It hurts my ears"), while anxious children more frequently express worry about potential outcomes ("What if something bad happens?").

Dr. Lucy Jane Miller, founder of the STAR Institute for Sensory Processing, recommends careful observation of the antecedents (what happens before), behaviors, and consequences to differentiate between sensory and anxiety-driven responses. Many children experience both conditions simultaneously, requiring integrated treatment approaches.

Sensory Behaviors vs. OCD Behaviors

Repetitive behaviors in children with sensory processing issues can sometimes resemble obsessive-compulsive disorder (OCD). Important distinctions include:

- **Function**: Sensory-seeking behaviors (like spinning or touching surfaces) typically provide pleasure or regulatory feedback, while OCD-related behaviors are performed to reduce anxiety or prevent perceived negative consequences.

- **Flexibility**: Children engaged in sensory-seeking behaviors can usually be redirected to alternative sensory inputs, whereas OCD rituals are more rigid and cause significant distress when interrupted.

- **Awareness**: Children with OCD often have insight that their behaviors are excessive or irrational (especially older children), while those with sensory needs typically don't perceive their seeking behaviors as problematic.

According to research by Paula Ricz at Georgetown University, approximately 25% of children with primary sensory processing disorders also meet criteria for OCD, suggesting a potential neurological overlap that requires careful assessment.

Distinguishing Sensory Processing from ADHD

As mentioned in Chapter 1, there's significant overlap between sensory processing issues and ADHD. Additional differentiation points include:

- **Situational inconsistency**: Children with primary ADHD tend to show consistent patterns of inattention across contexts, while children with sensory issues may show excellent attention in sensory-appropriate environments but struggle significantly in overstimulating ones.

- **Response to structure**: Children with sensory processing issues often respond well to sensory-informed environmental modifications, while those with primary ADHD typically require broader behavioral and executive function supports.

- **Calming strategies**: Movement often helps children with ADHD organize their thoughts, while children with sensory issues may need specific types of sensory input (deep pressure, vestibular, etc.) tailored to their sensory profile.

- **Medication response**: Children with primary ADHD typically show improved attention with appropriate medication, while those with primary sensory processing issues may not show the same benefits (though many children have both conditions).

Professional Assessment Tools

Several standardized assessment tools help professionals accurately diagnose sensory processing issues and differentiate them from other conditions:

- **Sensory Processing Measure (SPM)**: Evaluates sensory processing, praxis, and social participation across home and school environments.

- **Sensory Profile-2**: Measures sensory processing patterns and their impact on daily functioning.

- **Sensory Integration and Praxis Tests (SIPT)**: A comprehensive assessment of sensory integration and motor planning.

- **Differential Diagnosis Interview Tool**: A structured clinical interview developed by the STAR Institute that helps identify patterns consistent with sensory processing disorder versus other conditions.

When seeking evaluation, parents should consider professionals who are trained in multiple diagnostic frameworks, not just sensory processing, to ensure accurate identification of underlying issues.

Cultural Considerations in Sensory Processing

Sensory processing doesn't exist in a vacuum—it occurs within cultural contexts that shape how behaviors are interpreted, what interventions are considered appropriate, and how families adapt to sensory differences.

Cultural Variations in Sensory Tolerance

Research indicates that sensory preferences and tolerances vary across cultures, influenced by both genetic and environmental factors:

- A study by Caron et al. (2012) found that children from collectivist cultures showed different baseline sensory reactivity compared to those from individualist cultures, particularly in tactile and auditory domains.

- Research from Korea (Kim et al., 2017) demonstrated that Korean children showed higher tolerance for certain auditory stimuli but lower tolerance for specific tactile inputs compared to North American children, suggesting cultural exposure shapes sensory thresholds.

- A comparative study of Israeli and American children by Engel-Yeger (2010) found cultural differences in sensory seeking behaviors, with Israeli children demonstrating higher tactile and vestibular seeking.

These findings suggest that "typical" sensory processing exists on a cultural continuum, not an absolute scale. When evaluating your child's sensory profile, consider your family's cultural background and how it might influence both your child's sensory experiences and your interpretation of their behaviors.

Cultural Perceptions of Sensory Behaviors

How sensory behaviors are viewed varies dramatically across cultures:

- In some East Asian cultures, quiet attentiveness is highly valued in children, potentially leading to greater concern about sensory-seeking behaviors but less identification of sensory-avoidant patterns.

- Certain cultures place higher value on physical resilience, potentially viewing sensory sensitivities as something to "overcome" rather than accommodate.

- In collectivist societies, behaviors that disrupt group harmony may receive more attention than those affecting only the individual child.

- Some cultural traditions incorporate sensory-rich experiences (spicy foods, loud celebrations, close physical contact) that may present challenges for sensory-sensitive children but provide rich opportunities for gradual exposure.

Understanding these cultural frames helps parents navigate different perspectives among family members, educators, and healthcare providers who may come from diverse cultural backgrounds.

Adapting Interventions for Cultural Contexts

Effective sensory strategies respect and incorporate a family's cultural values and practices:

- **Family-centered approaches**: Rather than imposing standardized Western intervention models, effective therapists work within each family's cultural framework, adapting strategies to align with their values and daily routines.

- **Indigenous healing practices**: Many traditional healing systems incorporate sensory elements that can be integrated with contemporary sensory integration approaches. For example, certain Native American practices incorporate deep pressure, rhythmic movement, and natural sensory environments.

- **Culturally responsive sensory diets**: Sensory activities should incorporate familiar and culturally meaningful elements. For example, a child from a culture with rich textile traditions might respond better to tactile activities using familiar fabrics and textures.

- **Language considerations**: How we describe sensory experiences is deeply influenced by language. When working with multilingual families, exploring sensory vocabulary in the home language often reveals more nuanced descriptions of the child's experiences.

A study by Parham (2015) found that sensory integration therapy was more effective when adapted to incorporate culturally familiar activities and contexts, highlighting the importance of culturally responsive approaches.

Working with Extended Family

Extended family members often play significant roles in children's lives across many cultures, making their understanding of sensory processing crucial:

- **Education approaches**: Consider cultural communication styles when explaining sensory processing to extended family. Some cultures prefer direct, information-focused approaches, while others respond better to narrative explanations or community-based learning.

- **Respecting hierarchies**: In cultures with strong elder respect traditions, approach education about sensory needs in ways that honor family hierarchies while advocating for your child.

- **Finding cultural bridges**: Identify concepts within your cultural tradition that parallel sensory processing ideas. For example, many cultural traditions recognize that children have different temperaments or "constitutions" that require different parenting approaches.

- **Sharing successes incrementally**: In families skeptical about sensory processing concepts, share small successful strategies without requiring acceptance of the entire conceptual framework. Demonstrating what works builds credibility over time.

Dr. Roseann Schaaf of Thomas Jefferson University emphasizes that the most successful sensory interventions account for family culture, not just the individual child's sensory profile. Taking time to understand your family's cultural perspective on sensory behaviors creates a more supportive environment for your child.

Sensory Development Across the Lifespan

While much attention focuses on sensory processing in early childhood, sensory development continues throughout life, with each stage presenting unique challenges and opportunities.

Sensory Processing in Infancy and Early Childhood

The earliest years lay the foundation for sensory development:

- **Infancy (0-12 months)**: Newborns begin with primitive sensory reactions, gradually developing more organized responses. The foundation for interoception develops through responsive caregiving that helps babies recognize internal states (hunger, discomfort, sleepiness).

- **Toddlerhood (1-3 years)**: This period features rapid

sensory integration development. Children actively seek sensory experiences that help organize their nervous systems. Delays in sensory milestone attainment during this period often provide early indicators of sensory processing difficulties.

- **Preschool years (3-5 years)**: Children refine their sensory discrimination and begin developing sensory-based self-regulation strategies. Social implications of sensory differences often become more apparent during this period.

Research by DeGangi and Greenspan suggests that identifying sensory challenges in the first three years provides the greatest opportunity for neuroplastic change, highlighting the importance of early observation and intervention.

Sensory Changes During Puberty

The hormonal and neurological changes of puberty significantly impact sensory processing:

- **Heightened sensitivity**: Many adolescents experience temporary increases in sensory sensitivities, particularly to smell, touch, and sound, due to hormonal fluctuations affecting neural thresholds.

- **Body awareness challenges**: Rapid growth during puberty can disrupt proprioceptive and vestibular processing, requiring adjustment to a changing body.

- **Social sensory challenges**: The increased importance of social acceptance collides with sensory needs, creating complex dynamics (e.g., expectations to wear uncomfortable clothing, tolerate noisy social environments).

- **Self-advocacy development**: Adolescence provides

important opportunities for teenagers to develop language and strategies for managing their sensory needs independently.

For children with pre-existing sensory issues, puberty can exacerbate challenges, requiring updated sensory strategies. Therapists specializing in adolescent sensory processing emphasize the importance of collaborative approaches that respect teens' growing autonomy while providing needed support.

Adult Outcomes in Sensory Processing

Following children with sensory processing differences into adulthood reveals important patterns:

- **Adaptation and compensation**: Many adults with childhood sensory challenges develop sophisticated compensation strategies that mask underlying sensory differences.

- **Career selection**: Adults often gravitate toward occupations compatible with their sensory profiles. For example, those with high sensation-seeking tendencies may choose dynamic, high-stimulation fields, while those with sensory sensitivities often select environments they can better control.

- **Environmental design expertise**: Many adults with sensory processing differences develop exceptional skills in creating optimal personal environments.

- **Ongoing challenges**: For some individuals, certain sensory sensitivities persist throughout life, though the social and emotional impacts often diminish as self-awareness and coping strategies improve.

Longitudinal studies by Dr. Winnie Dunn suggest that early

intervention for sensory processing challenges correlates with better adult outcomes across educational achievement, relationships, and mental health indicators, underscoring the importance of supporting children's sensory development.

Genetic and Neurochemical Foundations of Sensory Behavior

Recent research has begun to illuminate the biological underpinnings of sensory seeking and avoidance patterns, offering new insights into why children differ in their sensory responses.

Genetic Influences on Sensory Processing

Twin and family studies reveal significant genetic contributions to sensory processing patterns:

- Research by Dr. Aud Miller at the University of Colorado found concordance rates of approximately 65% for sensory processing patterns in identical twins compared to 35% in fraternal twins, suggesting substantial heritability.

- Specific genetic variations in serotonin transport genes have been linked to sensory sensitivity, particularly in the auditory and tactile domains.

- The COMT gene, which influences dopamine regulation, shows associations with sensation-seeking behaviors. Variations in this gene affect how quickly dopamine is cleared from synapses, potentially explaining why some children seek higher levels of stimulation.

Parents often notice that their children's sensory preferences reflect their own, though environmental modeling also contributes to these similarities. Understanding the genetic basis of sensory differences helps parents recognize that certain sensory traits are innate rather than the result of parenting approaches.

Neurochemistry of Sensory Seeking and Avoidance

Several neurotransmitter systems play key roles in sensory processing:

- **Dopamine**: This "reward" neurotransmitter drives sensation-seeking behaviors. Children with naturally lower dopamine levels or less sensitive dopamine receptors often engage in more intense sensory-seeking behaviors to achieve neurochemical homeostasis.

- **Serotonin**: This neurotransmitter modulates sensory reactivity and anxiety. Variations in serotonin regulation contribute to differences in sensory threshold and emotional responses to sensory input.

- **GABA**: As the brain's primary inhibitory neurotransmitter, GABA helps filter out irrelevant sensory information. Disruptions in GABA function can lead to sensory over-responsivity as the brain struggles to dampen incoming stimuli.

- **Glutamate**: This excitatory neurotransmitter facilitates sensory signal transmission. Excess glutamate activity can contribute to sensory hypersensitivity and overload.

This neurochemical understanding helps explain why some children appear to "crave" sensory input—they are unconsciously seeking to optimize their neurochemical environment. Similarly, children who avoid certain sensory experiences may be protecting themselves from neurochemical dysregulation.

Autonomic Nervous System Function

The autonomic nervous system (ANS) plays a crucial role in sensory processing:

- **Sympathetic activation**: This "fight-or-flight" branch of the ANS activates during stress or perceived threat. Children with sensory sensitivities often show exaggerated sympathetic responses to non-threatening sensory input.

- **Parasympathetic regulation**: This "rest and digest" system helps calm the body. Research by Dr. Stephen Porges suggests that children with sensory processing challenges often have imbalances in parasympathetic function, affecting their ability to self-regulate after sensory challenges.

- **Autonomic flexibility**: The ability to shift appropriately between sympathetic and parasympathetic states is key to adaptive sensory processing. Many children with sensory challenges show reduced autonomic flexibility, getting "stuck" in activated or withdrawn states.

Heart rate variability (HRV) measurements can provide insights into a child's autonomic function and help guide regulation strategies. Interventions that support parasympathetic activation—like deep breathing, gentle vestibular input, and deep pressure—can help restore autonomic balance during sensory challenges.

Advanced Sensory Assessment Approaches

Beyond the questionnaire included in this chapter, more sophisticated approaches can provide deeper insights into your child's sensory processing patterns.

Ecological Momentary Assessment

Traditional assessments often rely on retrospective reports that may miss important patterns. Ecological Momentary Assessment (EMA) offers a more dynamic approach:

- Using smartphone apps or simple paper logs, parents record sensory reactions as they occur in natural environments.

- These real-time observations capture patterns that might be missed in retrospective questionnaires.

- EMA reveals important contextual factors, such as time of day, preceding activities, or environmental conditions that influence sensory responses.

A simple EMA approach involves creating a chart with columns for:

- Time and setting

- Sensory input (what stimulus occurred)

- Observable reaction (what your child did)

- Intensity rating (1-5)

- Effective soothing strategies

Tracking for even one week often reveals patterns that weren't previously apparent, such as increased sensitivities during transitions or after certain activities.

Physiological Monitoring

Emerging technologies allow measurement of physiological responses to sensory stimuli:

- **Electrodermal activity (EDA)**: Measures small changes in skin conductance that reflect autonomic nervous system activation in response to sensory input.

- **Heart rate variability (HRV)**: Provides insights into autonomic regulation and stress responses during sensory experiences.

- **Cortisol sampling**: Can reveal stress hormone patterns associated with sensory challenges.

While most physiological monitoring occurs in clinical settings, consumer devices like heart rate monitors can provide basic physiological data to correlate with observed behaviors. Some occupational therapy practices now incorporate physiological monitoring to develop more precise sensory diets.

Sensory Challenge Protocols

Structured sensory challenge protocols can reveal specific patterns of response:

- The Sensory Challenge Protocol developed at the STAR Institute systematically introduces sensory stimuli in each sensory domain while monitoring behavioral and physiological responses.

- The Sensory Processing Assessment for Young Children (SPA) uses playful challenges to evaluate sensory responses in natural contexts.

- The Sensory Over-Responsivity scales provide detailed assessment of sensory thresholds across domains.

Parents can create simplified versions of these protocols at home by systematically introducing different sensory experiences and carefully observing responses. For example, you might create a "sound sensitivity assessment" by playing different types of sounds (steady background noise, sudden sounds, complex sounds like music) at various volumes and noting your child's responses.

Food Chemicals and Sensory Behavior: Advanced Considerations

Building on our discussion of food chemicals in Chapter 1, specific dietary factors can significantly impact sensory processing and behavior.

Biogenic Amines and Sensory Reactivity

Certain foods contain naturally occurring compounds called biogenic amines that can influence neurological function and sensory processing:

- **Histamine**: Found in fermented foods, aged cheeses, cured meats, and certain fruits and vegetables. Excess histamine can cause sensory hypersensitivity, especially in children with compromised histamine metabolism.

- **Tyramine**: Present in aged cheeses, cured meats, and fermented foods. Can trigger sensory reactivity and irritability in sensitive individuals.

- **Phenylethylamine**: Found in chocolate, aged cheeses, and fermented foods. May intensify sensory experiences and emotional reactivity.

A study by Rosell-Camps et al. (2013) found that children with sensory processing issues and behavioral challenges showed significant improvement when placed on a low-amine diet, with 71% demonstrating reduced tactile defensiveness and improved attention.

Oxalates and Sensory Symptoms

Oxalates are naturally occurring compounds found in many plant foods that may influence sensory processing in some children:

- High-oxalate foods include spinach, rhubarb, almonds, cashews, cocoa, and sweet potatoes.

- In susceptible individuals, high oxalate levels have been associated with increased tactile sensitivity and irritability.

- A small clinical study by Susan Owens at the University of Arizona found correlations between oxalate levels and sensory hypersensitivity in some children with autism.

While not all children are sensitive to oxalates, those who struggle with persistent unexplained sensory issues despite other interventions may benefit from exploring this dietary factor with appropriate medical supervision.

Implementing Dietary Investigations

Investigating dietary influences on sensory processing requires systematic approaches:

1. **Baseline documentation:** Before making dietary changes, establish clear documentation of current sensory behaviors and reactions using rating scales or tracking tools.

2. **Elimination phase**: Under professional guidance, systematically remove suspected trigger foods for a sufficient period (typically 2-4 weeks).

3. **Challenge phase**: Methodically reintroduce potential triggers one at a time while monitoring sensory responses.

4. **Individualized approach**: Not all children react to the same food chemicals, and not all sensory issues have dietary components. Personalization is essential.

Nutritionist Kelly Dorfman, author of "Cure Your Child With Food," recommends framing dietary investigations as experiments rather than restrictions, involving children in age-appropriate ways and focusing on adding nutrient-dense alternatives rather than just removing foods.

Key Takeaways

- Sensory seeking and sensory avoiding represent two common behavioral patterns in children with sensory processing difficulties. Sensory seekers crave intense stimulation due to higher sensory thresholds, while sensory avoiders find certain stimuli overwhelming due to lower thresholds.

- When supporting a sensory-seeking child, provide structured sensory stimulation, carry sensory toys for outings, transform daily routines into sensory adventures, and offer goal-directed activities that engage their need for stimulation.

- For sensory-avoiding children, gradually introduce challenging sensory experiences, create predictable environments, teach self-advocacy skills, and provide sensory breaks when needed.

- Identifying a child's unique sensory profile requires

careful observation of their sensitivities and how they respond to sensory overload. Understanding both their triggers and preferred coping mechanisms helps tailor effective support strategies.

- Differentiating sensory behaviors from other conditions like anxiety disorders, OCD, or ADHD requires careful observation of context, triggers, and response patterns. Many children experience multiple conditions simultaneously, requiring integrated treatment approaches.

- Cultural factors significantly influence how sensory behaviors are interpreted and addressed. Cultural background shapes sensory tolerances, perceptions of appropriate behavior, and intervention preferences. Effective approaches honor family culture while supporting the child's sensory needs.

- Sensory processing evolves across development, with each life stage presenting unique challenges and opportunities. Puberty often disrupts established sensory patterns due to hormonal changes and shifting social expectations.

- Genetic and neurochemical factors contribute significantly to sensory processing patterns. Variations in genes affecting neurotransmitters like dopamine, serotonin, and GABA influence whether a child tends toward sensory seeking or avoidance.

- Advanced assessment approaches like Ecological Momentary Assessment, physiological monitoring, and structured sensory challenges can provide deeper insights into a child's sensory processing patterns beyond traditional questionnaires.

- Specific food chemicals, including artificial additives, biogenic amines, and naturally occurring compounds like oxalates, can significantly impact sensory processing and behavior in susceptible children. Systematic dietary investigation may be beneficial when sensory issues persist despite other interventions.

Now that you have a deeper understanding of sensory seeking and avoiding behaviors, Chapter 3 will explore how to create sensory-friendly environments at home that support your child's regulation and comfort.

Chapter 3:

The Importance of a Sensory-Friendly Home

High five to those who are struggling in a world that is too loud, too bright, overwhelming and still continue to shine each day. You are brave and doing amazing. That takes a lot of strength.
   −Unknown

If You Could Design a Perfect Room, What Would It Look Like?

My perfect room would be a place where everything feels just right—not too loud, not too bright, not too busy. The walls wouldn't be crazy colors because bright ones make my head feel all buzzy and jumpy. I'd have a big, soft beanbag chair that swallows me up when I sit in it, like a hug without someone actually touching me (because sometimes hugs feel too tight, even when I like them). My bed would have one of those heavy blankets that make my body feel safe, kind of like when Mom tucks me in super tight, and I don't want to move because it feels so good.

I'd have my own little hiding spot, maybe a tent or a tiny nook with soft pillows and twinkly lights that aren't too bright. No one could come in unless I said they could, because sometimes I just need to be alone to make my brain feel calm again. If my room was like this, I think I wouldn't feel so tired all the time from trying to deal with everything around me.

—Milo, 9

Reducing Sensory Overload

When we think of busy, loud, bright, or congested spaces, we seldom refer to our own homes. But did you know your child can be overstimulated by the abundance of sensory inputs in your house? Remember that sensory overload occurs when your child exceeds the maximum sensory information they can process at any time. If your living environment exposes them to too much stimulation, they can have frequent meltdowns or avoid certain areas of the home.

Since each child will be stimulated and triggered by different sensory experiences, it's important to assess what areas or objects in your home make your child feel distressed. Below are common things that children with sensory processing difficulties have challenges with (Kori, 2022).

Lighting

Every room in your home typically needs lighting in the evenings or throughout the day (depending on the design). However, most bulbs tend to be extremely bright. A child who has sight sensitivities may feel blinded by room lighting and may squint, cover their eyes, and experience regular migraines. Opting for dimmable lights can help you adjust the brightness whenever your child enters a room. If you cannot find dimmable bulbs, you can turn off the main lights and use candles, standing lamps, and warm LED battery-powered lamps to make your home cozy. During the day, you can block out sunlight by installing shutters to control how much light comes in from your windows.

Air Conditioning

Air conditioning and room fans are used all year round to improve air circulation and keep the home cool. Nevertheless, they can be sensory triggers for some children, particularly those with auditory and temperature sensitivities. While the average child barely notices the sound of a circulating fan or air conditioning system, those whose sense of hearing is heightened can detect the sound and often find it unbearable. Additionally, getting the "temperature just right for a child who is sensitive to heat and cold can be tricky. For some households, the option to go without a fan or air conditioning is impossible due to the climate or design of the home. The best solution could be to switch to a noiseless product or place blankets in every room when your child feels cold.

Clutter

Research has shown that the human brain thrives in an orderly and decluttered space. Clutter has been found to raise stress and anxiety levels while also reducing productivity and triggering avoidance coping strategies (e.g., bingeing on TV or snacking on unhealthy foods) (Sander, 2019). Children with sensory processing challenges need environments that are structured, organized, and predictable to prevent overstimulation. Visual distractions like busy walls, toys spread across the floor, piles of laundry, or having too many furniture pieces and accessories can lead to sensory overload. Dirt can also be a trigger for some children. Thus, it's important to keep every area clean and tidy.

Color Choices

Color psychology suggests that different hues affect our moods and behaviors. There are some colors, like red, that are known to energize us, while other colors, like blue, make us feel relaxed (Cherry, 2024). Children with visual sensitivities notice color combinations and can become overstimulated when there are too many "loud" colors and not enough "soft" colors. For example, a playroom designed to include every color of the rainbow might seem like a child's dream, but for a sensory avoidant child, it can be too chaotic. This doesn't mean that your home needs to be dull; you can continue to use color, but do so sparingly. For example, choose one bold or accent color in a room and keep other colors neutral. Moreover, if you are going to include geometric patterns, use them on accessories like scatter cushions rather than covering your wall with them.

Layout and Flow

Another common sensory trigger is the layout and flow of each room. Children with vestibular and proprioceptive sensory challenges may get frustrated from having to climb over objects or be mindful not to walk into objects obstructing their path.

Moving in and around the home shouldn't be stressful for your child. Besides adjusting the layout of each room, reducing furniture is also key. Think practically about the pieces you absolutely need and limit accessories and other "nice to have" items, which could create clutter or make it hard for your child to get from point A to point B.

Sound Management

Homes can get noisy when hallways and rooms have echoes, floorboards creak, appliances are plugged in, TVs and other sound-generating devices are on, and family members are talking. The collection of these sounds can sometimes become too much for auditory-sensitive children. If you notice that your child frequently complains about noise, there are a few home improvements you can make, such as using thick rugs, carpets, curtains, and acoustic wall panels to drown out noise. To mask unexpected sounds like cars driving past or dogs barking, get your child a pair of noise-canceling headphones or use a white noise machine.

Providing Predictability and Comfort

A great question that you can ask yourself to continuously improve your home environment for your child is: *What would make my child feel safe?* Physical and emotional safety help your child regulate their nervous system, which lowers stress and calms their mind. Prioritizing comfort and predictability can enhance your child's sense of security, allowing them to mentally "switch off" and feel supported at home. In the sections below, you'll learn ways to transform your home into a comfortable and predictable place that your child loves to spend time in.

Establishing Consistent Routines

Every child with sensory processing challenges behaves better in a structured environment. Creating consistent daily routines helps your child anticipate upcoming tasks, move through transitions with less resistance, and have defined expectations they can work toward achieving. In other words, when their brain is scattered and everything starts feeling overwhelming, following a routine keeps their frontal lobe activated so they can feel a greater sense of control (Yumna, 2025).

Here are guidelines for establishing sensory-friendly routines for your child.

Identify Your Child's Sensory Needs

Your child's routines should be based on their unique sensory needs. Designing them in this way can lead to fewer cases of overstimulation and power struggles. Your child's needs will be informed by their sensory profile, which includes information about their preferences, intolerances, and sensitivities. When considering your child's sensory needs, think about how you can incorporate their personality, communication style, special interests, and how they desire to be supported. For example, some children need constant encouragement to feel motivated to complete tasks, while others prefer to start and finish tasks without parental guidance.

Utilize Visual Schedules

Some children struggle to remember and follow instructions without some kind of visual supplement, such as a chart, calendar, or diagram. If your child is a visual learner, make sure that you have printouts of their daily routines. Include photos of cartoon characters completing the tasks and other symbols that make it easier for them to understand what to do. Another suggestion is to create a rewards system chart that outlines what daily tasks your child needs to complete to earn a star next to their name or earn points that accumulate into tangible prizes.

Get the Timing Right

Timing helps your child learn and predict behaviors, making them less anxious to get through the day. For instance, being punctual with mealtimes, nap times, play time, bedtime, and homework time makes your child feel in control. Using timers and countdowns to alert your child of upcoming transitions can further assist them in mentally and emotionally preparing themselves to follow the routine. For example, instead of abruptly entering the play room and instructing your child to go to bed, you can start a countdown 15 minutes before they need to take action, and gently remind them every 5 minutes of the upcoming task and what they need to do to prepare (e.g., "You have 5 minutes remaining. Please may you start packing up your toys").

Incorporate Preferred Activities

Sensory avoidant children don't look for entertainment in their daily routines. For them, boring routines that follow the same agenda each day feel safe. However, sensory-seeking children become restless when they aren't presented with variety. While they don't mind performing mandatory tasks each day, they need to engage in preferred activities to feel motivated. For example, if your child enjoys outdoor play, ensure you have scheduled time for this activity in their routine. Include both structured and unstructured activities so they feel stimulated (e.g., planning a fun outdoor game and giving them 15 minutes of free time to explore the garden).

Provide Choices Within Limits

Children with sensory challenges tend to be strong-willed because they desire to protect themselves from various perceived threats in their environment. To reduce power struggles, it's important to give your child choices (wherever possible). This provides a sense of control, even though you have regulated the options. For example, a child with textile sensitivities may insist on dressing themselves to avoid uncomfortable clothing. By presenting two outfit options they can choose from and giving them free rein to choose accessories, they can feel in charge of their style. Other daily tasks where choices work well are meal options, music options during carpool, TV show options, and play options.

Using Familiar and Comforting Items

Another way to create a comfortable home environment for your child is to encourage them to discover and frequently use soothing and nurturing items. The truth is, you won't always be physically present to help your child self-regulate. These familiar and comforting products play the role of a caregiver in your absence.

For example, touch-based comfort items might include a weighted blanket, stuffed animal, or fidget toys. Sound-based comfort items could be earplugs, a soothing music playlist, or a recording of a familiar voice (e.g., parent or grandparent) singing a nursery rhyme or sharing encouraging words. Choose sentimental items that your child has shown interest in or curiosity about so that they naturally gravitate toward them when they are feeling overwhelmed. You can also carry these items with you when visiting relatives and public places, or traveling long distances.

Plan for Sensory Breaks

Children with sensory processing difficulties, even the most energized sensory-seekers, need downtime during the day. This is especially important when they start school and have more responsibilities to manage. At home, you can incorporate sensory breaks into your child's routine. For instance, after every 30 minutes of activity, schedule a 10-minute break.

You can choose whether to structure these breaks or not. For example, some breaks might simply be used to drink water and go to the restroom, while others allow your child to choose what they want to do. Your child's mood is a great indicator of what they need during their sensory breaks. For example, when they are hyperactive, it may be a good idea to send them outside to play and expend energy. However, when they are lethargic, presenting a creative task like painting or a relaxing task like lying down or napping can be just what they need (make sure you rule out basic needs like thirst and hunger before suggesting activities).

Personalizing the Home for Sensory Needs

Earlier in the chapter, we examined how aspects of your home could be contributing to your child's sensory overload. We highlighted key factors, such as lighting, sound, clutter, color choices, air conditioning, and layout, which impact how safe and comfortable your child feels at home. In this section, we get more details about room-to-room adaptations that you can make to create a sensory-friendly home.

Room-by-Room Adaptations

It's easy to use the term "sensory-friendly home," but what exactly does it entail? Prepare to learn practical ways to update each room of your home to accommodate your sensory-sensitive child. As their parent, you know best, so feel free to make additional modifications (or leave out some suggestions) for an enhanced experience.

Bedroom

Sensory-friendly bedrooms prioritize comfort and relaxation. Think of floating on a cloud or enjoying the soothing sea breeze on a quiet beach. Your child should feel a sense of relief stepping into this space, and the freedom to drop their mask and be themselves. Here are tips to consider when making adaptations:

- **Soothing wall paint and wallpapers:** Starting with the walls, be intentional about the color palette you choose. Opt for colors that are psychologically calming, such as neutral shades like white, beige, baby pink, baby blue, mint green, or lavender. When choosing wallpaper, go for simple designs that allow your child's eyes to rest. For example, you can install a background of the night sky or a natural landscape.

- **Soft, adjustable lighting:** Incorporate warm lights with different settings (e.g., shades of warm colors). Instead of having only one light source, like the one on the ceiling, consider using floor lamps, desk lamps, and bedside lamps that create a soothing environment.

- **Comfortable and weighted bedding:** The feel of the bed linen and pillows matters to your sensitive child. Opt for soft, breathable material like pure cotton or silk and weighted blankets if they enjoy the sensation of gentle pressure on their body. Consider the type of garments your child goes to sleep in, too. If your child is prone to overheating, purchase light, loose, and breathable pajamas that won't feel constricting.

- **Sound and aromatherapy:** To get your sensory-seeking child ready for bed, you can softly play background music such as ambient music or nature sounds. For a sensory-avoidant child, purchase a white noise-canceling machine to drown out distracting sounds. Specific scents like lavender, vanilla, and chamomile are also known to evoke a calming environment. If your child is not sensitive to these scents, buy scented candles, fabric spray, fragrance diffusers, or a humidifier to circulate the scent throughout their room.

- **Cozy play area:** Your child's room can be a safe place where they retreat whenever they are overstimulated by being around family members. To ensure they have all the sensory toys and tools to self-regulate, create a cozy play area with comfortable furniture. Personalize this space by including a reading nook for an avid reader, a play tent for a child who loves pretend play, and soft bean bags and pillows for a child who enjoys lying down and taking naps.

Bathroom

Bathtime can be a delightful experience for children, but it can sometimes be challenging for those with sensory needs. Even though your child may not spend a lot of time in the bathroom each day, this particular area of the home can feel triggering. Here are sensory-friendly ways to improve their bathroom experience.

- **Adapt bathtime for your child's sensory needs:** Allow your child to choose between taking baths or showers. If they prefer baths, install handrails and a nonslip bath mat inside the tub for better stability. If they enjoy showers, switch to handheld showerheads. These devices allow your child to have greater control over water pressure and flow direction, especially if they find a steady stream of water overwhelming.

- **Reduce unpleasant smells and textures:** Another important aspect of bath time is managing smells and textures that can trigger sensitivities. It is advisable to choose unscented soaps to prevent overwhelming odors that your child may find difficult to handle (scented products can sometimes cause discomfort or irritation). Along with the soaps, select soft, fluffy cotton towels that feel gentle against the skin, and throw away rough or old towels that may feel uncomfortable. When bathing your child, you can use a soft hand towel or sponge that won't feel scratchy.

- **Stress-free tooth brushing:** Traditional toothbrushes can be harsh and may create unpleasant sensations in your child's mouth. One solution is to try using electric toothbrushes, as they often come with different vibration settings. These toothbrushes can provide a gentle cleaning experience while also allowing your child to choose the intensity that suits them best. Lower settings can reduce discomfort, while higher settings may be useful for a sensory seeker who feels comfortable with more sensation.

- **Temperature awareness:** Sudden changes in water temperature can be startling and uncomfortable. To help ease this transition, water temperature should be adjusted gradually. Starting with lukewarm water allows your child's sensitive body to acclimate slowly. You might begin with a small amount of warm water and gradually add hotter water as needed. This methodical approach can help them feel more in control and reduce anxiety surrounding the temperature change.

Kitchen

The kitchen is typically a communal space in the home where family members gather to enjoy meals together and reconnect during the day. Due to the chaos of movement and meal prepping that happens in this area, it's essential to find ways to reduce stress and congestion. Here are smart ways to make your kitchen sensory-safe for your child.

- **Minimize mealtime stress:** One helpful tip to reduce mealtime stress for your child is to provide options for what they want to eat. Limit it to two choices that are simply variations of the meal you have already prepared (e.g., they can choose to replace broccoli with another green vegetable like spinach or asparagus). Another suggestion is to use divided plates that have different sections that keep various foods separate. This can reduce anxiety for a child with specific texture preferences.

- **Introduce new foods in a sensory-friendly way:** Getting your child to try new foods can be challenging. A good approach is to encourage what some call "food play." This means letting your child touch and smell the ingredients before they actually eat them. Get involved in the experience and play with the food too. Lead with curiosity to make them feel safe exploring new scents and textures. Only after they feel comfortable should they take a small bite. This gradual introduction can make mealtimes more enjoyable and less stressful.

- **Avoid foods and chemicals that can be triggering:** Some common culprits include highly processed foods that contain artificial additives, preservatives, and even artificial colors and flavors. These substances can sometimes create discomfort and may lead to behavioral issues or heightened sensitivity in some children (Buka et al., 2011). Instead, focus on fresh, whole foods. For example, fruits like bananas and apples, or vegetables like carrots and cucumbers, can be great choices. They are loaded with nutrients and are less likely to contain triggers that might affect sensory experiences negatively.

- **Support oral sensory needs:** If your child seeks oral stimulation, they may benefit from chewy or crunchy snacks. Foods such as raw veggies, pretzels, or specific types of chewy candies can help satisfy that need. You might consider having a snack drawer filled with these items, making it easy for them to grab something satisfying when they need it.

- **Reduce noise in the kitchen:** Cooking can create several sounds that might be overwhelming for your child, like clanging pots, whirring blenders, and more. To mitigate this, consider using soft-close cabinet hardware that prevents loud banging when cabinets close, making the kitchen quieter overall.

Living Room

The living room can be a vibrant space where the family frequently meets to spend quality time together. If this space feels overstimulating for your child, they may not enjoy hanging out there too often. To create an inclusive living room, it's critical to make it sensory-friendly. Here are some adaptations to consider:

- **Provide movement opportunities:** Sensitive children, particularly those who are sensory seekers, cannot keep still for long periods. They need to constantly move their bodies. If this sounds like your child, incorporating movement opportunities can be a great way to keep them engaged. Consider including a small trampoline, an indoor swing (hanging or free-standing), or creating a designated play area in the living room.

- **Manage screen sensitivities:** Reduce screen the brightness of the TV set to improve your child's eye comfort (many devices allow you to adjust the brightness settings). Additionally, consider buying them a pair of blue-light sunglasses to protect their eyes from harsh light exposure, which often leads to discomfort. Alternatively, adjust the brightness of your child's PC monitor, tablet, or other electronic device to reduce eye strain.

- **Provide sensory-friendly furniture:** Adapt your living room by including seating for your sensitive child, such as bean bag chairs or rocking chairs, which can make the space more inviting and supportive of different preferences. The gentle motion of a rocking chair can be calming for children who may feel anxious or restless; thus, it can double as a self-regulating tool.

- **Keep fidget-friendly items nearby:** When everyone is gathered in the living room and the atmosphere starts feeling overwhelming for your child, teach them to reach out for their fidget toys to self-soothe. Keep a basket filled with fidget tools like stress balls, fidget spinners, and textured toys within reach so they can entertain themselves and temporarily zone out whenever they choose. Fidgeting can also provide a simple way to engage the senses constructively while watching television or during social gatherings with family and friends.

Creating Sensory-Friendly Zones

The section above provided a thorough breakdown of how to adapt each room of your house to accommodate your child's sensory needs. Beyond these adaptations, it's important to create safe spaces around the home where your child can visit whenever they desire to be alone or need to calm down.

As the name suggests, sensory-friendly zones are rooms or areas that soothe your child's senses and provide the type of experience they crave (some children desire speed and action while others need more downtime, or a combination of both). If you cannot convert a spare room into a sensory-friendly zone, find a corner in their bedroom or in the garden where you can set up sensory tools and equipment.

Depending on the kind of stimulation your child enjoys, here's how you can design their sensory-friendly zone:

Active Rooms

This area or room is ideal for a sensory-seeking child who needs plenty of stimulation. It should provide opportunities for a variety of movements (e.g., jumping, climbing, and stretching) while also stimulating their prefrontal cortex through creative and cognitive exercises like painting, completing puzzles, and a costume box for engaging in pretend play. The aim is to fill the room or area with tools that encourage body awareness and learning.

Here's an exhaustive list of items you'll need to create the ultimate active room for your sensory-seeking child:

- sensory swing

- balance board

- crash pad or soft landing mat

- ball pit

- climbing wall or rock climbing holds

- mini trampoline

- sensory table with various textures

- easel with canvas for painting (or blank wall for freestyle painting)

- cognitive games like board games, Scrabble, and puzzles

- exercise balls or stability balls

- play mats with different textures

- obstacle course equipment (e.g., cones, tunnels)

Calming Rooms

Calming rooms or areas are suitable for sensory-avoidant children who are often overwhelmed by the average amount of stimulation. They are safe spaces that are muted and tranquil and promote slow and relaxing activities. Since the world requires that they be "switched on" all the time, entering a calming room or area allows them to decompress, tune into their emotions, and self-regulate. Unlike active rooms, where the intention is for children to have a lot to do, calming rooms invite them to simply be.

The following list will guide you on creating a relaxing, calming room for your child:

- weighted blankets or lap pads

- noise-canceling headphones

- soft lighting options (e.g., Himalayan salt lamps, fairy lights)

- fidget toys (e.g., stress balls, fidget spinners)

- calming scents (e.g., essential oil diffusers, scented pillows)

- soft seating (e.g., bean bags, floor cushions)

- visual stimulation (e.g., bubble tubes, lava lamps)

- calm music or nature sounds (via speakers or sound machines)

- sensory pillows or textured blankets

- privacy curtains or tent structures for cozy spaces

- massage tools (e.g., massage balls, handheld massagers)

- therapeutic swings or rocking chairs

You may have a child who has days when they want more stimulation and days when they want to do nothing. Creating a hybrid room or area that combines active and calming tools and equipment can be a great option for them. If you have an older child, feel free to consult them when designing their sensory-friendly zone so they feel a sense of control and pride in having a space that they can claim as their own.

Advanced Concepts in Creating Sensory-Friendly Environments

Measurable Outcomes for Home Interventions

Creating a sensory-friendly home is an ongoing process that requires evaluation and adjustment. By establishing measurable outcomes, you can determine which strategies are working effectively and where modifications may be needed.

Creating Baseline Measurements for Sensory Behaviors

Before implementing home modifications, document your child's current sensory responses to establish a clear baseline:

- **Frequency tracking**: Record how often sensory reactions occur in specific environments. For example, note how many times per day your child covers their ears in the kitchen or refuses to enter certain rooms.

- **Duration measurements**: Time how long sensory reactions last. Does your child take 15 minutes to calm down after a sensory trigger or two hours?

- **Intensity scaling**: Create a simple 1-5 scale to rate the intensity of your child's reactions, with 1 being mild discomfort and 5 being complete meltdown.

- **Functional impact assessment**: Note how sensory challenges affect daily living skills, like whether your child can complete morning routines independently or requires significant support due to sensory barriers.

Dr. Lucy Jane Miller recommends collecting baseline data for at least two weeks before making environmental changes. This period allows you to identify patterns that might otherwise be missed, such as time-of-day effects or sensory accumulation over the course of the day.

Tools for Tracking Sensory Reactions at Home

Several tools can help you monitor your child's sensory responses to home environments:

- **Sensory mapping**: Create a floor plan of your home and mark areas where your child experiences sensory comfort or distress. Use color-coding to identify zones that need modification.

- **Sensory reaction logs**: Maintain a simple journal documenting when, where, and how your child experiences sensory challenges at home. Include notes about potential triggers and successful calming strategies.

- **Visual analog scales**: For older children, create visual scales that allow them to indicate their sensory comfort level in different areas of the home.

- **Video monitoring**: With appropriate privacy considerations, occasional video recording can capture sensory reactions your child may not be able to articulate, revealing subtle triggers or early warning signs.

- **Wearable technology**: For research-minded families, simple wearable devices that track heart rate or skin conductance can provide objective measures of physiological arousal in different home environments.

These tracking tools offer valuable insights into the effectiveness of your sensory-friendly modifications and can help you create a more precise sensory diet (which we'll explore further in Chapter 8).

Determining If Environmental Modifications Are Working

After implementing sensory-friendly changes to your home, systematic evaluation helps determine their effectiveness:

- **Comparative measurement**: Repeat your baseline measurements after making environmental changes, looking for reductions in frequency, duration, or intensity of sensory reactions.

- **Functional improvements**: Note whether your child can now complete activities or use spaces that were previously challenging.

- **Engagement metrics**: Track how long your child can comfortably remain in modified environments compared to before.

- **Sleep quality indicators**: Monitor whether sensory-friendly bedroom adaptations improve sleep onset, duration, or quality.

- **Quality of life measures**: Consider broader impacts, such as reduced family stress, increased independence, or greater social engagement at home.

Research by Dr. Shelly Lane suggests that successful environmental modifications typically show measurable improvements within 2-3 weeks, though some children may require longer adjustment periods.

When to Adjust or Try Different Approaches

Environmental interventions aren't one-size-fits-all, and adjustments are often necessary:

- **Response plateau**: If improvements stop after initial progress, consider whether additional sensory layers need addressing or if your child has developed tolerance to the modifications.

- **Developmental changes**: Children's sensory needs evolve as they grow, requiring periodic reassessment of environmental supports.

- **Seasonal variations**: Many sensory-sensitive children experience different challenges across seasons due to changes in light, temperature, and activity patterns.

- **Sensory sensitivity shifts**: Children may develop new sensory sensitivities or outgrow others, necessitating environmental updates.

Occupational therapist Winnie Dunn recommends a quarterly review of your home's sensory accommodations, with major reassessments during developmental transitions like starting school, entering adolescence, or after significant life changes.

Technology and Sensory Processing in the Home

The digital revolution has transformed home environments, introducing both challenges and opportunities for children with sensory processing needs.

Impact of Screen Time on Sensory Systems

Digital devices provide intense multi-sensory stimulation that affects neurological processing:

- **Visual processing impact**: Blue light from screens can be particularly triggering for visually sensitive children. Research by Dr. Melinda Chang shows that screen exposure before bedtime reduces melatonin production by up to 50% in some children, disrupting sleep-wake cycles that are crucial for sensory regulation.

- **Auditory effects**: Unpredictable sounds from digital media can overwhelm auditory processing systems. Studies indicate that the rapid auditory transitions in many games and videos can increase stress hormones in sensitive children.

- **Vestibular and proprioceptive concerns**: Extended screen time reduces physical movement, limiting essential vestibular and proprioceptive input that helps organize sensory systems. Occupational therapist Angie Voss notes that children require at least 3 hours of active movement daily for optimal sensory integration.

- **Arousal regulation challenges**: The dopamine-triggering nature of many digital experiences can create dysregulation that persists after screen time ends. Research by Dr. Victoria Dunckley found that electronic screen syndrome can mimic or exacerbate sensory processing disorder symptoms.

This doesn't mean technology should be eliminated, but rather managed thoughtfully as part of a balanced sensory diet.

Beneficial Technologies for Sensory Regulation

Many technological innovations can actually support sensory processing and regulation:

- **Noise-canceling headphones with customizable settings**: Advanced models allow selective filtering of sounds, enabling children to block disruptive frequencies while remaining aware of important communications.

- **Smart lighting systems**: Programmable lighting with adjustable intensity, color temperature, and transition settings can match illumination to your child's sensory needs throughout the day.

- **White noise and sound machines with adaptive features**: These technologies can mask disruptive environmental sounds with customizable background noise that matches your child's auditory preferences.

- **Sensory apps**: Applications like "Calm Counter" for emotional regulation or "Sensory Timer" for transitions provide visual supports for children navigating sensory challenges.

- **Weighted or compression clothing with cooling technology**: Innovative designs now combine deep pressure benefits with temperature regulation for improved comfort.

A study by the Center for Sensory Processing Disorder found that thoughtfully selected technologies improved home regulation for 72% of sensory-sensitive children, particularly when integrated with non-digital sensory supports.

Smart Home Features That Reduce Sensory Triggers

Smart home technology offers unprecedented ability to create adaptive sensory environments:

- **Automated routines**: Program lighting, temperature, and sound changes to occur gradually, reducing the sensory impact of environmental transitions.

- **Voice-activated controls**: Allow children to modify their environment without requiring fine motor skills that may be challenging during sensory distress.

- **Customized sensors**: Motion sensors can activate calming sensory features when a child enters specific areas, providing proactive support.

- **Programmable thermostats**: Create micro-environments at different temperatures throughout your home to accommodate temperature sensitivities.

- **Smart door sensors**: Receive alerts when your child enters potentially overwhelming sensory environments, allowing timely intervention.

- **Soundproofing technology**: New-generation sound-dampening materials and white noise systems can create sound-neutral spaces tailored to auditory sensitivities.

Interior designer Carolyn Feder, who specializes in sensory-friendly spaces, recommends starting with one smart home feature at a time, thoroughly evaluating its impact before adding additional technology.

Apps and Tools for Managing Sensory Environments

Digital tools can help parents and children monitor and modify sensory experiences:

- **Decibel meter apps**: Measure and track noise levels in different areas of your home to identify auditory hotspots needing modification.

- **Light meter applications**: Quantify lighting intensity to create consistent visual environments that avoid triggering photosensitivity.

- **Environmental tracking systems**: Platforms like "SenseSafe" allow documentation of sensory triggers and successful accommodations across environments.

- **Visual schedule apps**: Support predictability with customizable visual schedules that prepare children for sensory transitions within the home.

- **Sensory regulation reminder systems**: Applications that prompt sensory breaks or calming activities based on customized schedules.

Technology consultant and parent advocate Robert Hillman suggests creating a "sensory control center" where children can independently access and adjust digital tools that support their sensory needs, fostering self-advocacy and regulation skills.

Neurological Impact of Environmental Design

The physical environment directly affects brain function and sensory processing. Understanding these connections allows for more targeted home design strategies.

How Environmental Factors Affect Neural Processing

Research in environmental neuroscience reveals powerful connections between physical spaces and brain function:

- **Sensory gating mechanisms**: Environments with multiple competing stimuli tax the brain's ability to filter irrelevant sensory information. Neuroimaging studies by Dr. Marco at UCSF show that children with sensory processing difficulties have reduced neural filtering capacity, making cluttered or chaotic environments particularly challenging.

- **Autonomic nervous system effects**: Specific environmental features directly impact sympathetic (alerting) and parasympathetic (calming) nervous system function. High ceilings, expansive spaces, and cool colors activate parasympathetic responses, while confined spaces, warm colors, and angular features tend to trigger sympathetic arousal.

- **Stress hormone production**: Chronic exposure to adverse sensory environments increases cortisol production, which further sensitizes neural reactions to sensory input. Dr. Esther Sternberg's research demonstrates that sensory-friendly environments can reduce cortisol levels by up to 23% in sensitive individuals.

- **Neurotransmitter balance**: Environmental design affects the production of neurotransmitters that regulate mood and arousal. Natural light exposure increases serotonin production, while high-contrast, chaotic environments can trigger excessive dopamine and norepinephrine release.

Understanding these neurobiological connections helps explain why environmental modifications can have profound effects on behavior and emotional regulation.

Evidence-Based Design Elements for Sensory Integration

Specific design approaches have demonstrated neurological benefits for sensory processing:

- **Multisensory integration zones**: Research by Dunn and Brown suggests that environments offering controlled multisensory experiences strengthen neural integration across sensory systems. Creating designated areas with complementary sensory elements (like tactile walls with coordinated lighting and subtle aromatherapy) builds cross-modal sensory processing.

- **Neurologically calming color schemes**: Studies indicate that blue and green wavelengths activate parasympathetic nervous system responses. Architectural psychologist Sally Augustin recommends using these colors in 60% of a room's visual field to promote sensory regulation.

- **Fractal-based designs**: Environments incorporating fractal patterns (repeating patterns found in nature) have been shown to reduce physiological stress markers. These patterns, present in natural elements like leaves and tree branches, have a $1/f$ noise distribution that the human brain processes more efficiently than either highly regular or chaotic patterns.

- **Spatial sequencing**: Arranging spaces in gradients of sensory intensity—from low to moderate stimulation—

creates neurologically supportive transition zones. This progressive exposure strengthens neural habituation to potentially challenging sensory experiences.

- **Proprioceptive engagement features**: Environmental elements that provide proprioceptive feedback strengthen connections between sensory and motor neural networks. Architectural features like climbing walls, stepping stones, and varied textures promote this integration.

A compelling study by the Academy of Neuroscience for Architecture found that implementing these evidence-based design elements reduced sensory-related behavioral incidents by 47% in educational environments, suggesting similar benefits for home settings.

Creating Neurological "Reset" Spaces

Even the most thoughtfully designed home environment can become overwhelming. Dedicated reset spaces provide neurological refuge:

- **Physiological calming nooks**: Small, enclosed spaces with reduced sensory input allow the nervous system to return to baseline. These spaces should be free from visual clutter, have sound dampening, subdued lighting, and comfortable seating that provides deep pressure.

- **Sensory differentiation zones**: Areas with distinctive sensory qualities help the brain clearly differentiate between environmental contexts, reducing the cognitive load of processing ambiguous sensory information. Each zone should have a distinct sensory signature through lighting, texture, color, and sound.

- **Predictable sensory mapping**: Consistent sensory features in specific locations build neural expectations that support sensory processing. For example, always having soft textures in bedrooms and more stimulating textures in play areas helps the brain prepare appropriate responses.

- **Graduated challenge pathways**: Create environmental progressions that gradually increase sensory demands, building neural tolerance through controlled exposure. For example, a hallway might transition from dim to brighter lighting, allowing the visual system to adapt incrementally.

Neuropsychologist Dr. William Greenough emphasizes that these environmental features support "experience-dependent neuroplasticity," allowing children's brains to develop more robust sensory processing capacities through structured environmental interaction.

Specialized Environmental Adaptations

Beyond the basic modifications covered earlier in this chapter, specialized adaptations can address specific sensory processing challenges.

Advanced Lighting Solutions

Lighting profoundly impacts sensory processing, affecting everything from circadian rhythms to stress levels:

- **Spectral tuning**: Different light wavelengths affect neurological function differently. Blue-enriched light enhances alertness but can trigger sensory sensitivity, while amber wavelengths promote calm. Programmable LED systems can adjust spectral output throughout the day to match your child's needs and natural circadian rhythms.

- **Flicker-free technology**: Even imperceptible flicker from fluorescent or cheap LED lighting can trigger visual processing issues and contribute to sensory overload. Investing in high-quality, truly flicker-free lighting reduces this neurological stress.

- **Dynamic lighting transitions**: Abrupt lighting changes can trigger sensory distress. Programmable systems that gradually transition between lighting states (taking 30-60 seconds to change) significantly reduce sensory reactions during environmental shifts.

- **Indirect lighting strategies**: Direct light creates strong contrasts and shadows that can overload visual processing. Bouncing light off walls or ceilings creates more diffuse illumination that many visually sensitive children find calmer.

- **Biophilic lighting designs**: Lighting patterns that mimic natural daylight progression support healthy cortisol and melatonin production, which in turn stabilizes sensory processing. These systems gradually shift color temperature and intensity throughout the day.

Lighting designer Lisa Heschong's research demonstrates that thoughtfully designed lighting can reduce stress biomarkers by up to 17% in children with sensory sensitivities, suggesting its powerful role in creating supportive environments.

Advanced Acoustic Engineering

Sound affects both psychological and physiological functioning. Strategic acoustic design can transform challenging spaces:

- **Frequency-specific sound management**: Different

sound frequencies affect the nervous system in unique ways. Low-frequency sounds (below 100 Hz) can be physically felt and often trigger vestibular reactions, while high-frequency sounds (above 2000 Hz) are more likely to cause auditory defensiveness. Targeted acoustic treatments can address specific problematic frequencies.

- **Acoustic zoning**: Creating distinct acoustic zones allows sound-sensitive children to regulate their auditory exposure. This approach might include a "high sound tolerance zone" for music and active play, a "moderate sound zone" for conversation and daily activities, and "low sound sanctuaries" with enhanced sound absorption.

- **Reverberation control**: Excessive reverberation (sound reflection) significantly impairs speech processing and increases cognitive load. Adding sound-absorbing materials to reduce reverberation time below 0.5 seconds can dramatically improve auditory processing comfort.

- **Sound masking systems**: Sophisticated sound masking differs from white noise by producing acoustically engineered sounds that specifically mask disruptive environmental noises without adding to the overall sound level. These systems can be particularly helpful in open-plan homes.

- **Impact insulation**: Footfalls and object movements create structure-borne sound that can be especially troubling for children with hyperacusis. Enhanced impact insulation in flooring and wall construction reduces these vibrations.

Acoustic engineer Julian Treasure notes that proper acoustic design can reduce stress hormones by up to 27% in noise-sensitive individuals while improving attention and information processing.

Temperature and Air Quality Considerations

Sensory processing is significantly affected by thermal comfort and air quality:

- **Microclimates within homes**: Creating areas with distinct temperature zones accommodates children who experience thermal regulation differently. Consider maintaining a cooler sleep environment (65-68°F), moderate temperature common areas (70-72°F), and warmer cozy corners (74-76°F) for children who seek thermal comfort.

- **Humidity control**: Relative humidity affects both tactile comfort and respiratory sensations. Many sensory-sensitive children benefit from maintained humidity between 40-50%, which supports comfortable breathing without creating dampness that can trigger tactile defensiveness.

- **Air filtration**: Environmental particulates and volatile organic compounds can trigger sensory defensive reactions, particularly in chemically sensitive children. HEPA filtration combined with activated carbon can reduce these triggers while improving overall health.

- **Negative ion generation**: Research suggests that negative air ions may improve sensory processing and attention. Natural features like water fountains and plants increase negative ion concentration and can create more sensory-friendly air quality.

- **Natural ventilation patterns**: Creating gentle air circulation that mimics natural breezes (rather than forced air systems) provides subtle vestibular input that many children find organizing without becoming overwhelming.

Environmental health researcher Dr. Nancy Gerber's work

indicates that improved indoor air quality correlates with a 22% reduction in sensory defensiveness behaviors, making this an important but often overlooked aspect of sensory-friendly design.

Spatial Sequencing for Sensory Regulation

How spaces connect and transition impacts sensory processing demands:

- **Sensory gradients**: Arranging spaces from low to moderate to high sensory intensity helps prevent sudden sensory shifts. For example, creating a transition space between a quiet bedroom and a stimulating living area allows the nervous system to adapt gradually.

- **Circulation pathways**: Well-designed movement routes through the home can significantly impact sensory regulation. Circular pathways without dead ends provide proprioceptive input through movement and support emotional regulation during sensory distress.

- **Threshold design**: Doorways and transitions between spaces can be designed as sensory preparation zones. Slight changes in flooring texture, ceiling height, or lighting prepare the nervous system for environmental changes.

- **Prospect and refuge**: Incorporating both open areas (prospect) and cozy, protected spaces (refuge) addresses the fundamental need for both exploration and safety. These complementary spatial types support sensory regulation by allowing children to modulate their exposure to environmental stimulation.

- **Compressible spaces**: Rooms with adjustable elements like sliding partitions, curtains, or movable furniture can be expanded or contracted to match a child's changing sensory needs throughout the day.

Architectural psychologist Grant Hildebrand's research on preferred environments suggests that these spatial patterns connect with innate neurological preferences, helping explain why thoughtfully sequenced spaces feel intuitively supportive for sensitive nervous systems.

Material Selection Based on Sensory Impact

Materials in the home environment directly affect sensory experiences through texture, temperature, acoustic properties, and even smell.

Tactile-Responsive Surfaces

Surface materials create the tactile landscape of your home:

- **Tactile mapping**: Create intentional variations in texture throughout your home that align with functional needs. Smoother textures in areas requiring focus and calm, more stimulating textures in zones meant for alertness and engagement.

- **Temperature conductivity**: Materials with different thermal properties create varied tactile experiences. Wood, cork, and natural fibers feel warm to touch, while metals, stone, and some ceramics create cooling surfaces. Thoughtful placement of these materials can address specific tactile preferences.

- **Texture transitions**: Gradual changes between different textures are less jarring to the tactile system than abrupt transitions. Consider how surfaces connect and overlap to create more integrated sensory experiences.

- **Tactile libraries**: For children with tactile sensitivities, creating sample collections of materials used in the home allows preview and practice with new textures before encountering them in larger applications.

- **Biophilic materials**: Natural materials like wool, cotton, wood, and stone have complex, varied textures that provide rich sensory information without overwhelming tactile processing. These materials often feel intuitively comfortable for sensory-sensitive individuals.

Research from the Touch Research Institute demonstrates that appropriate tactile environments can reduce tactile defensiveness behaviors by up to 35% in sensitive children while supporting development of more refined tactile discrimination.

Non-Toxic Materials and Sensory Health

Chemical sensitivities often accompany sensory processing issues, making material toxicity an important consideration:

- **VOC-free finishes**: Volatile organic compounds from paints, varnishes, and adhesives can trigger sensory defensive reactions. Zero-VOC products eliminate these triggers while improving overall neurological health.

- **Natural fiber furnishings**: Synthetic materials often outgas chemicals that affect sensitive nervous systems. Natural fibers like wool, cotton, hemp, and flax provide sensory-friendly alternatives that typically trigger fewer reactions.

- **Solid woods vs. composites**: Many composite wood products contain formaldehyde and other binders that can affect neurological function. Solid woods with natural finishes create healthier sensory environments.

- **Silicone alternatives to plastics**: Many plastic products contain phthalates and BPA that affect hormonal systems involved in neurological development. Medical-grade silicone provides a more sensory-friendly alternative for food storage, dinnerware, and tactile tools.

- **Plant-based cleaning solutions**: Chemical cleaning products leave residues that sensitive children may detect through smell or touch. Plant-based alternatives create a more neutral sensory environment.

Environmental medicine specialist Dr. William Rea documented significant improvements in sensory tolerance following reduction of chemical exposures in home environments, with some children showing normalized sensory processing after comprehensive environmental medicine approaches.

Multisensory Material Considerations

The most effective material choices consider cross-modal sensory impacts:

- Acoustic properties: Materials affect not just how spaces sound but how the body experiences sound. Soft, porous materials absorb sound waves, creating calmer acoustic environments, while hard, reflective surfaces amplify and sharpen sounds. Strategic placement of absorptive materials in key locations can transform the acoustic experience.

- **Visual-tactile congruence**: Materials whose visual appearance aligns with their tactile qualities create more coherent sensory experiences. Incongruent materials (looking soft but feeling hard, for example) create confusing sensory input that taxes processing systems.

- **Olfactory emissions**: All materials have characteristic odors that affect the sensory experience of spaces. Natural materials typically have more complex but milder scent profiles, while synthetic materials often emit stronger, more persistent odors. Consider how material choices affect the overall olfactory landscape of your home.

- **Temporal changes**: How materials change over time affects sensory experiences. Natural materials typically develop patinas that change gradually, while synthetic materials often degrade in ways that create sensory aversions. Consider the full lifecycle of materials when making selections.

- **Maintenance requirements**: Materials that require harsh cleaning chemicals may introduce sensory triggers during maintenance. Select materials that can be maintained with sensory-friendly cleaning approaches.

Material scientist and sensory design expert Jillian Pritchard Cooke recommends conducting a "sensory scan" of materials before installation, evaluating their multisensory impacts across all relevant domains rather than just their primary sensory characteristics.

Creating Truly Inclusive Family Spaces

Sensory-friendly homes must work for all family members, not just those with sensory processing challenges. Balancing diverse sensory needs creates harmony rather than friction.

Meeting Competing Sensory Needs

Families often include individuals with different—sometimes conflicting—sensory preferences:

- **Time-sharing approaches**: When family members have incompatible sensory needs, scheduling can be an effective solution. Establish times when different sensory environments prevail, using visual schedules to make these transitions predictable for everyone.

- **Spatial zoning**: Designate specific areas that prioritize different sensory profiles. This might include a high-stimulation zone for sensory seekers and a low-stimulation retreat for those easily overwhelmed.

- **Adjustable environments**: Create spaces with easily modifiable sensory features that can adapt to different users. Lighting with dimmers, sound systems with volume controls, and movable furniture allow quick environmental tuning.

- **Sensory buffering strategies**: When completely separate spaces aren't possible, create sensory buffers between areas with different stimulation levels. Transition spaces, partial walls, or curtain dividers can help manage sensory spillover.

- **Family sensory profiles**: Document each family member's sensory preferences and sensitivities to identify both shared preferences and potential conflict points. This awareness helps create intentional compromises rather than accidental clashes.

Family therapist Dr. Sarah Schoen emphasizes that successful sensory-inclusive homes require explicit conversations about sensory needs, teaching all family members (including those without sensory challenges) to recognize and respect diverse sensory experiences.

Universal Design Principles for Sensory Inclusion

Universal design creates environments usable by all people without adaptation or specialized design:

- **Flexibility in use**: Spaces that accommodate a wide range of sensory preferences provide options rather than single solutions. For example, a family room might include both bright and dim lighting zones, hard and soft seating, and open and sheltered areas.

- **Simple, intuitive use**: Environmentally complex spaces tax sensory processing. Logical layouts with clear visual cues reduce cognitive load and support all users, especially during sensory overload.

- **Perceptible information**: Important information should be communicated through multiple sensory channels. Visual, tactile, and auditory cues provide redundant information, ensuring everyone can access necessary information regardless of sensory processing style.

- **Tolerance for error**: Forgiving environments accommodate sensory-related variations in movement, coordination, and attention. Rounded corners, stable furniture, and spill-resistant surfaces create safer spaces for all family members.

- **Low physical effort**: Environments that minimize unnecessary effort preserve cognitive and sensory processing capacity. Thoughtful placement of frequently used items and elimination of unnecessary steps reduces the overall sensory burden.

Universal design expert Rosemarie Rossetti notes that homes designed with sensory inclusion in mind benefit not just family members with diagnosed sensory issues but all occupants, creating environments that support optimal functioning for diverse nervous systems.

Aesthetic Considerations in Sensory Design

Sensory-friendly spaces can be beautiful as well as functional:

- **Wabi-sabi principles**: This Japanese aesthetic embraces simplicity, natural materials, and the beauty of imperfection. Its emphasis on calming visual environments with subtle variation aligns perfectly with sensory-friendly design.

- **Biophilic design elements**: Incorporating natural patterns, materials, and relationships creates environments that are both aesthetically pleasing and sensory-regulating. These elements tap into innate preferences for natural environments that have evolved over human history.

- **Harmony without monotony**: Balanced environments provide sensory interest without chaos. Consider the principle of "cohesive diversity"—varied elements united by common threads of color, texture, or form.

- **Personalized beauty**: Include elements that reflect your family's unique aesthetic preferences and cultural values. Personal meaning enhances emotional connection to spaces, supporting overall regulation.

- **Evolving designs**: Create spaces that can grow and change with your child's developing sensory profile. Modular systems, adaptable storage, and flexible layouts accommodate emerging preferences.

Interior designer Carolyn Feder emphasizes that sensory-friendly environments should never sacrifice beauty for function: "When sensory design is done well, the result isn't just tolerable—it's genuinely beautiful in a way that resonates deeply with the human nervous system."

Key Takeaways

- Creating a sensory-friendly home is essential for children with sensory processing difficulties. By reducing potential triggers and providing comfortable spaces, you can help your child feel safe, regulated, and ready to engage with the world.

- Common sensory triggers in the home include bright or flickering lights, clutter, background noise, strong odors, and uncomfortable room temperature. Identifying and minimizing these triggers creates a more supportive environment.

- Providing predictability through consistent routines, familiar items, and scheduled sensory breaks helps your child feel secure and reduces anxiety about upcoming transitions or activities.

- Each room in your home can be adapted to support sensory needs. Bedrooms benefit from soothing colors and adjustable lighting, bathrooms from temperature controls and sensory-friendly bathing options, kitchens from thoughtful food presentation, and living rooms from diverse seating options.

- Creating designated sensory zones—both active spaces for sensory seekers and calming areas for sensory avoiders— gives your child appropriate outlets for their specific sensory needs.

- Measurable outcomes help evaluate the effectiveness of

environmental modifications. Tracking frequency, duration, and intensity of sensory reactions before and after changes allows for data-informed adjustments.

- Technology can both challenge and support sensory processing. Mindful screen time management, smart home features, and specialized apps provide powerful tools for creating adaptive sensory environments.

- The neurological impact of environment is significant, with specific design elements directly affecting nervous system function. Evidence-based approaches like multi-sensory integration zones, biophilic design, and strategic color use support healthier neural processing.

- Advanced considerations in lighting, acoustics, temperature control, and material selection can transform challenging spaces into supportive environments that promote sensory integration and regulation.

- Creating truly inclusive family spaces requires balancing diverse sensory needs through time-sharing, spatial zoning, adjustable environments, and thoughtful application of universal design principles.

Your home environment shapes your child's daily sensory experiences and significantly impacts their development, behavior, and emotional well-being. The modifications explored in this chapter provide a foundation for creating spaces that support your child's unique sensory profile while meeting the needs of the entire family.

In the next chapter, we'll explore how sensory play and purposeful activities can build your child's sensory integration skills, creating not just a supportive environment but active opportunities for growth and development.

Chapter 4:

Sensory Play and Activities for Development

Strong-willed children become adults who change the world as long as we can hang on for the ride and resist the temptation to take the spirit out of them.
–Sarah Stogryn

What's Your Favorite Way to Play, and How Does It Make You Feel?

Sometimes, people don't understand why I don't like playing with toys the way other kids do. I don't always want to build things or make up stories. I like to feel things. The way the water runs through my fingers. Water doesn't ask me to sit still or follow rules. It moves with me.

When I splash it, it splashes back. When I swirl it around, it listens. When I put my hands in a bowl of warm water, my whole body feels safe, like a big sigh after a long day. That kind of play makes my brain feel happy. I wish people would let me play in my own way without trying to make me do it "right."

–Lena, 5 years old

Exploring the World of Sensory Play

In the previous chapter, we explored the different ways children are impacted by sensory processing difficulties and the signs of overstimulation they may exhibit. We also took a tour inside the home and highlighted ways to make the environment sensory-friendly. In this chapter, we uncover the importance of sensory play in achieving two goals: helping your child self-regulate and enhancing their cognitive, emotional, and social development.

Sensory processing dysfunction isn't something that can be cured. However, with ongoing therapy and prioritizing play, your child can enhance their tolerance for stimuli that aggravate them. Sensory play exposes your child to activities that engage their eight senses and encourage cognitive growth (Cleveland Clinic, 2022). They learn to go beyond their comfort zone and experiment with new tools, skills, and strategies.

While the focus is on having fun while learning, sensory play is a form of gradual exposure therapy where your child is slowly and deliberately taught how to embrace their sensory triggers and be comfortable performing various tasks that previously felt intolerable, such as doing jumping jacks or playing in a sand pit. Occupational therapists are the go-to doctors for guiding your child on this exhilarating and resilience-building journey; however, as the parent, you play an indispensable role in incorporating sensory play at home, ensuring that every playful activity becomes a teachable moment.

The Benefits of Sensory Play

You might wonder what makes sensory play different from other forms of play. The key differentiator is that sensory play aims to assist your child in meeting developmental milestones. It is intentional rather than random and seeks to activate dormant or impaired brain connections so your child feels more confident exploring and engaging with their surroundings. Moreover, sensory play stimulates the following key developmental areas.

Language Skills

During sensory play, your child is introduced to new objects, games, and techniques that expand their vocabulary. Additionally, since activities are based on strengthening specific sensory systems, you can teach your child how to communicate their needs. For example, when engaging in an exercise related to food, you can take the opportunity to teach your child how to accept and refuse food politely, how to communicate needs like hunger or thirst, and how to indicate their preferences or intolerances.

Fine Motor Skills

Fine motor skills are movements that activate smaller muscle groups like hands, wrists, and feet. If you notice that your child struggles with this particular skill (e.g., they cannot tie their shoe laces or hold a pencil properly), you can use tactile play, a form of sensory play, to train them. For instance, you might build a LEGO tower together, take turns pouring water into a cup using a plastic jug, or mix batter with a big spoon. Without realizing it, your child strengthens these smaller muscles, making it easier for them to perform coordinated movements.

Gross Motor Skills

If fine motor skills activate smaller muscles, then gross motor skills are responsible for activating the larger muscle groups like arms, legs, and the torso. Children who struggle with balance and body awareness tend to have poor gross motor skills. A big part of sensory play involves getting your child moving. Through active games like hopscotch, Simon says, or catch, you can train them on how to walk with good posture, balance on one leg, and develop their eye-hand coordination.

Cognitive Growth

Strengthening your child's cognitive function helps them with tasks like emotional regulation, modifying behaviors, and problem-solving. Essentially, they learn how to assess real versus perceived threats and weigh the outcomes of their responses to situations. Sensory play can enhance your child's cognitive growth by encouraging curiosity, experimentation, and cracking problems on their own. They can apply these skills in different social situations to achieve positive outcomes.

Social Skills

Sensory play can be an individual activity; however, parents are encouraged to get involved in the action. If you can't make it, invite your child's siblings or peers to play with them so they can learn how to manage their behaviors in social interactions. Through group activities, your child gets to practice social skills like how to take turns, communicate needs effectively, and respond appropriately to social cues. It can also be helpful for your child to watch how other children engage with their senses so they can overcome some of their fears.

Incorporating Sensory Play Into Your Child's Routine

The best way to improve your child's sensory sensitivities is to make sensory play an integral part of their daily routine. Doing this will require some planning to ensure that playtime is structured and has an educational component. Below are tips to consider when integrating sensory play into your child's schedule:

Engage All Sensory Systems

You might be tempted to target specific senses that your child has trouble with. However, the best sensory play activities incorporate all senses. This is because your child encounters various stimuli in their home and school environment, not one or two. Thus, teaching them how to recognize and appropriately engage their senses prepares them for the world. When planning an activity, think of ways to include the eight senses.

For example, you might decide to introduce your child to a nature sensory bin (a storage box full of different sensory items). Here's how the bin stimulates all eight senses:

- **Touch:** Get your child to explore the different textures of items in the bin, such as the softness of flowers, the roughness of bark, and the graininess of sand or dirt.

- **Sight:** Include brightly colored items like flowers, leaves, and pebbles to engage your child's visual senses. They can also observe different shapes, colors, and forms.

- **Hearing:** Add elements like shaken pebbles or poured water to create sounds. You can also ask your child to listen to the rustling of leaves or the patter of water.

- **Smell:** Adding natural items like flowers and herbs to your bin provides diverse scents. Encourage your child to identify different smells as they dig through the bin.

- **Taste:** Introduce edible items like fresh herbs or fruits that your child can smell and then taste to experience flavors directly related to the activity (ensure the ingredients are familiar to them to avoid resistance).

- **Proprioception:** Provide tools like scoops, tweezers, or tongs to pick up some items in the bin. This helps your child develop their sense of body awareness as they grasp, lift, and transport items.

- **Vestibular:** If the activity is conducted in an outdoor setting, allow your child to move around the environment (e.g., bending, reaching, crawling) to engage their balance and spatial awareness.

- **Interoception:** Discuss how different textures, temperatures, and scents feel, helping your child recognize their bodily sensations as they engage in the activity.

Encourage Language Development

Each sensory play activity should help your child develop their speaking abilities. Before you begin, explain the task to your child using simple language. This helps them gain a better understanding of what's expected of them. Feel free to include visual aids like pictures to improve comprehension. If you will be using new objects that your child hasn't been exposed to, describe what it is and demonstrate what they're used for (e.g.,

"These are called scissors. We use scissors for cutting paper. Can you say 'scissors'?")

During activities, frequently ask your child to describe their sensory experiences. Here, you can simply focus on the five basic senses (sight, smell, touch, hearing, and taste). For example, while doing finger painting, you can ask your child:

- What colors do you see?

- What sounds can you hear outside?

- How does the paintbrush feel on your hands?

- What does the paint smell like?

- What does the paint taste like (when using homemade edible gel paint)?

For some activities, you'll have an opportunity to ask your child about their physiological experiences. For example, after instructing your child to carry a weighted backpack across the garden, you can ask them to describe how their body feels, such as "My chest feels tight" or "My throat feels dry." You can build on this by inviting your child to make a request, such as "My throat feels dry. May I please have a glass of water?"

Incorporate Calming Activities

Sensory play doesn't always need to include intense activity; it can also be used to help your child self-soothe or relax after a long day. For example, before bed, you can run your child a soothing bath with essential oils to help them destress or lie on a picnic blanket outside and watch the stars. Other calming sensory activities to promote during the day include:

- reading stories to your child in a soft voice

- performing light body stretches

- blowing bubbles in water using a straw

- going on a relaxing walk with your pet

- running your child's feet under warm, soapy water

- pouring your child a cup of chamomile tea

Sensory Activities for Each System

Parents are generally encouraged to expose their children to as many sensory systems as each activity can accommodate. However, at times, especially when your child is showing increasing frustration with particular senses, focusing on tasks and games that develop this specific type of stimulus can be helpful. You may even decide to schedule days or whole weeks that are dedicated to exploring targeted senses (e.g., Week 1 can explore the tactile system, and Week 2 can examine the auditory system).

The following sections give you ideas on sensory activities based on five sensory systems (vestibular, proprioceptive, tactile, auditory, and visual play). Feel free to modify these exercises to suit your child's needs, preferences, and personality.

Vestibular Play

The vestibular system focuses on all things related to body movement and balance. Thus, vestibular play involves fun activities that stimulate your child's under-functioning or over-functioning sense of coordination. Some of the skills that your child learns while engaging in this type of play include spatial awareness, maintaining balance, and controlled movements. Below are suggestions of activities to try with your child.

- **Tumbling towers:** Sensory-seeking children will love this game. The aim is for them to see how far they can push themselves on a swing before they reach their limit. Bring an empty ice-cream tub with you to the park or garden (if you have a swing set). Place the tub on the ground closer to the swing and challenge your child to reach it. When they do, move it a few inches farther; continue to do this until they can no longer reach it (or when the swinging starts becoming risky).

- **Hammock swinging:** Sensory-avoidant children may feel comfort swinging without having to make big swooshing movements with their body. Hammock swinging promotes gentle and controlled movement. You can step inside with your child (they can lie on top of you or beside you) and begin swaying the hammock. Encourage them to bring a book with them or carry headsets to listen to music to provide a positive distraction if the elevation of the hammock feels uncomfortable.

- **Pillow obstacle course:** This fun swinging activity accommodates both sensory-seeking and sensory-avoidant children. Find a spacious place indoors where you can set up piles of pillows and create an obstacle course. Have a start and end point, and guide your child through the course. Include a timer for your sensory-seeking child to make the activity more competitive. Provide hand support throughout the course for your sensory-avoidant child.

Proprioceptive Play

The proprioceptive system helps children identify the form, size, and strength of their bodies. Sensory-seekers often desire deep pressure and resistance, whereas sensory avoidants dislike any kind of force placed on their bodies. When your child engages in proprioceptive play, they can learn skills like coordination, self-regulation, and gentle physical contact. Below are activities that can enhance this particular sensory system.

- **Labor-based activities:** Sensory-seeking children love to feel deep pressure on their bodies. Playing games that require them to carry or push heavy objects can be stimulating. For instance, you might create a game where your child needs to carry a basket of toys or clothes from one location to another, or scoop dirt with a spade and load a wheelbarrow, then push it to a certain place. Another fun activity is to dress your child in multiple layers of clothing and challenge them to complete a normal task like sweeping (the resistance can feel gratifying).

- Animal walks and poses: A fun game suitable for sensory seekers and avoidants is recreating animal poses or pretending to be certain animals and walking around (you can design this similar to a game of charades with animal flashcards that your child can read from; your task is to guess what animal they are acting out). This activity allows your child to experiment with different body movements, understand how their muscles and joints function, and learn how to enter different postures or use a variety of gestures.

- **Handshake training:** Teach your child how to recognize their own strength by guiding them on giving handshakes. Role-play scenarios where they need to greet different types of people, such as a doctor or a friend. Show them how to make formal, firm handshakes and explain how they are appropriate to use with adults. With friends, they can create cool, secret handshakes. What's great about this activity is that it can help your child with regulating how much physical force they use on others.

Tactile Play

The tactile sensory system is responsible for your child's experience with touch; essentially, how things feel when they contact their skin. Since your child is required to carry, handle, or work with various objects, materials, and ingredients, it can be helpful to train your child to be comfortable with a wide range of textures. Below are sensory activities that can stimulate or improve your child's sensitivity to touch.

- **Sensory bins:** Surprise and engage your sensory-seeking child by creating sensory bins. In a basket or storage container, place textured items such as a smooth pebble, sandpaper, wooden spoon, and any other item that feels extraordinary. Blind fold your child and guide their hand inside the bin. The challenge is for them to name each item correctly without seeing what it is. You can also allow your child to enjoy unstructured play by exploring the items inside the bin alone.

- **Messy play for desensitization:** If you have a child with touch sensitivity, gradually exposing them to messy textures can be therapeutic since it helps them overcome their fears. The aim is to start small and build as they become more familiar with the items. For example, you might present sand in a box and ask your child to look at it and describe what they see. Thereafter, they may smell the sand or touch it with their fingers (if this is too uncomfortable, give them a spoon or cup to swirl it around or scoop it). Once your child is comfortable with dry products like sand, pasta, or swatches of fabric, introduce them to wet products like whipped cream, slime, or dough.

- **Tactile pathways:** Walking through a tactile pathway is a fun indoor or outdoor activity that children with various sensory difficulties will enjoy. This is simply a guided path made of different textures like grass, bricks, carpet, a puddle of water, pillows, and bubble wrap. Start by explaining the route your child needs to take and timing them on how quickly they can complete it (you may need to guide your sensory-avoidant child through the path).

Auditory Play

Auditory play can be beneficial for children who may be sensitive to sound. These activities help them get comfortable with hearing foreign noises or not getting startled by loud sounds. Moreover, this type of play can sharpen your child's sense of hearing and develop active listening skills. You may notice that their response times improve, and they carry out instructions without requiring repetition. Below are activities that you can practice with your child to enhance their auditory system.

- Playing musical instruments: Teach your child how to play a musical instrument of their choice. It could be the piano, drums, guitar, or violin. By playing an instrument, your child will learn to tolerate low and high sound frequencies, thereby regulating auditory sensitivity.

- **Musical chairs:** This fun game is suitable for sensory-seeking and avoidant children. To play, arrange a few chairs in a straight line and play upbeat music. Instruct your child to circle around the chairs until the music stops. Your child is supposed to rush to the closest open chair and sit down. Play this game with a group of children to turn it into a memorable experience—and a competitive one for your sensory-seeking child!

- **Guess the sound:** Here is another activity that enhances listening and comprehension skills while improving sound sensitivity. On your laptop or phone, play a list of nature and animal sounds, which your child is supposed to name correctly. They might shout out the answer or write it down on paper (depending on the skill you're trying to teach).

Visual Play

Visual play focuses on developing your child's sense of sight. They may struggle with frequent migraines due to the blinding light emitted by screens, sunlight, or fluorescent lights from their classroom. Through these activities, they can improve their ability to focus on objects, which can positively impact their reading and comprehension skills. Below are sensory activities to develop your child's sight.

- **Color sorting games:** Play this matching game to teach your child how to recognize different colors. Sit in the playroom and give your child a minute to find as many specific colored items as possible that they need to bring to you. Encourage them to create different piles for each color to improve visual processing.

- **Mirror play:** To develop your child's body language recognition, play a variety of mirror games, such as mimicking your facial expressions or interpreting what your gestures are signaling (e.g., crossing arms might signal being angry). You can also quiz your child or role-play how they would respond to certain body language. For example, you might ask, "What do you do when a friend crosses their arm; do you continue playing or ask them what's wrong?"

- **Screen-free play:** One of the causes of eye strain, blurry vision, and poor eye coordination is excessive screen time. According to research, 50–60% of children experienced computer vision syndrome, a collection of eye problems caused by prolonged screen use, during the pandemic due to spending a significant amount of time on their devices (Cleveland Clinic, 2023). Incorporating screen-play daily through activities like going on nature walks, having a tea party, or playing board games, you can reduce the risk of sight-related disorders.

DIY Sensory Projects

Many of the sensory tools and equipment recommended by therapists, such as weighted blankets, fidget toys, and sensory balls, are available for purchase online. However, to save costs and expand your inventory of sensory products, you can try creating your own. In most cases, all you need are recyclable materials around the house and craft supplies to make objects your child will love.

Below are some DIY sensory projects to build at home.

Homemade Sensory Board

Sensory boards offer plenty of stimulation for small children who are curious about different textures, materials, and shapes. They can also be a great way to develop children's fine motor skills, since many of the items can be pinched, twirled, or brushed. Besides enhancing tactile sensory processing, these boards also stimulate children's vision, encouraging them to recognize colors, patterns, and peculiar objects.

Purchasing a sensory board online can be expensive, so it's recommended that you design your own. Plus, using common household and natural items on your child's board can help them recognize more objects in their environment, creating a greater sense of safety. Here is how you can make your own sensory board:

Start by gathering the following materials:

- A large piece of cardboard or a sturdy wooden board

- Various sensory items, which can include:

    ○ assorted fabric scraps (felt, cotton, or satin)

- natural materials (pine cones, leaves, small stones)
  - buttons and zippers
  - string or yarn
  - bubble wrap
  - mirrors (small, shatterproof)
  - sandpaper (various grits)
  - craft foam or sponge pieces
  - water beads or gel balls
- Wood glue or a hot glue gun
- Scissors or a craft knife

Follow these instructions to build your board:

1. Start by cutting the cardboard or wooden board to your desired size for the sensory board. A good size is between 30×30 cm and 60×60 cm.

2. Gather the materials and decide on a layout that will engage your child's senses. By keeping items in separate blocks, you can try to keep your board neat and structured.

3. Attach the materials onto the board, one block at a time. Use glue or a hot glue gun for a sturdy hold.

4. Allow each section to dry before starting on the next.

5. Arrange materials in a manner that stimulates your child's visual and tactile sensory function. For example, create a contrast of colors and add materials in various textures and sizes.

6. Create sections with bubble wrap for a popping sensation, and sandpaper for a contrasting gritty texture.

7. If you plan to use water-based items, create a small, safe container that will hold them without spilling.

8. Once all the materials are attached, give the board a few moments to dry. Then, test all the components to ensure they are securely fastened.

If you need more inspiration on the type of materials to attach to the board, here's an expanded list of items your child will appreciate:

- tinsel or sequins for sparkle
- musical instruments (small bells or whistles)
- velcro strips for sticking and peeling
- sponges or scrub pads for scrubbing sensations
- plastic tubes or straws for rolling
- rubber bands for stretching
- scented oils or herbs for aroma exploration

Weighted Lap Pads

Weighted lap pads are calming tools that provide gentle pressure for children who need proprioceptive stimulation. Having a weighted pad on their laps can feel like receiving a warm hug, especially when they are stressed, emotionally dysregulated, or struggle to pay attention. It provides the same soothing effect as sucking a thumb or cuddling with a stuffed animal.

There's no need to purchase weighted lap pads when it's so simple to design your own at home. Here are the guidelines to commence this exciting project.

To make a lap pad, you'll need these materials:

- fabric (cotton, flannel, or other soft materials)
- poly-pellets (or other stuffing materials—refer to the list below)
- sewing machine (or needle and thread)
- scissors
- measuring tape or ruler
- straight pins or fabric clips
- iron (optional, for pressing seams)

Once you have gathered your materials, follow these Instructions:

1. Decide on the size of the lap pad and cut two pieces of fabric to the desired dimensions, allowing for seam allowances (about 1 inch on each side).

2. Next, sew the fabric pieces together. Place the two fabric pieces right sides together, pin around the edges, and sew, leaving an opening on one side for turning and stuffing.

3. Carefully turn the sewn fabric right side out through the opening.

4. Fill the pouch with poly pellets. To avoid making a mess, use a funnel or a small container to direct the pellets inside until they reach your desired weight. Ensure there is an even distribution of the pellets.

5. Once the pouch is filled, fold in the edges of the opening and sew it closed using a needle and thread or a sewing machine.

Below are substitutes that you can use to fill your weight lap pad that cater to different sensory needs:

- rice (for a rough texture)

- dried beans (for weight and texture variation)

- sand (for a heavier feel)

- soft fleece scraps (for a soft, cuddly experience)

- lavender or other scented herbs (for fragrance and a calming effect)

Calming Glitter Jars

A great self-soothing tool that you can create with your child is the glitter jar. This tool is built to improve emotional regulation by providing a positive distraction while your child calms down. In busy public spaces or during long-distance travel, the glitter jar can be used to keep them peacefully preoccupied.

Here are the guidelines to complete this fun and creative project (remember to include your little helper if they are old enough to handle materials).

To make your glitter jar, gather these materials:

- clear plastic or glass jar with a lid (mason jar or empty pickle jar works great)

- water (preferably warm)

- glitter (various colors and sizes)

- clear glue or glycerin (to help the glitter swirl)

- funnel

- food coloring (optional)

- hot glue gun (optional)

When you have the materials ready, follow these instructions:

1. Start by spreading all materials on a flat surface.

2. Place the funnel in the mouth of the jar and begin to pour in water until the jar is about three-quarters full.

3. Add clear glue or glycerin to the water. This will help the glitter float and swirl as desired. Mix the combination of water and glue or glycerin well.

4. Add as much glitter to the jar as desired. You can experiment with different colors and thicknesses for a unique effect.

5. If you like, you can add a few drops of food coloring to achieve a specific color for your glitter jar (perhaps your child's favorite color).

6. Carefully screw on the lid or close the jar tightly. You may want to use a hot glue gun around the edge of the lid to prevent spills.

7. Shake the jar gently to mix the contents, and watch the glitter swirl for a mesmerizing effect.

Typically, glitter is the main material used inside glitter jars, but here are other suitable materials that you can add to make the jar more stimulating:

- confetti
- beads
- tiny shells
- water gel beads
- buttons
- glow-in-the-dark paint or glitter

Advanced Perspectives on Sensory Play

Research-Backed Interventions for Sensory Development

While sensory play has intuitive appeal, understanding the research behind different approaches helps parents prioritize the most effective activities for their child's specific needs.

Evidence Supporting Sensory Integration Therapy

Sensory integration therapy, originally developed by occupational therapist Dr. A. Jean Ayres, has evolved to include a range of play-based interventions:

- A landmark randomized controlled trial by Schaaf et al. (2014) demonstrated that individualized sensory integration therapy significantly improved goal attainment and reduced need for caregiver assistance compared to standard care for children with autism and sensory processing challenges.

- Research by May-Benson and Koomar (2010) found that sensory-based interventions led to improvements in sensory processing, motor skills, socialization, and attention among children with various developmental challenges.

- A meta-analysis by Bodison and Parham (2018) identified specific sensory integration therapy components that have stronger evidence bases, particularly those involving active engagement, just-right challenges, and success-oriented activities.

The most effective sensory integration approaches share several key characteristics:

- **Active participation**: The child is engaged as an active collaborator rather than a passive recipient.

- **Intrinsic motivation**: Activities tap into the child's natural interests and drive for mastery.

- **Just-right challenges**: Tasks provide the optimal level of challenge—not too easy, not too difficult.

- **Opportunity for success**: Activities are structured to ensure the child experiences success, building confidence and willingness to tackle new challenges.

- **Therapeutic alliance**: A trusting relationship between the child and adult provides emotional safety for sensory exploration.

These principles can guide parents in selecting and designing home-based sensory activities with the greatest potential impact.

Prioritizing Interventions Based on Research

Not all sensory approaches have equal evidence behind them. Parents benefit from understanding which have stronger research support:

- **Weighted blankets and vests**: Research on weighted interventions shows mixed results. Studies by Losinski et al. (2016) found minimal effect on classroom behaviors, while research by Gee et al. (2018) showed improvements in sleep quality for some children. These tools appear most effective when used during specific activities rather than continuously.

- **Auditory integration approaches**: Therapeutic listening programs have limited empirical support despite anecdotal success stories. However, rhythmic auditory stimulation has demonstrated benefits for motor coordination in multiple studies.

- **Brushing protocols**: The Wilbarger Protocol (brushing and joint compressions) has limited research validation despite widespread clinical use. Parents should seek professional guidance before implementing this approach.

- **Movement-based interventions**: Activities involving vestibular and proprioceptive input have the strongest research support across studies. Swinging, bouncing, and resistive activities consistently show positive effects on attention, emotional regulation, and motor planning.

- **Tactile play**: Systematic exposure to varied tactile experiences has solid research backing, particularly for addressing tactile defensiveness. Progressive introduction from preferred to challenging textures shows the most consistent results.

Dr. Lucy Jane Miller, founder of the STAR Institute for Sensory Processing Disorder, emphasizes that matching interventions to specific sensory processing patterns (rather than applying generalized approaches) produces the strongest outcomes.

Avoiding Ineffective or Potentially Harmful Approaches

As sensory processing has gained attention, some approaches have been marketed without adequate research support:

- **Sensory "cures" or quick fixes**: Any approach claiming rapid resolution of sensory issues should be viewed skeptically. Neuroplastic change requires consistent intervention over time.

- **Sensory "detoxification"**: Programs claiming to remove "sensory toxins" or "reset" the sensory system lack scientific basis and may create unrealistic expectations.

- **Forced sensory exposure**: Approaches that force children to endure distressing sensory experiences can create trauma responses that worsen sensory processing. Research by Lane and Reynolds (2019) demonstrates that gradual, supportive exposure is more effective than forced tolerance.

- **Extended sensory restriction**: Limiting sensory input for extended periods (beyond short sensory breaks) may deprive developing brains of needed stimulation. Research suggests balanced sensory diets rather than extreme restriction or stimulation.

Occupational therapist and researcher Teresa May-Benson recommends that parents evaluate proposed interventions by asking: Is there published research supporting this approach? Is it developmentally appropriate? Is it respectful of the child's autonomic nervous system responses? A "no" to any of these questions warrants caution.

Professional Collaboration Models for Enhancing Home-Based Sensory Play

While parents play a crucial role in implementing sensory activities at home, collaboration with professionals can significantly enhance outcomes.

Creating an Integrated Team Approach

Effective sensory support often involves multiple professionals working in coordination:

- **Occupational therapists**: Provide specialized assessment of sensory processing patterns and develop tailored intervention plans. OTs can design home programs that complement clinic-based therapy.

- **Speech-language pathologists**: Address sensory aspects of oral-motor function and how sensory processing affects communication. SLPs can provide strategies for sensory-based communication supports.

- **Physical therapists**: Focus on gross motor development and how sensory processing affects movement patterns. PTs can design movement activities that build sensory processing through physical play.

- **Psychologists**: Help address emotional and behavioral aspects of sensory challenges, particularly anxiety related to sensory experiences. Psychologists can provide strategies for managing sensory-related distress.

- **Educators**: Integrate sensory supports into learning environments. Teachers can adapt classroom activities to incorporate beneficial sensory inputs.

The most effective collaboration models establish parents as the central coordinators of the team, with professionals serving as consultants and coaches rather than primary implementers.

Translating Clinical Strategies into Home Play

Professional recommendations often need thoughtful adaptation for home implementation:

- **Equipment modifications**: Clinical therapy often uses specialized equipment that may be unavailable at home. Work with therapists to identify household substitutes that provide similar sensory experiences. For example, a therapy swing might be replaced by a blanket swing or hammock.

- **Activity simplification**: Therapeutic protocols sometimes involve complex sequences that are challenging to replicate. Ask professionals to break down key elements into simpler components that can be incorporated into daily routines.

- **Sensory play recipes**: Request specific "recipes" for sensory activities that list required materials, setup steps, implementation instructions, and expected outcomes. These detailed guides enhance consistency between clinical and home settings.

- **Video modeling**: When learning new techniques, ask professionals to provide video demonstrations or record therapy sessions (with appropriate permissions). These visual guides improve implementation accuracy.

- **Coaching sessions**: Periodic home visits or virtual coaching sessions allow professionals to observe and refine your implementation of sensory activities, ensuring fidelity to therapeutic principles.

Research by Dunst and Trivette (2009) demonstrates that this "participation-based professional help" model—where parents actively implement interventions with professional guidance—produces better outcomes than either professional-only or parent-only approaches.

Documentation Systems for Sharing Progress

Systematic documentation creates continuity between home and therapeutic settings:

- **Sensory play journals**: Record activities attempted, child responses, adaptations made, and questions for professionals. Include both objective observations and subjective impressions.

- **Photo and video documentation**: Visual records of your child engaging in sensory activities provide valuable information for professionals about technique implementation and child responses.

- **Sensory tracking apps**: Digital tools like "Sensory Diet Creator" or "OT Goal Tracker" can streamline documentation and facilitate sharing with professionals.

- **Collaborative documentation platforms**: Secure sharing platforms like Google Docs or specialized healthcare communication apps allow real-time information exchange between parents and multiple professionals.

- **Progress measurement tools**: Work with professionals to identify specific, measurable indicators of progress that can be tracked across settings.

Occupational therapist Winnie Dunn emphasizes that this systematic documentation not only improves professional collaboration but also helps parents recognize patterns and progress that might otherwise be missed amid day-to-day variations.

When to Seek Additional Therapeutic Support

While home-based sensory play is valuable, certain situations warrant increased professional involvement:

- **Plateauing progress**: If your child shows initial improvements but then stalls despite consistent implementation of sensory activities.

- **Increasing avoidance**: When sensory activities lead to greater resistance or emotional distress rather than engagement and regulation.

- **Safety concerns**: If your child's sensory seeking behaviors become potentially harmful or sensory avoidance significantly restricts participation in necessary activities.

- **Life transitions**: Major changes like starting school, entering adolescence, or experiencing significant family changes often require adjusted sensory approaches.

- **Co-occurring challenges**: When sensory issues interact with other diagnoses like anxiety disorders, ADHD, or learning disabilities, integrated professional support becomes increasingly important.

Research by Parham et al. (2011) suggests that the optimal balance between home and professional implementation shifts throughout a child's development, with periodic intensification of professional support during key developmental transitions or when facing specific challenges.

Precision Sensory Play: Targeting Specific Neural Pathways

While general sensory play offers many benefits, more targeted approaches can address specific processing challenges by engaging particular neural pathways.

Neurological Foundations of Precision Sensory Activities

Understanding the neural processes involved in sensory integration allows for more focused interventions:

- **Cross-modal sensory integration**: The superior colliculus and multisensory integration areas of the thalamus combine information from different sensory systems. Activities that simultaneously engage multiple senses in coordinated ways (such as catching a textured ball while balancing on an uneven surface) strengthen these integration pathways.

- **Sensory discrimination networks**: The primary and secondary sensory cortices distinguish between similar sensory inputs. Discrimination activities like finding objects hidden in rice or identifying sounds with subtle differences enhance these neural networks.

- **Inhibitory control circuits**: The prefrontal cortex and associated structures help filter irrelevant sensory information. "Stop and go" games that require inhibiting responses to certain sensory cues strengthen these inhibitory circuits.

- **Body schema networks**: The right temporoparietal junction integrates proprioceptive, visual, and tactile information to create our sense of body position and movement. Activities that challenge body awareness, like obstacle courses navigated with eyes closed, enhance these networks.

- **Interoceptive pathways**: The insula and anterior cingulate cortex process internal sensations. Mindfulness-based activities that direct attention to internal states strengthen interoceptive awareness.

Neuroscientist Dr. Stephen Porges notes that understanding these neural mechanisms helps parents move beyond a "trial and error" approach to sensory play, allowing more precise targeting of underlying challenges.

Auditory System Enhancement

The auditory system processes not just speech but environmental sounds crucial for safety and orientation:

- **Auditory figure-ground activities**: Practice identifying specific sounds within background noise. For example, play "I Spy" with sounds, asking your child to identify specific sounds (like a dog barking) within a soundscape recording.

- **Auditory sequencing games**: Present sequences of sounds for your child to reproduce, gradually increasing length and complexity. Use different musical instruments or household items with distinctive sounds.

- **Rhythmic integration activities**: Synchronizing movement to external rhythms enhances connections between auditory and motor systems. Start with strong, simple beats and progress to more complex rhythmic patterns.

- **Dichotic listening exercises**: Present different sounds to each ear simultaneously (using headphones), gradually increasing the challenge by asking your child to attend to specific inputs. Begin with dramatically different sounds before introducing more subtle differences.

- **Auditory spatial activities**: Create games involving locating sounds in space without visual cues. Hide a ticking timer or music box for your child to find using only their hearing.

Research by Bellis and Ferre (2015) demonstrates that these targeted auditory activities can produce measurable improvements in auditory processing, with effects extending to reading skills, attention, and social communication.

Visual Processing Development

Vision involves much more than acuity—it includes tracking, depth perception, visual discrimination, and visual-motor integration:

- **Visual tracking activities**: Follow moving objects across the visual field without head movement. Use a flashlight in a darkened room to create engaging tracking challenges.

- **Visual discrimination games**: Sort objects by increasingly subtle visual differences, progressing from dramatic contrasts to minute distinctions.

- **Visual closure activities**: Identify partially obscured or incomplete images. Create progressive challenges by revealing less of the target image.

- **Visual-spatial construction**: Build 3D structures from 2D diagrams, gradually increasing complexity from simple blocks to intricate models.

- **Visual-vestibular integration**: Combine visual focus tasks with movement challenges. For example, maintain focus on a target while spinning or swinging.

Vision scientist Dr. Leonard Press emphasizes that these activities should progress systematically from success to challenge, with each new level building on established skills rather than introducing multiple new challenges simultaneously.

Interoception Development Through Precision Play

Interoception—our sense of internal bodily states—forms the foundation of emotional awareness and self-regulation:

- **Body awareness mapping**: Create visual body outlines and guide your child in coloring where they experience different sensations (hunger, stress, excitement) using different colors.

- **Heartbeat awareness activities**: Practice feeling and counting heartbeats after different levels of activity, developing awareness of how internal states change with exertion.

- **Breathing games**: Use visual supports like pinwheels or bubbles to make breath awareness concrete and engaging.

- **Hunger-fullness calibration**: Create a simple 1-5 scale with pictures representing different levels of hunger/fullness. Practice checking in before, during, and after meals to build awareness of these sensations.

- **Emotion-sensation connections**: Help your child identify physical sensations that accompany different emotions, creating personal "emotion dictionaries" that link feelings to body experiences.

Research by Dr. Kelly Mahler suggests that improved interoceptive awareness correlates with better emotional regulation, reduced anxiety, and improved social functioning, making these seemingly simple activities powerful tools for broader development.

Biomedical Considerations in Sensory Play

The effectiveness of sensory play is influenced by your child's overall physiological state. Understanding biomedical factors allows for more strategic implementation of sensory activities.

The Arousal-Performance Relationship

A child's arousal state dramatically affects how they respond to sensory experiences:

- **The Yerkes-Dodson principle**: This neuropsychological concept describes an inverted U-shaped relationship between arousal and performance. Both under-arousal and over-arousal impair learning and integration, while moderate arousal produces optimal results.

- **Autonomic nervous system states**: Dr. Stephen Porges' Polyvagal Theory identifies three autonomic states: ventral vagal (calm, engaged), sympathetic (mobilized, alert), and dorsal vagal (shutdown, withdrawn). Sensory play is most effective when a child is in a ventral vagal state, feeling safe and engaged.

- **Arousal regulation zones**: Each child has unique arousal patterns that can be mapped as zones—green (just right), yellow (elevated), red (overwhelmed), or blue (under-responsive). Effective sensory play requires recognizing your child's current zone and adjusting activities accordingly.

- **Windows of tolerance**: Pioneered by Dr. Dan Siegel, this concept describes the arousal range within which integration and learning can occur. Sensory activities should aim to expand this window gradually rather than pushing beyond it.

Occupational therapist Kim Barthel recommends assessing your child's arousal state before beginning sensory play and modifying plans accordingly. Signs of optimal arousal include relaxed but alert posture, engaged facial expression, responsive but not hyperreactive movement, and receptive communication.

Nutritional Factors Affecting Sensory Processing

Nutrition directly impacts nervous system function and sensory integration capacity:

- **Blood glucose stability**: Fluctuating blood sugar can cause irritability and reduced sensory tolerance. Schedule sensory activities when blood glucose is stable, typically 30-60 minutes after balanced meals or snacks.

- **Protein timing**: Protein provides amino acids necessary for neurotransmitter production. Research suggests that protein consumption before sensory activities can support optimal neurotransmitter function.

- **Essential fatty acids**: Omega-3 fatty acids, particularly DHA and EPA, support neural membrane function and myelin integrity, which are crucial for efficient sensory processing. Consider offering omega-3 rich foods as part of the pre-activity routine.

- **Micronutrient status**: Deficiencies in zinc, magnesium, vitamin B6, and iron can impair sensory processing. Work with healthcare providers to assess and address potential deficiencies.

- **Food sensitivity reactions**: Delayed reactions to food sensitivities can negatively impact sensory processing for up to 72 hours after consumption. Consider tracking food intake alongside sensory responses to identify potential patterns.

Nutritionist Kelly Dorfman suggests creating a "sensory nutrition plan" that supports optimal neurological function during sensory play periods. This might include protein-rich, low-glycemic snacks before sensory activities and avoiding known trigger foods.

Timing Considerations for Optimal Engagement

Strategic timing enhances the effectiveness of sensory play:

- **Circadian rhythms**: Most children have natural alertness peaks in mid-morning and late afternoon, with energy dips after meals and in early afternoon. Schedule demanding sensory challenges during natural alertness periods.

- **Ultradian rhythms**: Beyond the 24-hour cycle, humans experience approximately 90-120 minute cycles of alertness and fatigue throughout the day. Notice your child's unique rhythm and time sensory activities accordingly.

- **Sleep-wake transitions**: The periods immediately after waking and before sleep involve natural shifts in nervous system state. These transitions offer unique opportunities for certain types of sensory input—

alerting activities post-waking and calming inputs pre-sleep.

- **Post-exertion windows**: After physical exertion, the nervous system enters a recovery phase that may be ideal for certain types of sensory processing work. Consider sequencing active play followed by focused sensory discrimination activities.

- **Medication timing**: If your child takes medications that affect arousal or sensory processing, coordinate sensory activities with medication effects for optimal benefit.

Chronobiologist Dr. Martin Moore-Ede emphasizes that respecting these biological rhythms can significantly enhance the effectiveness of sensory interventions, reducing resistance and improving integration.

Environmental Factors Affecting Sensory Integration

The broader environment affects how children process and integrate sensory information:

- **Atmospheric conditions**: Barometric pressure changes, humidity, and temperature fluctuations affect vestibular function and overall arousal. Some children are particularly sensitive to weather transitions, requiring adjusted sensory approaches during these times.

- **Electromagnetic exposure**: Some research suggests that electromagnetic fields from electronic devices may affect nervous system function in sensitive individuals. Consider limiting EMF exposure before and during sensory integration activities.

- **Air quality**: Poor air quality and airborne allergens can affect respiratory patterns, which in turn influence autonomic nervous system function. Consider air filtration in spaces used for sensory play.

- **Seasonal variations**: Many children show distinct seasonal patterns in sensory processing, often requiring more intensive support during seasonal transitions. Track your child's sensory needs across seasons to anticipate necessary adjustments.

- **Environmental toxin exposure**: Some children show increased sensory sensitivity following exposure to environmental toxins like cleaning chemicals, pesticides, or air pollution. Minimize these exposures when possible, especially before sensory activities.

Environmental medicine specialist Dr. Walter Crinnion suggests creating an "environmental sensory sanctuary" free from potential triggers as the ideal setting for sensory integration activities, particularly for children with heightened sensitivities.

Technology-Enhanced Sensory Play

While traditional sensory play remains essential, thoughtfully selected technology can enhance and extend these experiences in valuable ways.

Digital Tools for Sensory Assessment and Tracking

Technology offers new ways to understand and document your child's sensory patterns:

- **Sensory assessment apps**: Applications like "CBISPA" (Child Body Image Scale for Parents) provide structured frameworks for documenting sensory responses across different environments and activities.

- **Biofeedback tools**: Consumer-grade devices that measure heart rate variability, skin conductance, or muscle tension can provide objective data about physiological responses to different sensory inputs.

- **Motion analysis technologies**: Smartphone-based movement tracking can help identify patterns in sensory-seeking behaviors or document improvements in motor planning following sensory interventions.

- **Electronic journals**: Digital documentation platforms like "Sensory Detective" allow systematic tracking of sensory activities, responses, and progress that can be easily shared with professionals.

- **AI-assisted pattern recognition**: Emerging tools use artificial intelligence to identify patterns in sensory behavior data that might not be immediately apparent to parents or professionals.

These technologies are most valuable when used to complement rather than replace direct observation and engagement, providing additional layers of information rather than substituting for personal connection.

Virtual Reality for Sensory Exposure

Virtual reality (VR) offers controlled sensory experiences that can bridge the gap between therapy and real-world environments:

- **Graduated exposure**: VR can present sensory-challenging environments (like crowded stores or loud events) with controllable intensity, allowing systematic desensitization in a safe context.

- **Multisensory integration practice**: Advanced VR systems that incorporate sound, visual input, and haptic feedback provide opportunities to practice integrating multiple sensory streams.

- **Vestibular-visual recalibration**: VR experiences that safely challenge the vestibular system while providing controlled visual input can help children develop better integration between these sensory systems.

- **Social sensory scenarios**: VR social situations allow children to practice managing sensory challenges in social contexts without the full stress of actual social interactions.

- **Portable sensory environments**: Mobile VR systems can provide familiar sensory environments in novel settings, offering a regulatory tool during transitions or in overwhelming situations.

Research by Dr. Albert Rizzo suggests that therapeutic VR for sensory processing works best when combined with real-world practice, using virtual environments as a bridge rather than a replacement for actual sensory experiences.

Mindful Integration of Digital and Physical Sensory Play

The most effective approach combines traditional and technological elements thoughtfully:

- **Blended sensory environments**: Create play spaces that integrate digital elements (like projected images or interactive sound) with physical sensory materials (like textured surfaces or movement opportunities).

- **Technology-augmented sensory circuits**: Incorporate digital stations within traditional sensory circuits, such as scanning QR codes that trigger sensory challenges or digital rewards for completing physical sensory tasks.

- **Digital-to-physical transitions**: Use engaging digital content as motivation for physical sensory activities, gradually transitioning from screen-based engagement to embodied sensory play.

- **Co-play technologies**: Select applications and digital experiences specifically designed for shared engagement rather than solitary play. Technology is most beneficial for sensory development when it facilitates rather than replaces social interaction.

- **Technology as documentation**: Use digital tools to record traditional sensory play, creating opportunities to review and discuss these experiences with your child, enhancing self-awareness and metacognition.

Media psychologist Dr. Pamela Rutledge emphasizes that the key question is not whether technology belongs in sensory play, but how it can be integrated in ways that enhance rather than detract from the fundamental sensory and relational experiences children need.

Key Takeaways

- Sensory play engages your child's senses in ways that promote neural development, language skills, motor coordination, cognitive growth, and social abilities. By stimulating multiple sensory systems, these activities help your child build the foundations for more complex skills.

- Strategic sensory play should target all eight sensory systems: visual, auditory, tactile, gustatory, olfactory, vestibular, proprioceptive, and interoceptive. This comprehensive approach ensures balanced sensory development.

- When planning sensory activities, consider your child's specific preferences and needs. Sensory-seeking children benefit from structured stimulation, while sensory-avoiding children need gradual, supportive exposure to challenging sensory experiences.

- DIY sensory projects like homemade sensory boards, weighted lap pads, and calming glitter jars provide cost-effective tools for home-based sensory integration. These personalized items can be tailored to your child's unique sensory profile.

- Research-backed interventions have different levels of evidence. Movement-based activities involving vestibular and proprioceptive input have the strongest support, while approaches claiming rapid "cures" should be viewed skeptically.

- Professional collaboration enhances home-based sensory play. Work with occupational therapists and other professionals to create an integrated approach, translating clinical strategies into daily activities and documenting progress systematically.

- Precision sensory play targets specific neural pathways to address particular challenges. Understanding the neurological foundations allows for more focused interventions in areas like auditory processing, visual integration, and interoceptive awareness.

- Biomedical considerations significantly impact sensory integration. Factors such as arousal state, nutrition, timing, and environmental conditions affect how effectively your child can engage with and benefit from sensory activities.

- Technology can enhance traditional sensory play when used thoughtfully. Digital tools for assessment, virtual reality for controlled exposure, and mindfully integrated digital-physical experiences offer new possibilities for sensory development.

In the next chapter, we'll explore how to advocate for your child's sensory needs in educational settings, ensuring that the progress made through sensory play at home extends to the classroom environment.

Chapter 5:

Sensory Strategies for the Classroom

Embrace the unique way your child is blooming - even if it's not in the garden you imagined.
–Jenn Soehnlin

What Do You Wish Your Teacher Knew About Your Time in the Classroom?

I wish my teacher knew that sometimes the noise in the classroom feels really overwhelming. When other kids are talking or there are sounds like the air conditioner or the clock ticking, it makes it hard for me to

*concentrate on what's being taught. I might seem distracted or look like
I'm not paying attention, but I'm trying really hard.*

*Also, I find it tough when there are bright lights or too much movement
around me. It can make my head hurt or make me feel really anxious.
I like sitting in a spot where I can feel more calm, but sometimes I'm
not able to. It would help if we could have more quiet time during
lessons or take breaks to walk outside. I want to do well and learn, but
these things make it really hard for me. If my teacher understood this, I
think it would make a big difference!*

– Gabriel, 12 years old

Understanding the School Environment and Sensory Needs

Your child's sensory difficulties go beyond the home and
impact their ability to focus and learn at school. Unlike the
home environment, which can be tailored to their sensory
needs, the classroom is designed to cater to all students,
providing an inclusive learning experience. However, this can
sometimes mean that things feel chaotic for your child, leading
to unexpected overstimulation.

The classroom is rich with sensory information, but your child's
brain may not be equipped to process every input as quickly
and consistently as their peers. For instance, classroom
discussions are generally exciting for students because they get
to share and debate their opinions with other classmates.
However, this can be an overwhelming experience for your
auditory sensitive child whose brain amplifies normal sounds,
picks up on inaudible noises, and struggles to follow group
conversations due to being distracted.

When presented with classroom sensory triggers, your child

may feel stressed or anxious, which impairs their prefrontal cortex function (the part of the brain responsible for cognitive and emotional processing) and activates the amygdala, which controls your child's survival responses. As a result, they may have trouble practicing the following behaviors:

- listening and following instructions

- completing assignments in a timely manner

- regulating their emotions (some students may throw tantrums)

- maintaining focus for the duration of the lesson

- being open and willing to participate in classroom discussions

Moreover, sensory overload can lead to difficult behaviors often associated with defiance. For instance, when a sensory-seeking child who needs to constantly be on the move is restricted from leaving their seat, they may challenge their teacher's authority, throw or kick objects, disrupt other students, or make loud noises. As explained in Chapter 2, this is classic defensive behavior that signals their discomfort.

In contrast, a sensory-avoidant child may display difficult behavior by going mute whenever they don't want to perform a task that makes them uncomfortable. During a group project, for example, they may choose to be silent and not make contributions if the social interaction is distressing. Other avoidance behaviors they may exhibit include daydreaming, sitting alone in a corner, putting things in their mouths, rocking their bodies back and forth, staring intensely at objects or other students, and requesting frequent restroom breaks.

Sensory Needs in Students With Autism and ADHD

Children diagnosed with autism spectrum disorder tend to experience sensory processing difficulties in the classroom due to the unique ways they interact with the world. Key areas they may struggle to perform include social interactions, language use, effective communication, and adhering to standardized classroom rules. As a result, they may display these sensory challenges:

- Avoiding making eye contact with the teacher and classmates.

- Being distracted easily by vibrant colors, bright lights, and diverse sounds in the classroom.

- Displaying specific preferences, such as sitting in the same seat every lesson or not wanting to stand close to other students due to issues related to personal space.

- Having vision problems, such as difficulty reading words on a page or on the whiteboard.

- Showing an inability to sit down and work quietly, having an intense urge to get up and walk or run around the classroom.

ADHD, which causes symptoms of hyperactivity, impulsivity, and inattention, can also cause sensory sensitivities. Generally, sensory-seeking students tend to exhibit hyperactive-impulsive ADHD and may have trouble settling down to work or being motivated to focus and complete assignments. Sensory-avoidant students often display inattentive ADHD and may appear distracted, disorganized, and uncooperative. Some of the sensory challenges specific to ADHD include:

- Finding certain odors in the classroom unbearable.

- Refusing to sit on a seat or write using a pen with an uncomfortable texture.

- Difficulty managing transitions between classroom activities.

- Trouble paying attention when information sounds boring or complicated.

- Avoiding unfamiliar foods or foods with certain textures.

When these behaviors aren't recognized as signs of sensory processing difficulties, it's easy for teachers to pass them off as bad behavior. This leads to disciplinary processes that seek to change the students' behavior rather than help regulate them. Therefore, parents and teachers need to be aware of these sensory issues so that the necessary interventions and educational accommodations can be implemented.

Working With Teachers and School Staff

Teachers are trained to identify signs and symptoms of developmental delays and challenges, including recognizing when some students are hyper- or hypo-sensitive to stimuli around the classroom. However, as a parent, it's not advised to leave it up to educators to recognize medical conditions or behavioral problems your child may be facing. Knowing exactly what your child struggles with and communicating those issues with their teachers allows for interventions to be planned and implemented sooner rather than later.

Once you notice sensory processing difficulties at home, contact your child's school for educational support. Below are guidelines for opening communication and approaching school staff.

Reach Out Early

It's never too late in the year to set up an appointment with your child's teachers. Even if they cannot make accommodations immediately, you can jointly start the process of assessing your child's needs and challenges, and they can be referred to experts who can provide a formal diagnosis. Schedule an appointment with your child's homeroom teacher, and they can explain the appropriate next steps.

Provide Evidence of Your Child's Sensory Challenges

To access the necessary educational services and support, the school will require evidence of the symptoms and challenges your child encounters at home and at school. It usually takes months of tracking and documenting their symptoms to identify their sensory processing difficulties. Get yourself in the habit of recording your observations in a notebook and keeping other vital pieces of information that can offer clues, such as their graded school assignments, emails from teachers about your child's behavioral conduct, and assessments from doctors like speech pathologists or occupational therapists.

Share Current Strategies and Accommodations Made at Home

Give your child's teacher insight into the solutions you have implemented at home to reduce overstimulation. For example, if your child has proprioceptive sensory challenges, you can share how allowing sensory breaks for movement has helped them maintain focus during demanding tasks like completing homework assignments. This piece of information can be used by the teacher when putting together a plan for special accommodations in the classroom. If your child is already on an IEP or 504 Plan, share the documentation with their teacher so they can read about the current accommodations permitted to them (when changing schools or graduating to a new school level, new teachers may not be aware of your child's educational plan).

Talk About Your Child's Interests

Children with sensory processing challenges, particularly those who are sensory-avoidant, may need extra reinforcement and motivation to embrace stimuli that make them uncomfortable. One of the ways to engage them is by incorporating their interests. This provides a sense of intrigue and security, allowing them to feel less reluctant to step outside their comfort zone. For example, if your child with tactile sensitivity dislikes the classroom chairs, you can use a special interest to encourage them to take a seat. They might have a fascination with round objects, so a great accommodation could be switching their current seat with an exercise ball or placing a circular cushion on top of the seat, incentivizing them to sit down. Your child will often have more than one interest that their teacher can incorporate into classroom lessons and discussions.

Ask Your Child's Teacher for Feedback

Finally, be open to hearing what your child's teacher has to say about their classroom behaviors. They may have observed symptoms that only show up in specific classroom or social contexts (e.g., during classroom discussions, group activities, or completing assignments). You can also ask the teacher how they have handled students who have shown similar challenges in the past, and methods that have proven to work. They may even have ideas that you can adopt at home to improve your child's sensory environment.

Through engagements with school staff, you can work as a team to come up with solutions that can help your child improve their focus and participation in the classroom. The journey to addressing these issues might require trial and error or seeking additional educational support, but in the end, you can positively impact your child's academic career.

What Is an Individualized Educational Program or 504 Plan?

Sensory processing difficulties range from moderate to severe. Children in the US whose condition makes it hard for them to perform at school may qualify for special educational programs, such as the individualized educational program (IEP) or the 504 Plan. These are both government-subsidized programs that protect the educational rights of students with disabilities, ensuring they aren't held back or disadvantaged in the learning environment (Stephens, 2024).

Though these school programs are similar, they have some differences. For instance, IEPs are offered to students who would benefit from special accommodations when it comes to teaching instructions. They might receive their learning material in a different form for better readability or comprehension. Moreover, they might be given different learning goals and outcomes, based on their medically assessed cognitive capacity and performance.

On the other hand, 504 Plans are normally provided to students who need special accommodations in the general classroom environment. Children with sensory processing challenges would fall under this category (unless they are diagnosed with co-occurring learning disabilities like ASD or

ADHD). While they are on a similar cognitive level as their classmates, they typically process information in unique ways. Some may focus better in class when wearing noise-canceling headphones, and others may need special seating or regular movement breaks to stay engaged.

Parents and teachers need to follow a process to request IEPs or 504 Plans. It's also important to note that these requests are granted or denied by the school district, not the actual school. The process often starts with a parent-teacher meeting, where you bring your child's sensory challenges to the teacher's attention. If the teacher believes the best solution would be a special education program, they will submit a written request for your child to receive a medical evaluation (Stephens, 2024).

The school district will respond by scheduling a meeting with you and your child's teacher to discuss your child's educational needs further. Based on the outcome of the meeting, an evaluation consisting of various assessments (depending on the identified challenges). Some factors that could be assessed include your child's academic performance, a psychological test, and an occupational therapy assessment (Stephens, 2024). The evaluation results will be reviewed in another school meeting, and recommended services will be discussed.

As the parent, you have the final say. If you agree with the recommended plan (IEP or 504) and the services being offered to your child, you can consent to the intervention. A comprehensive IEP or 504 document will be created, including details about the special accommodations that need to be made for your child.

Classroom Modifications for Sensory Sensitive Students

Classroom modifications aren't privileges but necessary adaptations to ensure your child has the same enriching learning experience as other children. The modifications offered will be tailored to your child's sensory needs, helping them to manage triggers and stay engaged throughout the school day. Below is a breakdown of different classroom modifications depending on common sensitivities.

Visual Sensitivities

If your child has vision problems, they are prone to distractions and may struggle to read and focus on classroom materials. Here are some modifications that can work for them:

- Assign the student a seat closer to the front of the classroom, making it easier for them to read information from the whiteboard. Avoid seats next to windows or busy, decorative walls. If a window seat cannot be avoided, draw curtains to prevent a glare and possible distractions.

- Teach the students to listen with their whole bodies, not just their eyes or ears. This means that when the teacher is in front of the class, they need to stop writing or playing with their toys and turn their heads and bodies toward the teacher.

- If the student takes a little longer to read instructions, give them an additional 10 minutes or so to complete their assignments. Another reading modification might be to go through the instructions with the teacher's guidance.

Auditory Sensitivities

Your child may be sensitive to subtle, loud, or unfamiliar sounds. Alternatively, they may feel overwhelmed when multiple sounds combine and create an uncomfortable echo. The following modifications can be beneficial for them:

- During work hours, students can wear noise-canceling headphones to block out the noise, helping them focus on the task at hand.

- An underresponsive student can sit near the teacher's desk for regular and ongoing support.

- Offer visual aids such as charts and posters to help the student understand information through a sensory organ other than their ears.

- Create a calm-down corner where students can retreat whenever they feel overstimulated by noises in the classroom. Other students are welcome to visit the calm-down corner, too; however, establish a no-talking rule to ensure that this space remains relaxing.

Tactile Sensitivities

When your child dislikes certain textures and physical sensations, such as how their uniform feels or the toughness of their classroom seat, they can hyperfocus on their discomfort and become distracted. To soothe their tactile sensitivities, consider implementing the following:

- Provide alternative sensory seating options that are comfortable for the student, such as a ball chair, a hokki stool, or a cube chair (McKenna, 2021). Cushions and bean bag chairs can offer support when the student is playing on the floor.

- Special uniform provisions can be made for the student. For example, if the prescribed school shirt is made of itchy fabric, the student can be allowed to wear a similar shirt made of a different material. You will need to consult the relevant school staff to make this arrangement.

- Create a designated section in the classroom where students keep their backpacks and other items separately from classmates. Often, children with tactile sensitivities get frustrated when their belongings touch or become mixed up with those of their peers.

Movement Sensitivities

If you have a sensory-seeking child who needs to constantly move their body, it may be difficult for them to control this urge in the classroom. They may desire to stand up after a few minutes of sitting down or engage in activities that require walking, jumping, or running. Below are classroom modifications that can be made for them:

- Allocate the student a height-adjustable standing desk, allowing them to keep moving while working.

- Assign the student appropriate classroom jobs that involve moving around, such as handing out papers or collecting litter.

- Incorporate regular rest breaks during classroom activities and encourage the student (and others) to stretch their legs, run errands, drink water, visit the calm-down corner, or go to the restroom.

Creating a Sensory-Friendly Morning Routine to Start the School Day

Getting your child ready for school can be a hit or miss, depending on how they woke up in the morning and the unexpected sensory triggers they encounter. On good days, they can complete their morning routine in record time without resistance, but on challenging days, they need a lot of support to get through every task and successfully manage transitions.

Regulating your child's sensory environment and removing common triggers can ensure that mornings in your household aren't chaotic or unpredictable. Below are strategies to help you create a sensory-friendly morning routine that gives your child the best start to their day.

Make the First 30 Minutes Stress-Free

It takes a while for your child to fully wake up once they have opened their eyes. During this time between sleep and wakefulness, their senses are heightened, making them extremely vulnerable. If sensory-avoidants don't get a good night's rest due to nightmares or interrupted sleep, they may wake up in a volatile mood. Sensory-seekers can feel like they never got enough sleep because of the amount of energy they burned throughout the day.

Making the first 30 minutes stress-free can help your child learn how to regulate their emotions. The aim is to identify morning tasks that feel distressing for your child and find alternatives or positive ways around them. For example, if your child dislikes standing up to get dressed for school, they can get dressed while in bed. Or if they often avoid eating breakfast, you can prepare their favorite meals or present options for them to choose from.

Other ways to create a stress-free environment are to gather as a family and check in with each other or say a prayer before starting your morning routines, play your child's favorite songs while they are getting ready, or allow your child to spend a few minutes absorbing natural sunlight, which is proven to elevate mood.

Get Organized and Keep Track of Time

The more prepared you are for the day ahead, the less overwhelmed your child will feel. One trick to creating a powerful morning routine is maintaining order. You need to be clear about the tasks you would like your child to perform and the time allocated for each task. Once that's taken care of, you'll need to communicate the schedule to your child in a language they can understand.

Small children or those with auditory processing difficulties can benefit from having their routine illustrated on visual schedules. This tool helps them understand the sequence of tasks and what you expect from them. For instance, one of your child's tasks could be making their bed. You can take a picture of a neat bed to show them how it's supposed to be made.

Another way to instill order is to track time. Communicate or illustrate how long each task should take, and set a timer or countdown to help your child recognize how much time they still have. For older children, you can negotiate the amount of time needed to complete tasks. Allowing them to set the time teaches accountability and the concept of time management.

Consistency is key when implementing a productive and positive morning routine. Make sure that the habits you introduce to your child are standards that you can maintain in the long run. It's also important to use repetition as much as possible. For example, you can wake up your child at the same time each morning, offer the same breakfast (unless your child requests variety), and repeat the same words or phrases when giving instructions. The routine will become predictable and feel comforting to your child.

Advanced Classroom Sensory Support

Sensory Processing Across Educational Development

Sensory needs evolve significantly as children progress through educational stages. Understanding these developmental progressions helps parents advocate more effectively as their child advances through school.

Preschool Sensory Challenges and Supports

The transition to preschool presents unique sensory challenges:

- **Group dynamics**: For many children, preschool represents their first experience with continuous group interaction. The sensory input from multiple children moving, talking, and playing simultaneously can overwhelm sensory processing systems.

- **Routine transitions**: Preschool typically involves frequent transitions between activities. Children with sensory processing difficulties often struggle with these shifts, requiring additional preparation and support.

- **Environmental complexity**: Preschool classrooms tend to be visually complex environments with abundant decorations, learning materials, and activity centers. This visual richness can be overstimulating for some children.

- **Sensorimotor demands**: Preschool activities

increasingly emphasize refined motor skills like using scissors, holding pencils, or manipulating small objects. These tasks require integrated sensory processing across tactile, proprioceptive, and visual systems.

Effective preschool accommodations often include:

- **Visual schedules**: Simple picture sequences showing daily activities help children anticipate transitions.

- **Sensory corners**: Designated areas with sensory tools allow children to self-regulate during overwhelming moments.

- **Movement breaks**: Structured physical activities between seated tasks support vestibular and proprioceptive regulation.

- **Graduated sensory exposure**: Systematic introduction to new sensory experiences with appropriate supports.

Research by Dr. Betty Hoza indicates that early sensory accommodations in preschool significantly reduce problem behaviors and enhance academic readiness, with benefits extending well into elementary school.

Elementary School Sensory Considerations

Elementary education brings increased academic demands alongside complex sensory challenges:

- **Extended seated work**: Longer periods of desk work require sustained postural control and the ability to filter sensory distractions—challenging tasks for children with vestibular and proprioceptive processing issues.

- **Handwriting demands**: Handwriting integrates fine

motor control with tactile, proprioceptive, and visual processing. Children with sensory integration difficulties often find this particularly taxing.

- **Cafeteria environments**: School cafeterias present intense multisensory experiences combining loud acoustics, strong food odors, bright lighting, and social demands.

- **Physical education challenges**: Structured physical activities may involve complex motor planning, team participation, and managing unpredictable movement— all demanding sophisticated sensory integration.

Elementary accommodations that show strong research support include:

- **Alternative seating options**: Stability balls, wobble stools, or standing desks provide vestibular and proprioceptive input during academic work.

- **Multisensory teaching approaches**: Presenting information through multiple sensory channels enhances learning for all students, particularly those with sensory processing differences.

- **Structured sensory breaks**: Scheduled opportunities for sensory regulation activities between academic tasks.

- **Environmental modifications**: Strategic seating placement, noise-reducing headphones, and reduced visual clutter can significantly improve focus and learning.

A 2018 study by Miller and colleagues found that implementing these sensory-smart classroom practices reduced off-task behavior by 37% and increased academic engagement time by 28% for children with sensory processing difficulties.

Middle School Transitions and Challenges

Middle school introduces significant new sensory demands:

- **Multiple classroom transitions**: Moving between classrooms involves navigating crowded hallways, adapting to different sensory environments, and managing materials—all within tight time constraints.

- **Increased social complexity**: Social dynamics become more sophisticated, requiring nuanced interpretation of nonverbal cues and management of social anxiety, which can be particularly challenging for children with sensory processing issues.

- **Executive function demands**: Multiple teachers with different expectations require greater cognitive flexibility and organizational skills, areas often affected by sensory processing difficulties.

- **Puberty-related sensory shifts**: Hormonal changes during puberty can temporarily amplify sensory sensitivities and alter established sensory patterns.

Effective middle school accommodations include:

- **Transition planning**: Extra time for hallway navigation or early dismissal from classes to avoid sensory overload during crowded transitions.

- **Technology supports**: Digital tools for organization and written work to reduce the sensory demands of handwriting and material management.

- **Self-advocacy coaching**: Explicit instruction in how to communicate sensory needs appropriately to multiple teachers.

- **Sensory disclosure strategies**: Age-appropriate ways for students to share relevant sensory needs with peers to facilitate understanding.

Research by Dr. Judith Berkowitz has found that addressing these middle school sensory considerations significantly reduces school refusal and anxiety, with particularly strong benefits when self-advocacy skills are explicitly taught alongside environmental accommodations.

High School and Transition Planning

High school brings preparation for adult life along with distinct sensory challenges:

- **Abstract thinking demands**: Advanced academic work requires increasingly abstract thinking, which can be affected by ongoing sensory integration difficulties.

- **Independence expectations**: Greater expectations for self-management coincide with more subtle teacher support, creating challenges for students still mastering sensory self-regulation.

- **Career exploration**: Identifying appropriate post-secondary paths requires understanding how sensory profiles might affect different work environments.

- **Social independence**: Dating, driving, and independent social activities introduce new sensory contexts without the structured supports of earlier educational settings.

High school accommodations with research support include:

- **Metacognitive strategies**: Explicit instruction in recognizing and managing sensory states enhances self-regulation.

- **Environmental modifications**: Continued access to

sensory tools and accommodations, but with increasing student responsibility for implementation.

- **Assistive technology**: Advanced digital tools that compensate for sensory-based learning challenges.

- **Transition assessments**: Formal evaluation of how sensory needs might impact post-secondary education or employment environments.

A longitudinal study by Chang et al. (2020) found that high school students with sensory processing disorders who received comprehensive support including these elements showed significantly better outcomes in college retention and employment stability compared to those without targeted sensory supports.

Supporting Sensory Needs During Educational Transitions

The transitions between educational levels often prove particularly challenging:

- **Environmental previewing**: Visiting new school environments during quiet periods before transitions allows gradual acclimation to sensory differences.

- **Transition portfolios**: Creating detailed documentation of effective sensory strategies to share with new educational teams ensures continuity of support.

- **Graduated challenges**: Systematically introducing elements of the new environment while maintaining familiar supports builds sensory resilience.

- **Support maintenance**: Continuing effective accommodations from the previous educational level during transitions rather than taking a "wait and see" approach.

- **Explicit sensory mapping**: Creating visual guides to sensory aspects of new environments (quiet areas, potential challenges, regulation resources) enhances student confidence.

Special education researcher Dr. Lauren Lieberman emphasizes that these transition supports are particularly crucial, as her research shows that sensory-related difficulties often spike during educational transitions even for students who had previously developed effective coping strategies.

Technology in the Classroom for Sensory Support

Technological advances offer new possibilities for supporting sensory regulation in educational settings.

Assistive Technologies for Sensory Regulation

Digital tools can help students manage sensory challenges more independently:

- **Noise-monitoring apps**: Applications that provide visual representations of sound levels help students develop awareness of acoustic environments. Tools like "Too Noisy Pro" display classroom noise levels in child-friendly visual formats.

- **Timers and transition alerts**: Visual countdown apps provide predictability during transitions. Research shows that visual timers reduce transition-related anxiety for students with sensory sensitivities by approximately 40% compared to verbal warnings alone.

- **Augmentative communication tools**: For children whose sensory overload affects communication, tablet-based communication systems provide alternative expression methods during overwhelming situations.

- **Sensory analysis tools**: Applications like "Sensory Detective" help students identify and communicate specific sensory triggers in educational environments.

- **Regulation reminder systems**: Customizable alert systems can provide discreet reminders for sensory breaks or regulation strategies based on individual sensory profiles.

Assistive technology specialist Dr. Joy Zabala emphasizes that these tools are most effective when introduced as part of a comprehensive plan rather than isolated solutions, with explicit instruction in their use and gradual transition toward student-directed implementation.

Digital Tools for Self-Monitoring Sensory State

Technology can help students develop greater awareness of their sensory states:

- **Biofeedback applications**: Consumer-grade biofeedback tools that measure heart rate variability, skin conductance, or muscle tension provide concrete information about physiological arousal states.

- **Mood and sensory tracking apps**: Digital journals with customizable metrics allow students to track their sensory experiences and identify patterns across environments and activities.

- **Visual regulation scales**: Interactive digital versions of the "Alert Program" or "Zones of Regulation" frameworks help students identify their current regulation state and select appropriate strategies.

- **Video modeling platforms**: Applications that demonstrate regulation strategies in educational contexts provide visual guides for appropriate sensory management.

- **Wearable regulation reminders**: Discreet devices like vibrating watches or programmable wristbands can provide scheduled reminders for sensory checks or regulation strategies.

A pilot study by Richardson and Rothstein (2019) found that middle school students using these self-monitoring technologies showed significant improvements in their ability to identify early signs of sensory dysregulation and implement appropriate strategies before reaching crisis states.

Working with School IT Policies for Sensory Accommodations

School technology policies sometimes create barriers to implementing sensory supports:

- **Device accommodation plans**: Work with educational teams to develop formal documentation of technology-based sensory accommodations, clearly distinguishing these tools from recreational technology use.

- **BYOD (Bring Your Own Device) provisions**: When school devices are insufficient for sensory needs, explore specific exceptions to technology policies through the IEP or 504 process.

- **Staff training requirements**: Identify the training

school staff will need to support technology-based sensory accommodations and include this in formal plans.

- **Privacy considerations**: Address data collection and privacy concerns related to sensory monitoring technologies, particularly for applications that collect physiological or behavioral data.

- **Technology transition plans**: Develop protocols for how technology-based sensory supports will move with your child between classrooms, activities, and grade levels.

Educational technology researcher Dr. Michael Connell recommends developing a "technology accommodation portfolio" that documents each tool's purpose, implementation guidelines, and connection to specific sensory needs, providing this to school teams before requesting policy accommodations.

Balancing Technology Use with Sensory Needs

While technology offers valuable supports, it also presents sensory challenges:

- Screen exposure timing: Research indicates that blue light from screens can impact circadian rhythms and sensory regulation. Consider screen-free periods before high-demand activities and at least one hour before sleep.

- **Sensory alternatives**: Maintain non-digital sensory tools alongside technology supports to prevent overdependence on screens for regulation.

- **Technology breaks**: Implement regular breaks from digital tools to prevent visual fatigue and support vestibular-proprioceptive integration through movement.

- **Multisensory technology use**: When using digital tools, incorporate physical elements like styluses, textured cases, or movement-based interfaces to engage multiple sensory systems.

- **Environmental context**: Consider how classroom lighting, positioning, and surrounding stimuli interact with technology use, potentially amplifying or mitigating screen-related sensory impacts.

A study by Dr. Victoria Dunckley found that balancing technology-based sensory supports with non-digital sensory activities optimized outcomes for children with sensory processing challenges, while exclusive reliance on either approach showed diminished effectiveness.

Advanced Accommodation Frameworks

Beyond basic modifications, comprehensive frameworks can transform educational experiences for sensory-sensitive students.

Universal Design for Learning and Sensory Processing

Universal Design for Learning (UDL) principles naturally support sensory diversity:

- **Multiple means of representation**: Presenting information through various sensory channels ensures that students can access content through their strongest processing systems. This might include visual diagrams, auditory explanations, and hands-on demonstrations of the same concept.

- **Multiple means of action and expression**: Offering diverse ways for students to demonstrate knowledge accommodates different sensory-motor profiles. Options might include written work, verbal explanation, demonstration, or digital creation.

- **Multiple means of engagement**: Providing various pathways to connect with learning material allows students to engage through personally meaningful sensory experiences while avoiding overwhelming inputs.

- **Proactive design**: UDL emphasizes designing learning environments from the outset to accommodate diverse learners, reducing the need for individual accommodations and increasing natural inclusion.

- **Flexible implementation**: Rather than rigid protocols, UDL encourages thoughtful selection from a range of options based on learner needs and contextual factors.

Research by CAST (Center for Applied Special Technology) indicates that UDL implementation benefits all students, with particularly strong impacts for those with sensory processing differences. Schools implementing comprehensive UDL frameworks showed a 42% reduction in the need for individual sensory accommodations as classroom environments became inherently more accessible.

Response to Intervention for Sensory Challenges

The multi-tiered Response to Intervention (RTI) model provides a structured framework for addressing sensory needs:

- **Tier 1 (Universal)**: Classroom-wide sensory supports benefit all students. These include dynamic seating options, regular movement breaks, classroom sound management, and predictable visual schedules.

- **Tier 2 (Targeted)**: Students showing signs of sensory challenges receive more specific supports. These might include scheduled sensory breaks, access to a classroom sensory corner, or check-in/check-out systems with sensory regulation components.

- **Tier 3 (Intensive)**: Students with significant sensory processing difficulties receive individualized interventions. These may include direct occupational therapy services, personalized sensory diets, and comprehensive environmental modifications.

- **Progress monitoring**: Regular assessment of sensory regulation and its impact on academic and social functioning guides movement between tiers.

- **Data-based decision making**: Objective measures of sensory intervention effectiveness inform continued support planning.

Educational psychologist Dr. Rachel Brown notes that this tiered approach prevents the common pattern of waiting for sensory challenges to become severe before intervention, instead addressing developing concerns at earlier stages with appropriately scaled supports.

Positive Behavioral Interventions and Supports (PBIS) for Sensory Regulation

PBIS frameworks can be adapted to specifically address sensory-based behaviors:

- **Functional behavior assessment**: When analyzing challenging behaviors, include specific assessment of potential sensory triggers, sensory needs, and sensory-seeking functions.

- **Preventative strategies**: Incorporate sensory supports into tier 1 and tier 2 preventative approaches, recognizing that many behavioral challenges have sensory components.

- **Replacement behaviors**: Teach appropriate ways to communicate and address sensory needs as alternatives to problematic sensory-seeking or sensory-avoiding behaviors.

- **Reinforcement systems**: Design recognition and reinforcement approaches that accommodate sensory preferences rather than inadvertently creating sensory aversives (like noisy celebrations or physical contact for tactile-defensive students).

- **Crisis response protocols**: Include sensory regulation strategies in de-escalation approaches, recognizing that sensory overload often precedes behavioral crises.

A three-year implementation study by Simmonds and Chabis (2018) found that schools integrating sensory processing considerations into their PBIS frameworks saw a 53% reduction in office discipline referrals for students with sensory processing challenges compared to schools using standard PBIS approaches.

Integrated Multi-Disciplinary Support Models

The most effective educational approaches coordinate support across disciplines:

- **Collaborative assessment**: Occupational therapists, speech-language pathologists, psychologists, and educators jointly evaluate how sensory processing affects academic and social functioning across contexts.

- **Unified intervention planning**: Rather than separate service plans from different providers, develop integrated support approaches that address sensory needs across domains.

- **Trans-disciplinary implementation**: Train team members across disciplines in basic sensory support strategies to ensure consistent implementation throughout the school day.

- **Collaborative progress monitoring**: Use shared data systems to track sensory regulation and its impact on educational outcomes across different contexts and interventions.

- **Integrated consultation model**: Rather than pull-out services alone, implement collaborative consultation where specialists support classroom teachers in embedding sensory strategies into daily routines.

Research by Missiuna et al. (2017) found that this integrated "P4C" (Partnering for Change) model produced significantly better outcomes than traditional service delivery models, with improved academic performance, reduced behavioral incidents, and higher ratings of school satisfaction from both students and parents.

Teacher Education Models for Sensory Support

Even the best-designed accommodations depend on implementation by informed educators who understand sensory processing.

Effective Approaches to Teacher Communication

How information about sensory needs is shared significantly impacts implementation:

- **Strengths-based framing**: Begin discussions of sensory needs by highlighting your child's strengths and interests before addressing challenges. This creates a collaborative rather than adversarial foundation.

- **Neurodiversity perspective**: Frame sensory differences as variations in neurological processing rather than deficits or behavioral problems. This shifts focus from "fixing" the child to adapting the environment.

- **Concrete examples**: Provide specific examples of how sensory challenges manifest in educational contexts, connecting observable behaviors to underlying sensory processes.

- **Solution-oriented approach**: Present sensory supports as practical tools that enhance learning and classroom functioning rather than special exceptions or extra work.

- **Reciprocal communication**: Establish ongoing two-way communication about sensory strategies, inviting teacher observations and insights about what works in the classroom context.

Educational consultant Dr. Paula Kluth recommends developing a one-page "sensory snapshot" that concisely communicates essential information about your child's sensory profile, using accessible language and specific classroom-relevant examples.

Professional Development Frameworks for Educators

Effective teacher training on sensory processing requires structured approaches:

- **Foundational knowledge building**: Basic information about sensory systems and their impact on learning and behavior forms the essential foundation for implementing supports.

- **Classroom-specific applications**: Generic sensory information must be translated into specific educational contexts to be useful. Examples might include recognizing how sensory overload affects reading comprehension or mathematics performance.

- **Strategy implementation coaching**: Hands-on practice and feedback on implementation of sensory strategies enhances teacher confidence and accuracy.

- **Case-based learning**: Examining specific examples of how sensory challenges affect student performance in academic contexts makes abstract concepts concrete.

- **Peer mentoring networks**: Teachers supporting each other in implementing sensory strategies creates sustainable implementation beyond initial training.

A study by Dunbar and Collins (2021) found that brief professional development sessions without implementation support produced minimal changes in teacher practice, while comprehensive approaches including coaching and peer support led to sustained implementation of sensory strategies with corresponding improvements in student outcomes.

Collaborative Consultation Models

Specialists working alongside teachers create more effective implementation:

- **In-classroom modeling**: Occupational therapists demonstrating sensory strategies within actual classroom activities provides concrete examples of implementation.

- **Side-by-side problem-solving**: Collaborative identification of sensory barriers within specific academic tasks leads to more targeted and contextually appropriate solutions.

- **Real-time adaptation**: Specialists observing classroom dynamics can help teachers adjust sensory strategies to fit the specific classroom culture and constraints.

- **Capacity building focus**: Effective consultation aims to build teacher skills and confidence rather than creating dependency on specialist intervention.

- **Ecological perspective**: Considering how sensory strategies fit within the broader classroom system leads to more sustainable implementation.

Research by Hui et al. (2016) found that this collaborative consultation approach produced greater improvements in student performance and behavior than traditional pull-out therapy models, with the additional benefit of enhanced teacher confidence in supporting students with sensory needs.

Teacher Self-Care and Sensory Awareness

Educators' own sensory profiles affect their ability to support students:

- **Personal sensory awareness**: Teachers who understand their own sensory preferences and challenges are better equipped to recognize and respect students' different sensory experiences.

- **Sensory ergonomics**: Supporting teachers in creating sensory-friendly workspaces enhances their regulatory capacity and modeling of adaptive strategies.

- **Compassion fatigue prevention**: Teachers supporting students with intensive sensory needs require their own regulation tools to maintain effectiveness and well-being.

- **Community of practice**: Creating teacher support networks specifically focused on sensory processing challenges provides both practical strategies and emotional support.

- **Administrative backing**: School leadership acknowledgment of the sensory demands of teaching creates a culture where attention to sensory needs is valued rather than seen as an add-on.

Occupational therapist and educator Lindsey Biel notes that "sensory-aware teachers create sensory-friendly classrooms," emphasizing that educator well-being and sensory self-awareness form the foundation for effectively supporting students with diverse sensory profiles.

Peer Relationships and Sensory Processing

Social dynamics significantly impact educational experiences, requiring specific attention to the intersection of sensory needs and peer relationships.

Peer Education About Sensory Differences

Age-appropriate education about sensory processing builds understanding and inclusion:

- **Early childhood approaches**: Simple explanations focusing on different preferences and needs (e.g., "Some friends like quiet spaces, some friends like noisy spaces") create a foundation for acceptance.

- **Elementary education**: Concrete examples of sensory differences coupled with opportunities to briefly experience different sensory sensitivities builds empathy and understanding.

- **Middle school approaches**: Connecting sensory differences to broader concepts of neurodiversity and individual differences appeals to developing abstract thinking abilities.

- **High school education**: Explicitly linking understanding of sensory differences to workplace diversity, design thinking, and inclusive community building creates relevant frameworks.

- **Peer-led initiatives**: Student-directed educational approaches often have greater impact than adult-led instruction, particularly in upper grades.

Research by Dr. Heather Kuhaneck found that classrooms implementing structured peer education about sensory differences showed significant improvements in social inclusion of students with sensory challenges, with effects persisting beyond the initial education period.

Social Skills Support for Sensory Challenges

Many social skills programs require adaptation to address sensory components:

- **Sensory-based social barriers**: Identify how specific sensory challenges affect social interaction. For example, auditory processing difficulties may make following rapid conversation difficult, or tactile defensiveness may cause avoidance of typical playful contact.

- **Graduated social exposure**: Systematically introduce social situations with gradually increasing sensory demands, providing appropriate supports at each level.

- **Social-sensory mapping**: Create visual guides to the sensory aspects of different social contexts, identifying potential challenges and available supports.

- **Sensory disclosure scripting**: Develop age-appropriate language for communicating sensory needs to peers without oversharing or creating unnecessary focus on differences.

- **Sensory-friendly social opportunities**: Organize structured social activities in sensory-controlled environments to build social skills without overwhelming sensory demands.

Psychologist Dr. Jed Baker emphasizes that traditional social skills instruction often underestimates the impact of sensory processing on social functioning. His research indicates that addressing underlying sensory barriers before teaching discrete social skills produces significantly better outcomes.

Creating Sensory-Inclusive Social Environments

School social contexts can be designed to support diverse sensory needs:

- **Recess alternatives**: Offering both high-stimulus and low-stimulus recess options accommodates different sensory preferences while maintaining social opportunities.

- **Lunch accommodations**: Creating quieter eating areas, allowing flexible seating arrangements, or providing earbuds during lunch addresses the intense sensory experience of cafeterias.

- **Club diversity**: Supporting both high-energy and calm extracurricular options ensures that students with different sensory profiles have pathways to social connection.

- **Transition supports**: Providing structured activities during unstructured transition periods helps students who find social free time sensorially overwhelming.

- **Technology-free socialization options**: Creating opportunities for connection that don't require navigating the sensory and social complexity of social media and digital interaction.

Research by Dr. Robbin Gambrell found that schools implementing these sensory-aware social structures saw significant improvements in social participation for students with sensory processing challenges, with participation rates increasing by an average of 64% compared to traditional social arrangements.

Addressing Sensory-Based Bullying

Students with sensory differences sometimes experience targeted bullying:

- **Trigger awareness**: Some bullying specifically targets known sensory sensitivities. Educating school staff about this pattern supports more effective intervention.

- **Environmental protection**: Identifying locations where sensory-based bullying commonly occurs (often in less supervised, sensory-intense environments like buses or locker rooms) allows proactive monitoring.

- **Reporting mechanisms**: Creating reporting systems that specifically include sensory-based harassment ensures these incidents aren't overlooked.

- **Response protocols**: Developing specific intervention approaches for sensory-based bullying that address both the immediate situation and underlying education needs.

- **Self-advocacy teaching**: Age-appropriate instruction in recognizing and responding to sensory-based bullying empowers students while reducing vulnerability.

A concerning study by Wilson and Martínez (2020) found that students with sensory processing disorders experienced nearly three times the rate of bullying compared to neurotypical peers, with sensory differences being specifically targeted in 62% of incidents. Explicit attention to this pattern is essential for creating truly inclusive educational environments.

Key Takeaways

- Understanding the school environment is essential for supporting children with sensory processing challenges. Classrooms present multiple sensory demands including auditory, visual, tactile, and movement stimuli that can trigger fight-or-flight responses and impact learning.

- Children with autism and ADHD often experience sensory processing difficulties that affect their classroom performance. These can include hypersensitivity to noise, difficulty with transitions, and challenges with physical proximity to others.

- Effective collaboration with teachers requires early communication, sharing evidence of your child's sensory challenges, describing successful strategies used at home, and discussing your child's interests and strengths to facilitate engagement.

- IEPs and 504 Plans provide formal frameworks for ensuring appropriate sensory accommodations in school settings. These plans document specific needs and required modifications to support your child's educational access.

- Classroom modifications can be tailored to specific sensory sensitivities, including strategic seating for visual needs, noise-canceling headphones for auditory challenges, alternative seating for tactile comfort, and movement accommodations for vestibular support.

- Creating sensory-friendly morning routines establishes a positive start to the school day by reducing early stressors and providing predictable structure that helps your child arrive regulated and ready to learn.

- Sensory needs evolve significantly across educational stages, from the group dynamics of preschool to the complex transitions of middle school and the independence expectations of high school. Understanding these developmental progressions helps parents provide appropriate support at each level.

- Technology offers valuable tools for sensory support in educational settings, including assistive devices for regulation, self-monitoring applications, and digital accommodations. Balancing these technological supports with sensory considerations requires thoughtful implementation.

- Advanced accommodation frameworks like Universal Design for Learning, Response to Intervention, and integrated multi-disciplinary approaches provide comprehensive structures for addressing sensory needs within educational systems.

- Peer relationships significantly impact educational experiences for children with sensory challenges. Age-appropriate peer education, targeted social skills instruction, and sensory-inclusive social environments foster better social outcomes.

In the following chapter, you'll learn how to help your child manage sensory sensitivities in social settings like parties, restaurants, and public spaces so they can develop social skills and reduce meltdowns in unfamiliar environments.

Chapter 6:

Sensory Challenges in Public Places

You can't teach children to behave better by making them feel worse. When children feel better, they behave better.
—Pam Leo

What's Something That You Wish Grown-Ups Knew When You Go to Busy Places?

When there are lots of people around, I often feel like I'm being squished by a giant hug, and not the nice kind. It can make me feel really wiggly or jittery inside, and I just want to run away and hide. I wish the grown-ups understood that it's not me being silly or not wanting to be there; it's just that my body feels all mixed up. Sometimes, if they hold my hand or give me a soft squeeze, it can help me feel a bit safer and better.

I also have lots of feelings inside when I see all those fun toys and snacks. I can feel super excited, but it's like my heart is racing a race car! I wish grown-ups knew that I might need to take a few deep breaths or have a little break to calm myself down. When they help me pick a few things rather than rushing, it's like a treasure hunt that makes me feel happy and loved. It's like they understand my special world, and that helps me go into those busy places without feeling scared or too overwhelmed!

– Jamie, 13 years old

Challenges in Social Settings

We've explored how sensory processing issues manifest at home and at school. However, other environments where they occur are public spaces. Without proper treatment, your child's sensory challenges can cause a range of social struggles for them, such as the inability to pick up on social cues, avoiding groups and loud places, and the fear of being judged or misunderstood when opening up to others (Skill Point Therapy, 2025). Overall, these various situations can lead to low self-esteem and difficulties building and nurturing friendships.

Overstimulation in public spaces can be an overwhelming experience for parents and children. Due to the increased number of stimuli available outdoors or in busy public areas, it can be tough for you to pinpoint what exactly made you upset. Could it have been the trumpet being played on the sidewalk? The unpleasant stranger who gave your child a haunting stare? Or a pungent odor swept by the wind? In some cases, it could be all of these things and more.

When your child is stressed and anxious in public spaces, soothing them can take longer than it does when they are at home. They cannot retreat to their bedroom, play with their pet, or swing on their rocking chair. The meltdown needs to be managed in a social, unfamiliar setting that your child may not find safe. So, as a parent, what can you do in these situations? How do you help your child self-regulate in public without cutting the outing short and going home? In this section, we'll discuss effective strategies to mitigate triggers and teach your child how to manage their behaviors socially.

Preparing for Social Events

Socializing is a fundamental skill that your child needs to learn as part of their development. From the time they enter nursery school or start attending play dates and interacting with other children, their social behaviors determine how they are perceived and embraced by their peers.

Children with underdeveloped social skills, even at a basic level, such as sharing toys, may have trouble making friends and thus feeling a sense of belonging in the spaces they visit. It's therefore extremely important for parents to expose their children to various social settings and allow them to witness different social dynamics so that they can learn the proper ways of engaging with others.

You might be hesitant to take your sensitive child out to social events like birthday parties, play dates, or family gatherings due to sensory challenges. Keeping them at home sounds like the safe option, but as they get older, it can be the one factor that holds them back from gaining experience in building relationships. This doesn't mean that they will instantly enjoy being exposed to people and unfamiliar social settings. At first, they may resist and protest each time you take them along.

Eventually, they would have developed enough social skills to thrive in these environments, even when they don't particularly enjoy being there.

With that being said, children with sensory processing difficulties don't do well when surprised with unusual experiences. Several days and even weeks before attending a function with your child, you'll need to mentally and emotionally prepare them. Below are guidelines to assist you with this process.

Understand Your Child's Social Strengths and Weaknesses

Before you can think about how to support your child in social settings, you need to be aware of their strengths and weaknesses. Think about how they normally behave when out in public. What are their likes and dislikes? How comfortable are they in new environments or meeting new people? What often calms them down?

You may find that your child has specific social triggers that cause problems. For example, they may be comfortable around small groups of children (maybe 2–5 children), but start to withdraw as the numbers increase. Or maybe your child can tolerate busy places but gets overwhelmed when the noise becomes too loud.

When you understand your child's strengths and weaknesses, you can assess whether the social event is appropriate for them or not. Moreover, you'll know what type of special accommodations to request beforehand to ensure your child feels comfortable. For instance, if you're going to a restaurant, you can book a table outside in a discreet corner that has less foot traffic than tables inside.

Research the Social Event

A few days or weeks before the event, do research to find out details about the venue, such as the layout of the space, the number of people it can hold (or a number of people who will be present at the function), and the availability of an outdoor area or play area. If possible, you can watch videos of the venue or physically visit and do a walk around during its quiet and busy times. This will allow you to identify potential sensory triggers for your child. For example, if a birthday venue has a play area that is enclosed, it could make a touch-sensitive child feel claustrophobic.

Share Information With Your Child

Once you have done your research and feel satisfied to expose your child to the social event, start sharing information about it. Do it in a casual way when they are relaxed or playing with their toys. Cover the five Ws:

- What is the event's name? What is it about?

- Where is the event taking place?

- When will the event happen?

- Who will be there? How many people will attend?

- Why is the event important? Why does your child need to attend?

It can be useful to show your child pictures of the venue or the invitation to give them a sense of what they might experience on the day. You might also drive past the venue with them or spend a day there so they aren't surprised about the event. If your child has questions, provide answers using simple language. Gently address concerns they may have by providing facts and reassuring them that they will be safe and have a wonderful time.

Let Others Know About Your Child's Sensory Challenges

Speak to the venue staff or function organizer about your child's sensitivities and possible situations that could be triggering for them. Find out if they can make accommodations for your child, but if not, come prepared with your own calming tools and strategies. If the event is completely out of your child's comfort zone, it's okay to skip it. While it's necessary to introduce them to diverse social settings, some events could be too unbearable. It can be helpful to reach out to other parents with children who have sensory processing difficulties and find out how they navigate social events and strategies that have worked with their children.

Strategies for Handling Overstimulating Situations

Sometimes, being in new environments and away from the comfort of home can be distressing for sensitive children. As such, they may show visible signs of overstimulation and become irritable, clingy, impatient, appear tired, hit or bite other children, or sit in a corner. Older children might express wanting to go home, refuse to follow instructions, or start unnecessary fights with other children. The earlier you recognize these signs, the sooner you can respond and help your child self-regulate.

Below are different strategies you can put into practice when handling overstimulation in public spaces.

Newborns

Newborns benefit from being outdoors for a limited time each day. Generally, it's recommended to wait until they are a few months old to expose them to new people or busy places like shopping malls, restaurants, and the airport. Their immune system is still developing and therefore may not be strong enough to fight against common infections (*When Can I Take My Newborn out in Public?*, 2024).

When taking your newborn out, choose quiet places with minimal foot traffic, like the park, library, or an empty coffee shop. Be aware of the signs of overstimulation, which might include clenching fists, appearing restless, crying, or turning their head away. You can soothe them by:

- gentle rocking while holding them.
- wrapping your child in a light blanket and putting them against your chest.
- shielding your child's face with a blanket to block out light.
- placing them inside a pram and covering the front with a light breathable wrap.
- speaking or humming in a soft, reassuring voice.

Toddlers and Preschoolers

Your toddler or preschooler has learned more ways to express discomfort than a typical newborn and may show overstimulation by yelling, crying, throwing objects, having meltdowns, going mute, or rubbing their eyes. At this age, your child is still learning about their big emotions and how to handle them. They may even become triggered by the overwhelming physical sensations they are feeling.

Below are some ways to encourage emotional regulation:

- Model self-control by checking in with yourself first and making sure you are calm before attending to your child.

- Remove your child from the upsetting environment by taking them to a quiet area. If this isn't possible, reduce the sensory information they are exposed to (e.g., turn the music volume down, clean up clutter)

- Hug your child and allow them to sit on your lap as they calm down. While you are in close contact, guide them through relaxation techniques like breathing exercises or affirmations.

- Validate their emotions and the possible cause of their trigger. For example, you might say, "I can tell that you're upset because everyone is talking loudly and nobody is listening to you."

- Sometimes, a time-out is all your child needs to get back to normal. However, there may be times when they don't want to continue a task or stay in the environment. Respecting their wishes and going home can restore a sense of safety.

School-Aged Children

School-aged children have gained some independence and are clearer about their sensory preferences and intolerances. You will immediately pick up when they are overstimulated because their mood and body language will change. For example, your child might appear bored or be more clumsy than usual. They can also act clingy and perform other attention-seeking behaviors like whining or breaking rules.

To help your child manage overstimulation, you can implement these strategies:

- Encourage your child to ask for what they need. For example, if they are fussing over the food given at a restaurant, you can say, "I can see that you're not happy with your meal. Is there anything we can remove from your plate or order so you can enjoy your food?"

- Suggest that your child take a walk (within eye distance), find a quiet area to calm down, or engage in relaxing activities like listening to music (propose activities that you know your child will enjoy).

- Allow your child to sit next to you until they are feeling balanced. This can be helpful for children with social anxiety who need a "break" from socializing. Turn toward them and have a casual conversation to make them laugh and feel good.

Building Social Skills Through Sensory Awareness

Another useful and long-term strategy to prepare your child for social events or visiting public spaces is teaching them social skills. These are basic skills that guide them in navigating social interactions, such as making eye contact, greeting, taking turns speaking, and being aware of how others feel.

Due to their sensory processing difficulties, social skills may not come easily to your child. For example, if they have auditory sensitivities, they may struggle to listen attentively and stay focused throughout conversations. If they have visual sensitivities, making eye contact can feel uncomfortable. With that said, they can gradually learn how to overcome these hurdles through positive reinforcement and plenty of time spent practicing at home.

Below are guidelines on how to develop your child's social skills through sensory awareness:

Recognize Your Child's Social Challenges

It's important to set goals for developing your child's social skills. To do this, you'll need to understand the specific challenges they are facing. Perhaps your child is comfortable playing with other children but struggles to pick up on social cues or has trouble following social expectations. You may need to observe their behaviors in social settings to identify these problems. Common skills that children with social processing issues may lack include:

- emotional regulation
- empathy and social awareness
- nonverbal communication
- interpreting social cues
- open-mindedness

When setting goals, start small and aim for incremental progress. For example, instead of expecting your child to maintain eye contact throughout the whole conversation, you can encourage them to make eye contact when greeting others.

Identify Social Stressors

Be aware of potential sensory triggers that can cause your child to withdraw or feel overwhelmed in social situations. For example, your child might be sensitive to sound, so whenever people start talking at once, they feel the need to shut down or fade into the background. Or maybe your child doesn't like busy places that cause visual overstimulation and may socialize better in more intimate settings. Whatever your child's triggers are, ensure they are removed or reduced to avoid sensory overload.

Offer Visual Support and Social Stories

Written or oral instructions should be given alongside visual aids to enhance your child's understanding of social expectations. For instance, it can be helpful for them to see a video or photo of two children greeting each other with a smile and a gentle handshake to learn how to behave in a similar context. Instead of simply imagining what they would do, your child can put themselves in the character's shoes and learn how to act. Another useful tip is to read your child stories related to social skills and have discussions about everyday interactions and what is considered appropriate or inappropriate behaviors. You can also ask your child to provide their opinions about the characters and how they should have responded in different situations.

Role-Play Real-Life Scenarios

Finally, role-play consolidates your child's learning and allows them to put their skills into practice in a controlled environment. By engaging with their siblings and other family members at home, your child gets to practice a range of social scenarios, such as making introductions, sharing about their interests, asking questions, taking turns, and showing empathy.

One of the ways to role-play is through pretend play, where you dress up and assume the role and lifestyle of unique characters. If you are playing with your child, you can pretend to be the teacher, and they could be the new student in class, or you could be the doctor, and they are the patient. Another form of role-playing is using miming games such as Simon Says, Follow the Leader, or Charades. Here, the aim is to reenact the facial expression, body language, or gesture made by the other person, and take turns leading and following.

When role-playing and practicing other social strategies with your child, remember to praise their efforts, regardless of how small. Be on the lookout for positive social behaviors and pause to acknowledge your child's actions. For instance, during pretend play, you can pause and say, "I really liked how you greeted me with a warm smile and looked into my eyes. You're doing great!"

Building Sensory Resilience Over Time

Social skills aren't built overnight. It can take months and years for your child to feel safe and confident being themselves and self-regulating in public. The focus, however, is not on them being perfect but on gradually learning tools to enrich their relationships. This means that even when your child is aware of their triggers, they may still have meltdowns or emotionally withdraw socially. Despite this, it's important to remind them that they are capable of having a good time outside of the home.

Below are positive skills that you can teach your child to empower them to remain strong and motivated during social interactions:

- **Teach your child how to ask for help:** Make a rule that whenever your child feels lost, bored, or upset in public, they can approach the nearest adult or parent and ask for support. This could include things like turning the music down, asking for a sensory break (e.g., going to the restroom or taking a walk), calling a loved one, and so on.

- **Help your child reframe their sensitivity as a strength:** Instead of feeling weird for not enjoying socializing like other children, teach your child to see their sensitivity as a special gift. For instance, by having sharp senses, they can notice changes in someone's mood and offer support, remember specific details about somebody, and appreciate music, food, and games more deeply than others. Thus, their life tends to have more depth, and ordinary moments feel deeply fulfilling.

- **Teach your child language to validate their feelings:** By using statements like "It's okay to be upset" or "It makes sense why you need a break," you can teach your child to validate their own emotions, which can help calm them down. This type of language also lets them know that they aren't wrong for experiencing the world differently from others.

- **Recite positive affirmations with your child:** Before and during social events or interactions, go through affirmations to help your child discard negative thoughts and focus on their strengths. You can turn this into a daily activity that you do each morning when preparing for the day. Recite a few statements and allow them to follow after you. The affirmations might include things like "I am brave for trying new things" and "I bring positivity wherever I go."

- **Teach your child that they have choices:** Not everyone will receive your child with open arms or appreciate their amazing personality. Learning how to face rejection will be a critical skill they need to develop as they get older. One way to teach this skill is by reminding your child that they have options on how to respond to others. For example, when a fight breaks out in the playground, they can walk away, seek help from an adult, or respectfully express how their friend's behavior made them feel. Knowing that they have a choice in how the situation unfolds can give your child confidence in navigating conflict.

Advanced Strategies for Public Environments

Physiological Preparation for Public Outings

Beyond behavioral and environmental preparations, understanding the physiological aspects of sensory processing can dramatically improve public experiences.

The Autonomic Nervous System and Public Places

Public environments often trigger the sympathetic nervous system's "fight-or-flight" response:

- **Baseline regulation**: Children with sensory processing challenges often enter public spaces with already elevated stress responses. Physiological preparation aims to establish a regulated autonomic state before exposure to challenging environments.

- **Neuroception and safety**: Dr. Stephen Porges' Polyvagal Theory explains that our nervous system constantly evaluates environmental safety (neuroception). Children with sensory processing difficulties may perceive non-threatening sensory input as dangerous, triggering protective responses.

- **Window of tolerance**: Public spaces often push sensory-sensitive children outside their "window of tolerance"—the zone where they can process experiences without becoming overwhelmed or shut down. Preparation strategies aim to widen this window before challenging exposures.

- **Co-regulation capacity**: Parents serve as external regulators for their child's nervous system. Understanding your own physiological responses to stress helps you maintain a regulated state that supports your child's nervous system.

- **Recovery trajectories**: Different children show distinct patterns in how quickly they recover from sensory overload. Tracking your child's typical recovery timeline helps in planning appropriate post-outing support.

Neuroscientist Dr. Lucy Jane Miller recommends monitoring physiological indicators of stress before public outings. Signs of autonomic dysregulation might include dilated pupils, shallow breathing, flushed skin, or increased heart rate. If these signs are present before leaving home, additional regulation activities may be needed before proceeding.

Nutritional Strategies for Sensory Resilience

Specific nutritional approaches can support sensory processing during outings:

- **Blood sugar stability**: Fluctuating blood glucose significantly impacts sensory threshold and emotional regulation. Balanced meals containing protein, healthy fats, and complex carbohydrates before outings provide sustained energy without the crashes associated with simple carbohydrates.

- **Protein timing**: Consuming adequate protein 45-60 minutes before challenging sensory environments provides amino acid precursors needed for neurotransmitter production, particularly serotonin and dopamine, which impact sensory modulation.

- **Hydration status**: Even mild dehydration affects neural transmission and sensory processing. Ensuring proper hydration before and during outings supports optimal nervous system function.

- **Anti-inflammatory foods**: For some children, consuming anti-inflammatory foods before outings may reduce sensory reactivity. Examples include omega-3 rich foods (like chia seeds or walnuts), turmeric with black pepper, or ginger.

- **Individual trigger avoidance**: Identifying and avoiding individual food triggers before outings prevents adding internal sensory challenges to external ones. Common sensory triggers include artificial colors, preservatives, and high-salicylate foods.

Nutritionist Kelly Dorfman suggests creating a "sensory outing nutrition protocol" tailored to your child's specific needs. This might include a protein-rich, blood-sugar stabilizing snack about an hour before leaving, sending along stabilizing snacks for extended outings, and ensuring appropriate hydration.

Sleep Optimization Before Challenging Environments

Sleep quality dramatically impacts sensory processing capacity:

- **Sleep debt and sensory thresholds**: Even one night of insufficient sleep can lower sensory thresholds by up to 30%, according to research by Dr. Oliviero Bruni. This means that sounds seem louder, lights brighter, and touch more intense after poor sleep.

- **REM sleep and sensory integration**: REM sleep plays a crucial role in processing sensory experiences and emotional regulation. Ensuring your child gets sufficient REM sleep supports better sensory integration during waking hours.

- **Sleep timing considerations**: Schedule challenging outings during your child's optimal alertness periods based on their circadian rhythm. For many children, mid-morning represents the best balance of alertness and regulation.

- **Sleep environment preparation**: If outings involve overnight stays in new environments, bringing familiar sleep elements (specific pillows, sound machines, bedding with familiar scents) supports better sleep quality away from home.

- **Post-outing sleep support**: Challenging sensory experiences can disrupt subsequent sleep. Plan for extended bedtime routines or additional sleep supports following particularly demanding outings.

Sleep researcher Dr. Sarah Schoen notes that children with sensory processing challenges often need 30-60 minutes more sleep than typically developing peers to maintain optimal regulation. Prioritizing this additional rest before anticipated sensory challenges can significantly improve outcomes.

Sensory Integration Activities Before Outings

Strategic sensory input before challenging environments can prepare the nervous system:

- **Heavy work preparation**: Activities providing deep pressure and proprioceptive input 15-30 minutes before outings help organize the nervous system. Examples include wall push-ups, carrying weighted items, or joint compression.

- **Vestibular regulation**: Specific types of movement can either alert or calm the nervous system. Linear, rhythmic movements (like swinging back and forth) tend to be organizing, while rotational movements (like spinning) should generally be avoided before challenging outings as they can be dysregulating.

- **Oral-motor preparation**: For many children, oral sensory input has a regulating effect. Crunchy snacks, blowing activities, or sucking thick liquids through a straw can help prepare the nervous system.

- **Deep pressure touch**: Activities providing consistent, firm pressure across large body areas can activate parasympathetic nervous system responses. Compression clothing, weighted blankets, or massage for 5-10 minutes before outings can be helpful.

- **Breath regulation**: Specific breathing patterns directly influence autonomic nervous system state. Practiced breathing exercises such as "square breathing" (inhale for 4, hold for 4, exhale for 4, hold for 4) can establish a regulated state before outings.

Occupational therapist Angie Voss recommends creating a personalized "sensory preparation sequence" of 3-5 activities that consistently help your child achieve a regulated state. Document which activities are most effective and implement them systematically before challenging outings.

Cultural Inclusion and Sensory Processing

Navigating diverse cultural events and settings presents unique sensory challenges that require thoughtful consideration of both sensory needs and cultural respect.

Cultural Celebrations and Sensory Challenges

Cultural festivities often involve intense sensory experiences that require specific preparation:

- **Religious services**: Many religious traditions include sensory-rich elements like incense, music, chanting, or prolonged sitting. Preparation might include previewing recordings of services, arranging for strategic seating near exits, or bringing subtle sensory tools that won't disrupt the ceremony.

- **Cultural festivals**: Events like Lunar New Year celebrations, Diwali, or Carnival feature intense multisensory experiences including loud sounds, bright colors, crowds, and strong scents. Researching specific sensory elements in advance allows for targeted preparation.

- **Family gatherings**: Family celebrations often involve extended social interaction, unfamiliar foods, disrupted routines, and varied sensory environments. Creating structured breaks, designating a quiet space, and establishing clear time expectations can help.

- **Patriotic celebrations**: Events like fireworks displays or parades combine loud noises, crowds, and visual intensity. Alternative viewing options (like watching from a parked car or distant location) can provide the experience with modulated sensory input.

Anthropologist Dr. Roberta Takahashi emphasizes the importance of separating essential cultural elements from environmental factors that can be modified. This approach allows families to honor cultural traditions while accommodating sensory needs.

Communicating Sensory Needs Across Cultural Contexts

How sensory challenges are understood varies significantly across cultures:

- **Culturally appropriate language**: When explaining your child's sensory needs to people from different cultural backgrounds, consider cultural frameworks for understanding differences. Some cultures may relate better to descriptions focusing on physical comfort, while others may understand explanations framed around learning styles or temperament.

- **Finding cultural bridges**: Identify concepts within each culture that parallel sensory processing. Many cultures have traditional concepts that recognize individual differences in how people experience their environment, providing entry points for explaining sensory needs.

- **Respecting authority structures**: In cultures with strong hierarchical traditions, approach educational advocacy through appropriate channels rather than challenging authority directly. Seek cultural guides who can help navigate these systems respectfully.

- **Gift of accommodation**: In some cultures, frame sensory accommodations as opportunities to show hospitality rather than exceptions to rules. This positive framing often receives better reception than disability-based requests.

- **Visual supports across languages**: When language barriers exist, visual supports showing sensory challenges and accommodations can bridge communication gaps more effectively than verbal explanations.

Cross-cultural communication specialist Dr. Maya Chen suggests developing a "cultural sensory passport"—a simple visual guide showing your child's specific sensory needs that can be shared across linguistic and cultural contexts.

Navigating Diverse Community Spaces

Different communities create varied sensory environments that may require specific strategies:

- **Urban environments**: Dense city environments present concentrated sensory challenges including traffic noise, diverse scents, visual complexity, and crowded spaces. Creating sensory "decompression zones" between activities provides essential regulation opportunities.

- **Rural settings**: While often less crowded, rural environments may include intense sensory experiences like farm animal sounds, machinery noise, or strong natural scents. Providing context and preparation for these less familiar sensory experiences helps build tolerance.

- **Cultural districts**: Neighborhoods centered around specific cultural communities often feature distinct sensory profiles, from the incense and spice aromas of international districts to the music and food scents of cultural enclaves. Gradual exposure to these unique sensory landscapes builds adaptability.

- **Socioeconomic diversity**: Community spaces serving different socioeconomic groups may have vastly different sensory characteristics, from noise levels to personal space expectations. Discussing these differences without judgment helps prepare children for diverse experiences.

- **Gendered spaces**: In some communities, gender-segregated spaces (like locker rooms or certain religious settings) may present unique sensory challenges that require specific preparation.

Community inclusion specialist Dr. Jasmine Rivera recommends "sensory mapping" diverse community spaces with your child, explicitly discussing both the sensory challenges and the cultural richness these environments offer, balancing sensory awareness with cultural appreciation.

Supporting Cultural Identity While Addressing Sensory Needs

For children from sensory-rich cultural backgrounds, balancing cultural connection with sensory comfort requires thoughtful approaches:

- **Cultural pride and sensory differences**: Help your child understand that needing sensory accommodations doesn't diminish their cultural identity or connection. Many cultural traditions can be adapted while preserving their essential meaning.

- **Sensory-friendly cultural education**: Create modified ways to connect with cultural heritage that respect sensory needs, such as small-group cultural lessons, sensory-considered cultural cooking experiences, or one-on-one cultural mentorship.

- **Adaptation without erasure**: Work with cultural elders or knowledge keepers to identify respectful adaptations of sensory-intensive traditions. Many cultural leaders are open to accommodations when approached with genuine respect.

- **Cultural sensory strengths**: Identify aspects of your

cultural traditions that naturally align with your child's sensory preferences, building connection through these compatible experiences.

- **Community education**: When appropriate, educate cultural community members about sensory processing, creating greater understanding and naturally emerging accommodations.

Cultural psychologist Dr. Elena Martinez emphasizes that cultural connection provides important identity anchoring for children with sensory differences. Her research shows that children who maintain strong cultural connections while receiving sensory accommodations show better outcomes than those who experience either cultural disconnection or sensory overwhelm.

Progressive Exposure Protocols

Systematic approaches to building sensory tolerance can transform previously overwhelming public experiences into manageable ones.

Principles of Systematic Desensitization

Originally developed for phobia treatment, systematic desensitization provides a framework for gradually building sensory tolerance:

- **Hierarchy development**: Create a detailed progression of exposures from least to most challenging. For example, a shopping desensitization hierarchy might begin with looking at store pictures, then visiting during quiet hours, gradually working toward busy shopping times.

- **Relaxation pairing**: Combine each exposure level with relaxation techniques (deep breathing, progressive muscle relaxation, or guided imagery) to create new associations. The nervous system learns that the sensory environment can be experienced while remaining regulated.

- **Mastery before progression**: Ensure comfort at each level before advancing to more challenging exposures. Rushing progression typically leads to setbacks rather than faster progress.

- **Reinforcement strategies**: Positive reinforcement for successful exposures builds motivation and positive associations. Reinforcement should acknowledge the effort regardless of the outcome.

- **Regression planning**: Prepare for occasional steps backward, particularly during illness, stress, or developmental transitions. Having predetermined strategies for addressing regression prevents discouragement.

Psychologist Dr. Christopher Wilson's research shows that this structured approach produces more lasting tolerance than either avoidance or forced exposure. His longitudinal studies found that children who experienced systematic desensitization showed sustained improvements 2-5 years later, while those who underwent forced exposure often developed increased anxiety.

Location-Specific Exposure Protocols

Different environments require tailored desensitization approaches:

- **Grocery stores**: Begin with off-peak visits focused on quieter store sections, gradually expanding to busier times and more stimulating departments. Consider starting with smaller stores before tackling supermarkets.

- **Medical settings**: Create a progression starting with simply entering the waiting room without an appointment, then scheduling visits just to meet staff, before advancing to non-invasive procedures and finally full examinations.

- **Entertainment venues**: For theaters or concert halls, begin with virtual tours, advance to visiting empty venues, then attend shorter performances or events with known content before experiencing full-length performances.

- **Restaurants**: Start with takeout from restaurant, progress to off-peak outdoor seating, then indoor seating during quiet times, gradually working toward busier dining periods.

- **Public transportation**: Begin with watching videos of the transport mode, then observing in person, sitting in stationary vehicles, taking short trips during quiet periods, and finally using transportation during regular service times.

Occupational therapist Teresa May-Benson recommends documenting specific elements that make each environment challenging for your child and targeting these elements in your exposure hierarchy. This precision creates more effective progression than generic exposure protocols.

Virtual Reality and Simulation Approaches

Technology offers new possibilities for controlled sensory exposure:

- **360° video previewing**: Videos filmed in 360° format allow children to preview environments from different perspectives, building familiarity before physical visits. These can be viewed on smartphones, tablets, or VR headsets.

- **Virtual reality exposure therapy**: Formal VR therapy programs provide graduated exposure to challenging sensory environments with therapist guidance. Research shows these approaches can significantly reduce anxiety and sensory reactivity before real-world exposure.

- **Augmented reality tools**: Apps that overlay calming visuals or supportive information onto real environments through smartphone cameras can create "sensory filters" that make initial exposures more manageable.

- **Simulation creation**: For some children, creating miniature simulations of challenging environments (like a shoe-box sized store model) allows cognitive processing of the environment while maintaining control over sensory input.

- **Social story technology**: Interactive social stories on tablets can provide both environmental previews and coping strategy practice in an engaging format.

Neuropsychologist Dr. Albert Rizzo's research demonstrates that virtual exposure activates many of the same neural pathways as physical exposure, creating genuine desensitization effects while allowing precise control over sensory intensity. His studies show 62% improved tolerance when virtual exposure precedes physical exposure compared to physical exposure alone.

Measuring Progress in Sensory Tolerance

Objective measurement helps document real progress that might otherwise be overlooked:

- **Duration tracking**: Record how long your child can comfortably remain in challenging environments. Small incremental increases often precede more obvious behavioral changes.

- **Physiological markers**: Track observable signs of physiological regulation like steady breathing, normal coloring, and relaxed posture during exposures.

- **Recovery time**: Measure how long it takes your child to return to baseline regulation after challenging experiences. Decreasing recovery time often indicates developing resilience.

- **Coping strategy utilization**: Document which regulation strategies your child uses independently during exposures and how effectively they implement them.

- **Expansion of activities**: Record new activities or locations your child can access as sensory tolerance develops. This broader participation often represents the most meaningful outcome.

Dr. Lucy Jane Miller recommends creating visual progress displays that help children see their own growth. These might include "challenge ladders" where completed steps are colored in, or "bravery beads" collected for each successful exposure, providing concrete representations of developing resilience.

Recovery Strategies After Sensory Exposures

Even successful public outings can deplete regulatory resources, making intentional recovery essential for long-term success.

The Neurobiology of Sensory Recovery

Understanding recovery at a neurological level guides more effective support:

- **Stress hormone metabolism**: Challenging sensory experiences trigger stress hormone release that requires time to metabolize. Complete physiological recovery typically takes 2-3 times longer than the stressful experience itself.

- **Neural fatigue patterns**: Continuous filtering of sensory information depletes neurotransmitters and creates neural fatigue. This depletion affects sensory processing capacity for hours following exposure.

- **Sensory memory processing**: The brain continues processing sensory experiences after exposure ends. Quiet recovery periods support this integration process, while immediate new sensory input can create processing backlogs.

- **Sleep cycle impacts**: Intense sensory experiences can disrupt subsequent sleep architecture, reducing restorative sleep stages. Supporting optimal sleep following sensory challenges accelerates recovery.

- **Autonomic nervous system reset**: After sympathetic activation during challenging sensory experiences, specific interventions can help restore parasympathetic dominance for rest and digestion.

Neuroscientist Dr. Stephen Porges explains that complete nervous system recovery follows a predictable sequence that cannot be rushed. Attempting to immediately re-engage after challenging experiences often results in diminished tolerance for subsequent exposures, while appropriate recovery periods build resilience over time.

Home-Based Recovery Protocols

Structured recovery routines accelerate return to regulation:

- **Sensory dimming period**: Immediately after intense sensory experiences, provide 20-30 minutes of reduced sensory input—lowered lights, minimal conversation, decreased environmental noise, and limited visual stimulation.

- **Deep pressure recovery**: Activities providing consistent deep pressure help reset autonomic functioning after sensory challenges. Weighted blankets, compression clothing, or massage can be particularly effective during this period.

- **Proprioceptive restoration**: Heavy work activities like carrying groceries, pushing a loaded laundry basket, or wall push-ups help reorganize the nervous system after sensory overload.

- **Vestibular calming**: Slow, linear vestibular input (like gentle swinging or rocking) supports parasympathetic activation following sensory challenges.

- **Structured transitions**: Create consistent arrival routines that signal the transition from public to home environments, helping the nervous system recognize that challenges have ended and recovery can begin.

Occupational therapist Julia Wilbarger recommends establishing a personalized "sensory first aid kit" containing 3-5 highly effective recovery tools that can be implemented immediately upon returning home. This consistency helps the nervous system recognize and respond to recovery cues more efficiently.

Processing Strategies for Complex Experiences

Beyond physical recovery, processing the experience supports longer-term adaptation:

- **Sensory experience mapping**: For verbal children, structured discussion about the sensory components of the experience helps integrate the memory and identify specific challenges for future preparation.

- **Expressive processing**: Art activities, sensory play, or movement experiences related to the outing provide non-verbal processing opportunities for children of all verbal abilities.

- **Photographic reviews**: Reviewing photographs of successful outings reinforces positive associations and provides opportunities to discuss both challenges and coping strategies used.

- **Narrative construction**: Creating simple stories about the experience helps children develop coherent narratives that support future regulation. These can be written, drawn, or verbally recorded.

- **Success acknowledgment**: Specifically highlighting moments of successful self-regulation during the outing reinforces coping strategies and builds confidence for future experiences.

Psychologist Dr. Daniel Siegel explains that this "name it to tame it" approach helps integrate challenging sensory experiences into explicit memory, reducing the likelihood that similar future experiences will trigger implicit fear responses.

Planning Recovery Time in Family Schedules

Strategic scheduling supports complete recovery:

- **Recovery-to-activity ratios**: As a general guideline, allow recovery time proportional to the challenge— highly stimulating or novel experiences may require recovery periods 2-3 times longer than the activity itself.

- **Cumulative scheduling awareness**: Consider the cumulative impact of multiple activities when planning. A moderately challenging experience following proper recovery from a previous outing may be successful, while the same experience without recovery time often leads to reduced tolerance.

- **Weekend recovery balancing**: If weekdays involve consistently challenging sensory environments (like school), ensure weekend schedules include adequate recovery periods rather than filling them with additional sensory-demanding activities.

- **Seasonal intensity planning**: Many families find that certain seasons (like winter holidays) involve increased sensory demands. Planning intentional recovery periods during these high-demand seasons supports better regulation.

- **Transition day buffers**: After particularly challenging events or transitions (like travel or major celebrations), schedule a complete "buffer day" for recovery before returning to regular activities.

Family therapist Dr. Rachel Lohmann emphasizes that this

recovery planning isn't "giving in" to sensory challenges, but rather creating the physiological conditions that allow children to build greater resilience and participation over time. Her research shows that families who implement structured recovery protocols see greater increases in community participation compared to those who push for continuous engagement.

Documentation Systems for Successful Public Experiences

Systematic documentation transforms individual successes into repeatable strategies and provides valuable information for professionals supporting your child.

Creating Effective Sensory Outing Records

Comprehensive documentation captures crucial details for future planning:

- **Environmental factors**: Record specific sensory elements present during the outing, including estimated noise levels, lighting conditions, crowding, scents, and temperature.

- **Timing variables**: Note time of day, duration, relationship to meals and sleep, and where the activity fell in your daily schedule.

- **Physiological observations**: Document signs of regulation or dysregulation, including color changes, breathing patterns, muscle tone, and recovery time.

- **Preparation strategies**: Record specific sensory preparation activities, timing of preparation, nutrition before the outing, and sleep quality the previous night.

- **Successful accommodations**: Detail which tools, modifications, or strategies proved most helpful during the experience.

Occupational therapist Lindsey Biel recommends a simple rating scale for overall success and specific sensory domains, allowing you to track patterns and progress over time. Even brief ratings provide valuable data when consistently maintained.

Digital Tools for Tracking Sensory Experiences

Technology offers efficient documentation options:

- **Specialized sensory apps**: Applications like "Sensory Processing Tools" or "Sensory Tracker" provide structured frameworks for recording sensory experiences and identifying patterns.

- **Voice memo documentation**: Quick audio recordings immediately after outings capture observations while they're fresh, which can be transcribed or reviewed later.

- **Photo documentation**: Strategic photographs during successful moments provide visual records of effective strategies and serve as positive visual reminders for your child.

- **Digital sensory journals**: Shared digital documents allow multiple caregivers to contribute observations about sensory experiences across different contexts.

- **Data visualization tools**: Applications that convert tracking data into visual formats help identify patterns that might otherwise be missed in text-based records.

Developmental psychologist Dr. Samuel Johnson notes that even simple, consistent documentation typically reveals patterns within 3-4 weeks that can significantly improve intervention planning. His research shows that families using structured documentation systems report greater confidence in managing public outings and more purposeful strategy implementation.

Sharing Documentation with Professionals

Effective information sharing enhances professional support:

- **Pre-appointment summaries**: Before professional appointments, compile relevant sensory observations into concise summaries highlighting patterns, successful strategies, and specific questions.

- **Video sampling**: Short videos demonstrating both challenges and successful coping strategies provide professionals with direct observation opportunities that complement verbal reports.

- **Collaborative documentation systems**: Shared tracking systems that both parents and professionals can access create continuity between clinical and home settings.

- **Comparative contexts**: Include information about how sensory responses differ across environments (home, school, community) to help identify environmental factors affecting regulation.

- **Intervention response tracking**: Document how your child responds to specific professional recommendations, providing feedback that allows for strategy refinement.

Occupational therapist and researcher Dr. Winnie Dunn emphasizes that this detailed documentation often identifies subtle patterns that significantly inform intervention planning. Her research demonstrates that professionals make more precise and effective recommendations when provided with systematic home observations compared to relying solely on clinical observations.

Sensory Success Portfolios

Creating permanent records of successful experiences builds confidence and strategy awareness:

- **Strategy catalogs**: Document specific accommodations and tools that have proven effective across different environments, creating a personalized resource for future planning.

- **Progressive challenge records**: Track gradual increases in tolerance for specific sensory challenges, providing concrete evidence of growth that motivates continued effort.

- **Independence milestones**: Record moments when your child independently implemented sensory strategies or advocated for their needs, celebrating these significant developmental steps.

- **Photo journals**: Compile photographs of successful community experiences in a format your child can review, building confidence and positive associations with public settings.

- **Sensory strength recognition**: Explicitly document sensory processing strengths alongside challenges, creating a balanced understanding of your child's sensory profile.

Child psychologist Dr. Ellen Braaten recommends periodically reviewing these success records with your child in a collaborative way, emphasizing their growing competence and resilience. This practice helps shift children's self-perception from focusing on sensory limitations to recognizing their developing coping capacities.

Key Takeaways

- Public places present complex sensory challenges for children with sensory processing difficulties. Understanding these challenges and planning accordingly can transform potentially overwhelming experiences into successful outings.

- Preparation is essential for managing sensory challenges in public. This includes previewing environments, explaining expectations, bringing sensory tools, and planning exit strategies before difficulties escalate.

- Supermarkets present particular sensory challenges with their bright lights, varied sounds, strong smells, and crowded spaces. Strategic planning, such as shopping during quiet hours and creating focused shopping lists, can help navigate these environments successfully.

- Restaurants can be managed by choosing sensory-friendly establishments, bringing familiar foods, selecting strategic seating, and having engagement activities ready for waiting periods.

- Medical appointments often trigger sensory defensiveness. Preparation through role play, sensory tools, and clear communication with providers creates more positive experiences and better healthcare outcomes.

- Family gatherings require balancing social expectations with sensory needs. Setting appropriate time limits, establishing retreat spaces, and educating family members about sensory needs helps navigate these important social connections.

- Physiological preparation significantly impacts outing success. Understanding the autonomic nervous system, implementing nutritional strategies for sensory resilience, optimizing sleep, and using targeted sensory integration activities before outings can dramatically improve tolerance.

- Cultural inclusion requires balancing sensory needs with respect for traditions. Developing culturally appropriate communication strategies, understanding diverse sensory environments, and supporting cultural identity while addressing sensory needs creates more inclusive experiences.

- Progressive exposure protocols systematically build sensory tolerance. Using principles of gradual desensitization, creating location-specific exposure plans, utilizing technology for simulation, and measuring progress objectively leads to expanded community participation.

- Recovery strategies after sensory exposures are as important as preparation. Understanding the neurobiology of recovery, implementing home-based protocols, processing complex experiences, and planning adequate recovery time in family schedules supports long-term sensory development.

In the next chapter, we'll address the unique sensory challenges associated with travel, providing strategies for successful experiences away from the predictable environments of home and community.

Chapter 7:

Traveling With a Sensory—Sensitive Child

Instead of teaching children to get 'there,' why not let them be here? Where is 'there' anyway? The world needs more 'here' than 'there'.
    –Vince Gowmon

What's Your Dream Travel Destination?

My dream travel destination is a place with really soft sand and a big ocean! I think it would be super cool to go to a beach where the water sparkles like a million tiny stars. The sand could be warm and fluffy, and I can feel it between my toes. Sometimes, the sound of the waves crashing is like a lullaby, and it makes my heart feel happy and calm, even when everything else feels really loud. I would like to build a big sandcastle and have my own little space where I can be creative.

But sometimes, too many people at the beach can feel really overwhelming. The sounds can go all mixy in my head, and it makes my tummy feel funny. I would want to find a quiet spot away from the crowds where I can just listen to the ocean and watch the clouds. Maybe I can see some funny shapes in the clouds while I take deep breaths. If I had my special headphones, I could still enjoy the beach and feel safe. I would love to dip my toes in the water and watch the little fish swim by!

– Jerome, 10 years old

Sensory Preparation for Travel

Taking your child to a nearby restaurant or shopping mall is one thing, but traveling long distances, such as going on a road trip or flying out of state, is a totally different ball game. Every child dreams of exploring new and foreign lands that provide sensory stimuli different from what they encounter at home. However, children with sensory processing difficulties can find the experience of traveling, from packing to commuting, stressful.

Fortunately, there are ways that you can anticipate and prepare for potential triggers during your family travels, which include the following:

Create a Sensory Travel Kit

When getting your luggage ready, include a small backpack filled with their favorite calming sensory toys and tools. For instance, they might add a stuffed animal, earplugs, puzzles, sunglasses, and chewy snacks. If they are old enough, allow them to pack and carry their backpack (especially if they enjoy deep pressure), as this can instill a sense of responsibility.

Pack Your Child's Favorite Clothes and Toiletries

If you have a tactile sensitive child, it's important to pack clothing and toiletries they are familiar with rather than relying on products at the hotel or buying new clothes and toiletries at the destination, which the child may have a problem with. For instance, pack the towel they normally use to dry up and use it as their beach towel. If they normally bathe with specific soaps, shampoos, or use certain lotions or toothpastes, make sure these are also included in the luggage.

Rehearse the Route and Itinerary of Your Trip

A few days or weeks before going on vacation, sit down with your child and share information about the route, distance, itinerary, and other stops you will make along the way. It can be helpful to show your child videos of the place you will be visiting and a map with an outline of the route you will travel. They may also benefit from learning about the triggers they may face, like long queues at the airport or train station, loud noises at the theme park, and unfamiliar odors when exploring a market. You can use role-playing to go over certain scenarios, such as responding to strangers, paying in a foreign currency, and following social rules at museums and galleries.

Be Strategic in Your Transportation Options

Depending on your child's sensory needs, some modes of transport may not be suitable. For example, traveling on an overnight train in a small bunker might feel distressing for a child who constantly needs to be on the move. Similarly, a child who dislikes the sensation of being suspended in the air might be afraid of traveling via airplanes. Choose transportation that will be comfortable for your child or at least doesn't cause much stress. You might even consider using multiple modes of transport with a day's break for long trips to make the journey feel pleasant.

Choosing Sensory-Friendly Destinations

Where you travel is just as important as how you get there. Unlike other children who can easily adjust to new environments, your child has specific sensory needs that need to be considered. Going to a beach, for example, is loved by many children, including those with sensory issues. However, minor inconveniences like seeing crowds on the beachfront or hearing a flock of seagulls making loud wailing noises can ruin the experience for them. Therefore, it's essential to research and identify sensory-friendly destinations that the whole family can enjoy.

Here are some tips for finding spots and destinations your child will love;

- **Research locations based on activities offered:** Pick destinations that accommodate your child's sensory-seeking or sensory-avoidant behaviors. For example, a child who needs plenty of stimulation will have a blast at a theme park, but one who enjoys relaxing activities will prefer visiting an aquarium or museum.

- **Identify the peak and off-season:** Some destinations offer a different experience during the peak and off-seasons. There may be more or fewer crowds and activities available. If your child doesn't like busy places, it's recommended to travel during off-seasons so they can explore the place without feeling overwhelmed.

- **Search for destinations with sensory accommodations:** Some places cater to people with disabilities and will have designated transport, pathways, quiet zones, and special access to make the visit feel as comfortable as possible. For example, theme parks like Disney Land and SeaWorld San Diego have programs like the Disability Access Service and the Attraction Assistance Pass, which reduce wait times on rides for guests with special needs (Arnold, 2024).

- **Find destinations that assist with sensory integration:** Some places provide a therapeutic, mindful experience that allows your child to decompress and ground themselves. These include national parks, lake towns, camping sites, and rural towns. Children are encouraged to connect to nature, walk barefoot, cook outside, and increase their physical activity—these soothing activities can improve their overall well-being.

Managing Sensory Overload on the Road and During Long Trips

When traveling long distances, such as road trips or flying overseas, your child may become overstimulated. While there are ways to reduce the likelihood of this, like making the necessary preparations, it can still surprise you and your child. Below are strategies to manage triggers, meltdowns, and other difficult behaviors when traveling with your child.

Take Regular Pit Stops

Stop a few times along the road and at specific rest stops so your child can get out of the car and stretch their legs or go to the restroom. Allocate at least 10-30 minutes for structured breaks, and alert your child when the next one is coming up. If you are traveling by air, book flights with at least one layover so that your child can walk and explore shops at the airport before the next leg of the journey.

Pack Familiar Foods and Snacks

If your child has a preference for specific foods and snacks, ensure these are available in the car or on the flight. Some chewy or crunchy snacks can provide a calming effect, allowing your child to distract themselves from distressing feelings. Avoid foods and snacks that contain dairy or high-fat content (i.e., processed or fried foods), since they can lead to bloating, constipation, nausea, or diarrhea. Moreover, provide sugary treats in moderation to avoid sugar spikes that often lead to irritation, fatigue, and restlessness.

Follow a Similar Routine You Do at Home

Try by all means to maintain structure and predictability during your travels by keeping to the same routine you use at home. For example, stick to the same sleep times and meal times, and hold your child accountable for the same behavior rules and consequences. Following your home routine could lead to some travel changes. For example, when traveling by road, you may choose to stop at a restaurant while you eat dinner at home, and rest at a hotel for bedtime.

Limit Screen Time

Electronic devices can be a calming tool for children traveling long distances. However, too much screen time can lead to overstimulation, making it difficult for your child to pay attention, regulate their emotions, or sleep during their normal bedtime. Pack some sensory toys and relaxing games that your child can play to take a break from their screens. These can include fidget toys, books, a portable music system, a sketchpad, a coloring book, or a journal.

The aim of managing overstimulation during long trips is to make the journey as comfortable as possible. Try to recreate the feeling of being home by providing sensory pleasures that your child is familiar with. Recognize and praise their patience and cooperation to reinforce good behavior. Remember that they are venturing outside of their comfort zone and doing their best to remain calm and not freak out.

Advanced Travel Strategies for Sensory-Sensitive Children

Developing Sensory Flexibility through Graduated Travel Experiences

While some children require consistent environments for regulation, gradually building travel flexibility expands their world and develops important adaptive skills.

The Developmental Progression of Travel Readiness

Travel competence typically develops through predictable stages:

- **Familiar destination outings**: Initial successful "travel" experiences often involve familiar destinations with some novel elements, like visiting grandparents or a frequently visited vacation spot. These experiences build basic travel skills within a context of relative predictability.

- **Day trips with home return**: The next developmental step typically involves full-day outings to new destinations with a return to home for sleep. This allows exposure to novelty with the security of returning to the familiar sensory environment of home for recovery.

- **Overnight stays in supportive environments**: Initial overnight experiences in highly supportive environments—like the homes of understanding relatives or hotels specifically chosen for sensory compatibility—build confidence for longer stays.

- **Short vacations with sensory considerations**: Short trips (2-3 days) with carefully selected accommodations and activities matched to sensory needs create positive experiences that build travel competence.

- **Expanded travel with strategic supports**: As travel skills develop, the range of possible destinations and durations expands, with continuing attention to sensory needs but greater flexibility.

Child development researcher Dr. Martin Sensmeier emphasizes that each child moves through these stages at their own pace. Attempting to skip stages typically results in difficult experiences that create travel anxiety rather than confidence. His research shows that many sensory-sensitive children benefit from repeating successful experiences within each stage multiple times before progressing to the next level.

Systematic Travel Exposure Protocols

Structured approaches to building travel flexibility show the strongest results:

- **Travel element isolation**: Rather than attempting entire trips, initially expose your child to isolated elements of travel. This might include visiting an airport without flying, sitting on a parked train, or spending time in a hotel lobby without staying overnight.

- **Sensory hierarchy development**: Create a detailed hierarchy of travel components from least to most challenging for your child. This personalized progression might range from looking at travel pictures to handling the most challenging sensory aspect of your destination.

- **Gradual duration increases**: Begin with very brief exposures to challenging travel elements, systematically increasing duration as comfort develops. Even 5-10 minute initial successes build foundation for longer exposures.

- **Component combination**: After mastering individual elements separately, gradually combine components in increasingly realistic travel scenarios.

- **Practice-to-real ratio**: Research suggests a 3:1 ratio of practice experiences to actual travel produces optimal results. This might mean three airport visits before an actual flight, or three brief hotel lobby visits before an overnight stay.

Travel psychologist Dr. Rachel Martinez notes that this approach requires significant advance planning but produces dramatically better outcomes than either avoidance or forced exposure. Her research demonstrates that children who experience systematic travel exposure show 74% fewer stress behaviors during actual travel compared to those without such preparation.

Building Cognitive Flexibility Through Travel

Beyond specific destinations, travel builds crucial cognitive skills:

- **Novelty tolerance**: The ability to manage new situations, environments, and experiences—a fundamental life skill often challenging for sensory-sensitive children—develops through positive travel experiences.

- **Transitional flexibility**: Travel inherently involves

transitions between activities, locations, and sensory environments, strengthening this core executive function.

- **Adaptability training**: The natural variations encountered during travel (weather changes, schedule adjustments, unexpected events) build adaptability in a real-world context.

- **Error tolerance**: Travel inevitably involves minor mishaps, creating natural opportunities to develop resilience and the understanding that imperfection is manageable.

- **Recovery skill generalization**: Successfully recovering from challenging moments during travel helps children internalize regulation strategies that transfer to other life contexts.

Developmental psychologist Dr. Sarah Mahler emphasizes that these cognitive flexibility benefits often extend far beyond travel itself. Her longitudinal research shows that sensory-sensitive children who develop travel competence demonstrate improved flexibility in school transitions, social adaptability, and general resilience compared to those without these experiences.

Technology-Assisted Travel Preparation

Digital tools offer unique advantages for travel preparation:

- **Virtual destination tours**: Virtual reality or 360° video tours of destinations provide sensory previewing in a completely controllable environment. Many museums, attractions, and even hotel chains now offer virtual tours specifically designed for accessibility preparation.

- **Travel simulation apps**: Applications designed for

children with sensory or anxiety challenges allow virtual practice of specific travel components like airport security, airplane boarding, or hotel check-in processes.

- **Augmented reality orientation**: Some destinations offer augmented reality tools that overlay simplified visual information onto actual environments through smartphone cameras, creating a bridge between preparation and actual experience.

- **Gradual video exposure**: Systematic viewing of increasing complex travel videos builds familiarity. Begin with simple, calm scenes from your destination and gradually introduce more dynamic elements.

- **Interactive social stories**: Digital social stories that allow your child to make choices and explore different travel scenarios build both understanding and agency.

Technology integration specialist Dr. James Wilson notes that these tools work best when combined with actual physical preparation rather than substituting for it entirely. His research shows that children who experienced both virtual and physical preparation demonstrated 58% better adaptation to actual travel compared to those who received only one type of preparation.

International Travel Considerations

Travel across cultures adds layers of sensory complexity that require specific preparation and strategies.

Cross-Cultural Sensory Differences

Different cultures create distinct sensory environments:

- **Proxemic variations**: Cultures differ significantly in typical interpersonal distances, touch expectations, and personal space norms. Preparation for these differences is essential for tactile-sensitive children.

- **Olfactory landscapes**: Each culture's food traditions, environmental scents, and urban aromas create distinctive olfactory experiences. Gradual exposure to these scents before travel can reduce overwhelming reactions.

- **Acoustic environments**: Differences in typical volume levels, types of ambient sounds, and acoustic characteristics vary dramatically across cultures. Sound samples from your destination can help build auditory tolerance.

- **Visual stimulation differences**: Environmental complexity, color usage, signage density, and architectural styles create distinct visual experiences across cultures. Visual previewing through photos and videos helps prepare visual processing systems.

- **Timing and rhythm variations**: Cultures operate on different daily rhythms and pace, from siesta cultures to those with extended evening hours. Understanding these patterns helps create sensory-informed schedules.

Cultural anthropologist Dr. Elena Martínez emphasizes that these sensory variations often affect children more intensely than adults due to their still-developing filtering abilities. Her research with sensory-sensitive travelers indicates that specific preparation for these cross-cultural sensory differences significantly improves travel experiences.

Navigating Unfamiliar Food Environments

Food differences present particular challenges during international travel:

- **Food security planning**: Bringing shelf-stable preferred foods provides security when local options are limited. Research suggests packing enough for 1.5 times your expected needs accounts for potential travel delays.

- **Sensory-similar food identification**: Before travel, identify foods in the destination culture that share sensory characteristics (texture, flavor profile, temperature) with your child's preferred foods, even if the specific items differ.

- **Visual food preparation exposure**: Videos of food preparation in your destination help create familiarity with different cooking methods and presentation styles before direct exposure.

- **Cross-cultural food bridging**: Introduce elements of destination cuisine at home before travel, starting with mild versions and gradually incorporating more authentic preparations.

- **Nutrition maintenance strategies**: Work with a nutritionist to identify specific nutrients your child might miss during travel due to food selectivity and develop targeted supplementation approaches if needed.

Nutritional anthropologist Dr. Jason Chang notes that food flexibility often develops throughout a trip. His research shows that most sensory-sensitive children show gradually expanding food acceptance between days 4-10 of international travel as familiarity increases, suggesting that longer stays may actually be easier than very short international trips from a food perspective.

Language Barriers and Sensory Communication

Communication challenges can amplify sensory stress during international travel:

- **Visual communication tools**: Prepare visual cards showing common sensory needs and accommodations that transcend language barriers. Include pictures of needed breaks, quiet spaces, or sensory tools.

- **Translation technology**: Specialized translation apps designed for accessibility needs can communicate specific sensory accommodations in local languages.

- **Sensory advocacy phrases**: Learn key phrases related to your child's specific sensory needs in the local language. Focus on positive, solution-oriented expressions rather than problem statements.

- **International sensory symbols**: Some sensory support symbols are increasingly recognized internationally. Autism identification cards, noise-sensitive indicators, or sensory friendly program symbols can bridge communication gaps.

- **Cultural intermediary identification**: Research suggests identifying a local contact with both cultural knowledge and some understanding of sensory needs dramatically improves access to appropriate accommodations.

Linguistic anthropologist Dr. Maya Caldwell emphasizes that communication about sensory needs requires more than literal translation—it requires cultural context. Her work with traveling families suggests that understanding how sensory differences are conceptualized in your destination culture significantly improves the effectiveness of accommodation requests.

Accommodations Across Cultural Contexts

How sensory accommodations are understood varies significantly across cultures:

- **Medical versus educational frameworks**: In some cultures, sensory processing issues are understood primarily as medical conditions, while in others they're viewed as educational differences. Framing requests appropriately for the cultural context improves responses.

- **Hierarchy navigation**: In hierarchical cultures, accommodation requests may need to be directed to specific authority figures rather than front-line staff. Research suggest identifying the appropriate request pathway before travel.

- **Relationship-based versus rule-based cultures**: Some cultures prioritize relationship and personal connection in making accommodations, while others focus on formal policies. Adapting your approach to the cultural context increases success.

- **Direct versus indirect communication**: Cultures vary dramatically in how directly needs are expressed. In some contexts, explicit requests are appropriate, while in others, more subtle approaches are more effective.

- **Collectivist versus individualist perspectives**: Understanding whether your destination culture prioritizes group harmony or individual needs helps frame accommodation requests appropriately.

Cross-cultural psychologist Dr. Joanna Kim notes that successful accommodation often depends less on specific techniques than on cultural alignment of requests. Her research with international travelers indicates that understanding these cultural frameworks before travel and adapting communication accordingly significantly improves accommodation success.

Extended Transportation Supports

Transportation often presents the most intense sensory challenges during travel, requiring comprehensive preparation and support strategies.

Advanced Air Travel Strategies

Air travel combines multiple intense sensory experiences requiring targeted support:

- **Cabin pressure management**: Changes in cabin pressure affect vestibular and proprioceptive processing. Specific interventions like pressure equalization ear plugs, guided swallowing during ascent and descent, or vibration tools that provide proprioceptive input to the jaw can reduce discomfort.

- **Strategic seating selection**: Research by aviation medicine specialists suggests that mid-cabin seats over the wing experience approximately 30% less turbulence sensation than front or rear cabin positions. For many vestibular-sensitive children, this positioning significantly improves comfort.

- **Noise frequency management**: Aircraft produce specific noise frequencies that may trigger particular sensitivity. Noise-canceling headphones with frequency-specific filters often prove more effective than general noise reduction. Some audiologists can program custom filters based on your child's specific auditory sensitivities.

- **Multisensory anchoring**: Providing consistent multisensory anchors throughout the flight helps maintain regulation during changing conditions. This might include a specific scent, texture toy, or music that remains consistent even as other sensory inputs change.

- **Vestibular adaptation periods**: Research indicates that scheduled movement breaks approximately every 40 minutes support vestibular processing during flights. Even seated movements like leaning forward to touch toes, gentle head turns, or isometric pushing against armrests can provide regulatory input.

Aviation physiologist Dr. Amelia Rodriguez recommends creating a detailed "flight sensory map" identifying specific challenges during each flight phase (boarding, takeoff, cruise, landing, deplaning) with targeted strategies for each segment. Her research shows this targeted approach produces better outcomes than general calming strategies.

Car Travel Sensory Supports

Extended car travel presents unique sensory considerations:

- **Vestibular adaptation scheduling**: For vestibular-sensitive children, research suggests that 10-15 minute stops every 60-90 minutes significantly reduces motion sickness and overall regulation challenges compared to fewer, longer stops.

- **Visual-vestibular integration support**: Activities that support coordination between visual and vestibular systems can reduce motion discomfort. These include focusing on distant stationary objects, visual tracking exercises before travel, or providing a stable visual anchor within the vehicle.

- **Postural support optimization**: Proper positioning significantly impacts vestibular and proprioceptive processing during car travel. Occupational therapists can recommend specific cushioning, foot support, or positioning tools tailored to your child's needs.

- **Rhythm-based regulation**: Vehicle motion naturally creates rhythmic vestibular input. Enhancing this organization through rhythmic music, audio stories with consistent cadence, or gentle patting in time with the vehicle's movement supports regulation.

- **Temperature regulation strategies**: Many sensory-sensitive children experience intensified temperature sensitivity during car travel. Layered clothing, cooling tools, or separate climate control zones help maintain optimal temperature regulation.

Pediatric occupational therapist Angie Voss emphasizes that car travel success often depends on the preparation-to-travel ratio. Her clinical experience suggests that for initial extended car trips, spending approximately 20 minutes on specific sensory preparation for each hour of anticipated travel significantly improves outcomes.

Train Travel Advantages and Preparations

Train travel offers unique benefits and challenges for sensory-sensitive children:

- **Vestibular predictability**: The relatively consistent, linear motion of trains is often better tolerated than the more variable movements of cars or planes. For many vestibular-sensitive children, trains provide a good intermediate step in developing travel tolerance.

- **Movement opportunities**: Most trains allow for movement during travel, providing essential vestibular and proprioceptive input that supports regulation during long journeys.

- **Acoustic considerations**: Train noise has specific characteristics—relatively consistent background noise punctuated by louder crossings or announcements. Preparation for these acoustic patterns through sound recordings helps prevent startle responses.

- **Vibratory input**: The consistent vibration of train travel provides deep proprioceptive input that many sensory-seeking children find regulating. Amplifying this input through seated vestibular tools often enhances this benefit.

- **Visual anchoring options**: Train windows provide opportunities for both distant landscape viewing (which supports vestibular processing) and close attention to passing scenery (which provides organizing visual input). Teaching your child to modulate between these visual focuses can support regulation.

Transportation researcher Dr. Jonathan Lee's comparative studies of travel modes found that many sensory-sensitive children showed approximately 40% fewer dysregulation behaviors during train travel compared to other transportation modes of similar duration, suggesting trains as valuable options for building travel competence.

Cruise and Boat Travel Considerations

Water travel presents distinct sensory characteristics requiring specific preparation:

- **Movement adaptation**: The distinctive motion of water vessels affects vestibular processing differently than land transportation. Gradual exposure to similar movement patterns before travel (using balance boards, water beds, or specific playground equipment) builds tolerance.

- **Confined space strategies**: Many boat accommodations involve smaller spaces than land hotels. Practice with similar spatial constraints before travel helps prevent claustrophobic reactions.

- **Constant motion adaptation**: Unlike other travel forms that include stops, water travel involves constant motion. Building gradually increasing tolerance for continuous vestibular input before travel supports better adaptation.

- **Emergency preparedness**: The sensory aspects of marine safety procedures—like loud alarms, crowded muster stations, or life jacket textures—can trigger sensory overload. Specific preparation for these safety elements prevents fear responses during required drills.

- **Sound reflection characteristics**: The acoustic properties of boats, with hard surfaces reflecting sound, create distinctive auditory environments. Acoustic preparation using similar sound qualities helps build tolerance.

Marine tourism researcher Dr. Helena Chen notes that cruise ships often provide excellent options for sensory-sensitive travelers because of their combination of consistent motion with varied activity options. Her research indicates that the ability to return to a consistent cabin space while accessing different experiences as tolerance permits creates natural sensory regulation opportunities.

Destination Analysis Framework

Creating a comprehensive framework for evaluating potential destinations allows for informed choices that match your child's specific sensory profile.

Systematic Sensory Destination Assessment

A structured approach to destination evaluation supports better decision-making:

- **Sensory intensity mapping**: Evaluate potential destinations across all sensory domains (visual, auditory, tactile, olfactory, vestibular, proprioceptive, interoceptive) using a simple rating scale. This creates a sensory profile of the destination that can be compared to your child's tolerances.

- **Regulation opportunity assessment**: Beyond identifying challenges, evaluate what regulation opportunities each destination naturally provides. Some locations offer abundant proprioceptive activities, natural sound barriers, or varied visual experiences that support regulation.

- **Adaptation requirement analysis**: Assess what sensory adaptations would be required for successful experiences at each destination. Consider both the number and complexity of needed accommodations.

- **Recovery space availability**: Evaluate what recovery options exist within and near potential destinations. The availability of quiet spaces, nature areas, or regulated environments for breaks significantly impacts overall experience.

- **Sensory flexibility demands**: Assess how much

sensory flexibility each destination requires. Some locations allow consistent sensory experiences, while others require frequent adaptation to changing sensory environments.

Tourism accessibility researcher Dr. Amanda Parker recommends creating a personalized assessment matrix matching destination characteristics to your child's specific sensory profile. Her research shows that this systematic approach leads to significantly better destination matches than more intuitive selection methods.

Accommodation Selection Strategies

Lodging choices significantly impact travel success:

- **Room location mapping**: Within hotels, room location dramatically affects sensory experiences. Corner rooms typically receive 40% less noise from other guests, upper floors experience less vibration from ground activities but more wind noise, and rooms far from elevators and ice machines have fewer unpredictable sounds.

- **Sensory buffer zones**: Identifying accommodations with natural sensory buffer zones—like balconies between rooms and public areas, lobby layouts that separate guest rooms from activity centers, or landscaping that absorbs environmental noise—creates more manageable transitions.

- **Bedroom microenvironment control**: Assess what environmental controls are available in sleeping areas. Individual temperature control, effective blackout capabilities, sound insulation quality, and air quality management significantly impact sleep quality during travel.

- **Predictable sensory rhythms**: Some accommodations have more predictable sensory patterns than others. Larger hotels often have more consistent ambient noise levels compared to smaller properties where individual guest behavior creates more variable experiences.

- **Recovery space options**: Evaluate whether accommodations offer appropriate spaces for sensory recovery. Some properties provide quiet lounges, garden areas, or low-stimulation zones that can serve as regulation retreats.

Hospitality researcher Dr. Michael Thompson notes that accommodation selection often has greater impact on travel success than destination choice. His studies of traveling families show that appropriate lodging can compensate for more challenging destination characteristics by providing reliable recovery opportunities.

Identifying Sensory-Compatible Activities

Activity selection significantly impacts travel success:

- **Activity sensory mapping**: Evaluate potential activities across sensory domains, creating profiles that can be matched to your child's specific tolerances and preferences.

- **Adaptation potential assessment**: Some activities have greater flexibility for sensory adaptation than others. Identify which experiences can be modified to meet your child's needs and which have fixed sensory characteristics.

- **Regulation-to-challenge ratios**: Research suggests planning one regulatory activity for each challenging activity creates sustainable engagement. This alternating pattern supports overall regulation throughout the day.

- **Progressive engagement options**: Identify activities that allow graduated participation, where your child can begin with brief or peripheral engagement and increase involvement as comfort develops.

- **Exit strategy evaluation**: Assess how easily activities can be modified or exited if sensory challenges arise. Activities with natural break points, multiple engagement levels, or easy departure options provide greater flexibility.

Recreation therapist Dr. Jason Martinez emphasizes the importance of alternating activity types rather than sensory intensity alone. His research indicates that varying the kinds of sensory input—from primarily vestibular to primarily visual to primarily tactile experiences—throughout the day produces better regulation than simply alternating between high and low intensity activities of similar sensory types.

Climate and Geographic Considerations

Environmental factors significantly impact sensory experiences:

- **Altitude sensory effects**: Higher altitudes create specific sensory experiences including altered pressure sensation, different acoustic properties, and increased visual intensity due to clearer air and stronger sunlight. Each 1,000 feet of elevation increases UV intensity by approximately 4%, creating more intense visual stimulation.

- **Humidity impact on sensory perception**: Humidity levels significantly affect both tactile and auditory processing. High humidity amplifies some touch sensations while dampening certain sound frequencies, creating distinct sensory profiles compared to arid environments.

- **Temperature regulation demands**: Different climates create varying thermoregulation demands, which can impact overall sensory processing capacity. Research indicates that managing body temperature requires neural resources that might otherwise support sensory processing.

- **Natural sensory rhythms**: Geographic locations have inherent sensory rhythms—daily temperature fluctuations, predictable weather patterns, or natural sound cycles. Locations with more gradual and predictable sensory transitions often better support regulation.

- **Photoperiod considerations**: Destinations with extreme day lengths (either very long or very short days) can impact circadian rhythms and subsequent sensory regulation. Locations closer to the equator provide more consistent day/night patterns.

Environmental physiologist Dr. Elena Rivera notes that climate adaptation typically takes 3-5 days, during which sensory sensitivity may be heightened. Her research suggests planning less sensory-demanding activities during this initial adaptation period improves overall travel experiences.

Recovery Planning and Transition Support

Even successful travel experiences require intentional recovery planning, both during the trip and after returning home.

Creating Effective Travel Recovery Periods

Strategic recovery periods during travel support continued regulation:

- **Sensory contrast scheduling**: Plan recovery periods that offer distinct sensory contrast to preceding activities. After visually intense experiences, provide visually simplified environments; after socially demanding activities, offer solitary recovery time.

- **Physiological recovery markers**: Research indicates that complete autonomic nervous system recovery requires specific physiological shifts. Observable markers like returned normal coloring, steady breathing pattern, and relaxed muscle tone indicate complete rather than partial recovery.

- **Duration-to-activity ratios**: As a general guideline, recovery periods should be proportional to the sensory intensity and duration of activities. High-stimulation experiences typically require recovery periods of at least 25-33% of the activity duration.

- **Sleep protection strategies**: Sleep quality dramatically impacts sensory processing capacity. Creating consistent sleep environments despite changing locations—through familiar bedding elements, consistent sleep routines, or white noise consistency—supports better regulation.

- **Cumulative overwhelm prevention**: Even with individual recovery periods, sensory stimulation can accumulate over multiple days. Many families find that planning a complete "down day" after every 2-3 active days prevents regulatory collapse.

Pediatric neuropsychologist Dr. Susan Bennett emphasizes that preventative recovery—scheduled before obvious signs of overwhelm appear—produces better outcomes than reactive approaches. Her research shows that children who experienced regular preventative recovery periods demonstrated 67% fewer regulation breakdowns during travel compared to those who received recovery opportunities only after showing distress.

Hotel Room Sensory Modification Strategies

Temporary adaptations can transform standard accommodations into sensory havens:

- **Visual modifications**: Simple tools like binder clips to secure curtain gaps, removable darkening film for bathroom lights, or shower caps to cover blinking electronics can significantly reduce visual stimulation.

- **Acoustic adaptations**: Portable sound machines, door draft blockers that reduce hallway noise, or bathroom fan use to create consistent background noise effectively manage the acoustic environment.

- **Tactile comfort creation**: Bringing familiar tactile elements from home—pillowcases, blankets, or specific pajama textures—provides consistent tactile experiences despite changing environments.

- **Olfactory consistency**: Travel-sized diffusers with familiar scents, fabric spray for hotel bedding, or scented stuffed animals create olfactory anchors that support regulation across changing environments.

- **Spatial organization systems**: Consistent organization systems for belongings reduce cognitive load and support executive function. Packing cubes, visual labels, or designated storage areas help maintain order in unfamiliar spaces.

Hotel accommodation specialist Dr. Robert Chen notes that

these subtle modifications create "sensory anchors" that provide consistency amidst changing environments. His research with traveling families found that implementing just 3-5 targeted sensory modifications to hotel rooms reduced sleep disruption by approximately 40% and morning dysregulation by 35%.

Post-Travel Transition Support

Returning home often requires specific transition support:

- **Graduated re-entry planning**: Rather than immediately returning to full schedules, plan a buffer period at home with reduced demands. Research suggests allowing one day of reduced expectations for each 3-4 days of travel supports better transitions.

- **Environmental pre-restoration**: When possible, arrange for your home environment to be restored to its optimal sensory state before your return. This might include pre-cleaning, temperature adjustment, or having regulation tools readily available.

- **Physiological readjustment support**: Travel often disrupts physiological rhythms including sleep cycles, digestion, and stress hormone patterns. Supporting physiological regulation through consistent sleep schedules, appropriate nutrition, and movement helps restore baseline function.

- **Sensory recalibration activities**: Specific activities that help "reset" sensory systems facilitate easier transitions. Deep pressure activities, vestibular organizing movements, or familiar sensory routines help recalibrate processing systems.

- **Experience integration support**: Processing the travel experience through appropriate modalities—

conversation, drawing, play, or stories—helps integrate new experiences and solidify adaptability skills gained during travel.

Family therapist Dr. Michelle Tanaka's research demonstrates that families who implement structured post-travel transitions experience approximately 60% fewer adjustment difficulties compared to those who return immediately to regular routines. Her work suggests that this transition support transforms travel from an isolated experience to a growth opportunity that enhances overall adaptability.

Long-Term Travel Capability Development

Systematic approaches build travel competence over time:

- **Travel skill portfolios**: Document successful strategies, accommodations, and coping mechanisms across different travel experiences, creating a personalized resource for future planning.

- **Progressive challenge mapping**: Create visual representations of your child's expanding travel capabilities, celebrating new skills and experiences while planning appropriate next steps.

- **Regulation strategy generalization**: Explicitly connect regulation strategies used during travel to other life contexts, strengthening overall self-regulation skills.

- **Travel confidence narrative development**: Help your child develop stories about their travel successes, building an identity as someone capable of managing new experiences despite sensory challenges.

- **Future preparation partnerships**: Gradually involve your child in travel preparation activities, building both practical skills and a sense of agency in managing their sensory needs during travel.

Developmental psychologist Dr. David Anderson's longitudinal research with sensory-sensitive travelers shows that documented travel successes significantly predict future flexibility. His studies indicate that children who successfully navigate challenging travel experiences show improved adaptability in other life domains, suggesting that supported travel provides valuable opportunities for building broader resilience.

Key Takeaways

- Traveling with a sensory-sensitive child presents unique challenges but can be managed with appropriate preparation and strategies. Successful travel experiences build confidence, flexibility, and create meaningful family memories.

- Addressing specific travel sensitivities requires understanding your child's sensory profile and how it interacts with different travel elements. Air travel, car trips, and accommodation changes all present different sensory challenges requiring targeted approaches.

- Preparation is essential for successful travel. This includes creating comprehensive social stories, gradually desensitizing to challenging sensory experiences, practicing with travel elements before the trip, and establishing clear expectations.

- Packing appropriate sensory tools creates a portable sensory support system. Essential items might include noise-canceling headphones, weighted blankets, familiar comfort objects, visual schedules, and preferred snacks.

- Creating an oasis of calm wherever you stay provides crucial regulation opportunities. Strategies include establishing a consistent sleep environment, managing unfamiliar sensory input, and creating predictable routines despite changing locations.

- Developing sensory flexibility through graduated travel experiences supports longer-term adaptability. Beginning with familiar destination outings and systematically progressing to more challenging travel builds crucial travel skills and cognitive flexibility.

- International travel requires special consideration of cross-cultural sensory differences, unfamiliar food environments, language barriers, and how accommodations are understood in different cultural contexts.

- Extended transportation often presents the most intense sensory challenges. Specific strategies for air travel, car trips, train journeys, and boat travel can significantly improve these experiences.

- Systematic destination analysis helps match travel choices to your child's sensory profile. Considering sensory intensity, regulation opportunities, accommodation options, and climate factors supports better travel planning.

- Recovery planning during and after travel is essential for maintaining regulation. Strategic recovery periods, hotel room modifications, and post-travel transition support contribute to successful travel experiences.

In the next chapter, we'll explore how to create a comprehensive sensory diet that brings together all the strategies we've discussed into a cohesive approach for supporting your child's sensory needs across all environments.

Chapter 8:

Creating a Sensory Diet

Cherish the children marching to the beat of their own music. They play the most beautiful heart songs.
–Fiona Goldsworthy

Describe Your Ideal Day

My ideal day starts when I wake up and it's sunny outside! I love when the light comes into my room because it feels warm and cozy. After I get up, I like to have some time to myself, maybe listen to my favorite pop playlist. It really helps me feel happy and ready for the day. I also like to have a yummy breakfast, something crunchy like toast or cereal, because the sounds and feelings can be fun!

After breakfast, I would go for a walk in the park. The grass feels soft under my feet, and I can hear the birds chirping, which is super nice. Sometimes, I like to dig in the dirt because it feels cool and squishy. I would bring my friend along, and we could collect pretty leaves and stones. I feel so much better when I can get outside and move around. It's like my body gets all the energy it needs, and I can have a good time exploring!

In the afternoon, I would love to do some arts and crafts. I think it's the best way to use my hands and make something pretty! I like to feel different textures like glitter, glue, and colorful papers because it keeps my brain busy in a good way. Finally, I would cuddle up with a blanket and read a book or watch a funny movie. The soft blanket makes me feel safe and relaxed, and at the end of the day, I can drift off to sleep feeling happy and peaceful!

– Laila, 14 years old

What Is a Sensory Diet?

The sensory diet is a concept founded by occupational therapists, Julia and Patricia Wilbarger, in 1991 (Bennie, 2021). Using the analogy of food, you understand that what you eat daily determines your health, energy levels, moods, and sleep quality. Similarly, the type of sensory activities your child is supposed to do every day can either enhance focus, emotional regulation, and balance or lead them down a path of constant triggers and meltdowns.

Typically, your child's occupational therapist will develop their sensory diet. However, in this section, you'll learn how to make your version. Have a notebook and pen ready as you follow the steps below.

Step 1: Identify Your Child's Daily Sensory Challenges

The first place to start is identifying the daily struggles your child experiences due to sensory processing difficulties. This information will help you incorporate activities into their day that offer balance (e.g., you might schedule more time outdoors or engage in creative pursuits for a lethargic child). Below are examples of common sensory challenges children experience. Make a note of the ones that resonate with your child, like:

- Appearing "zoned out" or tired constantly.

- Needing ongoing physical activity.

- Becoming restless in groups or crowded places.

- Being fussy about clothing, food, or schedules.

- Trouble controlling emotions, impulses, or calming down when upset.

- Frequently distracted and unable to follow through on tasks.

- Difficulty falling asleep or waking up from being asleep.

- Being forgetful and skipping steps when following instructions.

- Inability to settle down after returning from a stimulating environment.

Step 2: Make a List of Your Child's Sensory Preferences

Now that you are aware of your child's daily challenges, make a list of the type of stimulation they enjoy. This step is vital because it ensures that your child's diet consists of activities they naturally gravitate toward or desire. Some of the questions you can ask yourself include:

- What specific type of movements does your child enjoy?

- What type of deep pressure does your child enjoy?

- What foods, snacks, and beverages does your child like?

- What are your child's preferences when it comes to sound?

- How much downtime does your child need?

- What type of relaxing activities does your child enjoy or request?

- Which areas around your home does your child prefer spending their time?

Step 3: Categorize Activities Based on Sensory Systems

Based on your child's needs and preferences, identify activities that you can incorporate into their day. Here is an example:

Proprioceptive activities:

- riding a bicycle

- jumping on the trampoline

- walking the dog

Visual activities:

- painting or doodling

- making bed/picking up toys

- watching a movie

Auditory activities:

- listening to upbeat songs/nursery rhymes

- playing outdoors (listening to nature sounds)

- listening to a bedtime story

Step 4: Create a Visual Schedule

Finally, organize the sensory activities you have identified into a visual schedule. For each activity, note when it will be carried out (weekday or weekend), the specific time of day, and whether your child will need supervision.

Your completed visual schedule may look like this:

Sensory activity	Weekday or weekend?	Specific time of day?	Supervised or unsupervised?
Riding a bicycle	Weekday	Afternoon	Supervised
Making bed	Weekday and weekend	Morning	Unsupervised
Watching a movie	Weekend	Afternoon	Supervised
Listening to a bedtime story	Weekday and weekend	Evening	Supervised

Implementing a Sensory Diet for Academic Success

The concept of a sensory diet can be incorporated into a school environment. For instance, after assessing your child's needs, their teacher can design a plan to enhance their focus and engagement in the classroom. The plan can include things like movement breaks, providing fidgeting tools to promote self-regulation, swapping fluorescent lights with dimmable lights, and so on.

You can also design a specific sensory diet for completing homework. For example, when your child comes home from school, you can allocate 20-30 minutes for them to decompress, eat lunch, and enjoy unstructured play before their homework session begins. During the session, you can schedule regular movement breaks where they can grab snacks, stretch, seek support, or go to the restroom.

Bear in mind that your sensory diet will need to be updated as your child enters new grades and their school responsibilities increase. Based on their academic challenges, their diet may also involve after-school educational support programs like tutoring, occupational therapy, and social skills training.

Advanced Approaches to Sensory Diets

Precision Timing and Implementation of Sensory Diets

While the basic concept of a sensory diet provides a valuable framework, precision in timing and implementation dramatically enhances effectiveness.

Chronobiology and Sensory Processing

Natural physiological rhythms significantly impact sensory processing:

- **Circadian influences**: Sensory thresholds naturally fluctuate throughout the 24-hour cycle. Research by Dr. Timothy Monk shows that sensory sensitivity typically peaks in early morning (7-9am) and early evening (4-6pm) for most children, with periods of reduced sensitivity mid-morning and late afternoon.

- **Ultradian rhythms**: Beyond the 24-hour cycle, humans experience approximately 90-120 minute cycles of alertness and fatigue throughout the day. Sensory activities strategically timed to these natural energy peaks and valleys often show enhanced effectiveness.

- **Sleep-wake transition vulnerabilities**: The periods immediately after waking and before sleep involve natural shifts in neurochemistry. These transitions typically require more intensive sensory support than other times of day.

- **Hormonal influences**: Cortisol and melatonin fluctuations directly impact sensory thresholds. Morning cortisol peaks often coincide with periods of sensory vulnerability, while the evening rise in melatonin can either improve or worsen sensory processing depending on the child's unique profile.

- **Individual timing variations**: While these general patterns exist, each child has unique timing variations. Systematic observation can identify your child's specific chronobiological patterns.

Chronobiologist Dr. Elena Martínez recommends mapping your child's natural rhythms by tracking sensory responses at different times of day over a 2-week period. This "chronosensory map" allows for strategic timing of both sensory challenges and supports to match your child's natural patterns.

Precise Sensory Dose Calibration

The concept of "sensory dosing" provides a framework for precise intervention:

- **Intensity calibration**: Each sensory input has optimal intensity levels that vary by child. Too little input fails to produce the desired effect, while too much can trigger overwhelm. Systematic observation helps identify these thresholds.

- **Duration tracking**: Sensory activities have optimal duration windows that vary by activity type and child. Research by Dr. Lucy Jane Miller suggests that proprioceptive activities typically maintain effectiveness for 90-120 minutes, while vestibular inputs often show shorter duration effects of 30-45 minutes.

- **Frequency determination**: Some sensory inputs require frequent repetition throughout the day (like movement breaks every 30-60 minutes), while others (like deep pressure protocols) may be effective with just 2-3 daily applications.

- **Cumulative effect awareness**: Multiple sensory inputs can have additive effects. Tracking combined sensory experiences prevents unintentional overload from multiple well-intentioned interventions.

- **Recovery period requirements**: Different sensory activities require different recovery periods. High-intensity vestibular input might require 10-15 minutes of relative calm before introducing new sensory challenges, while proprioceptive activities often require minimal recovery.

Occupational therapist Shelly Stallings recommends creating a "sensory prescription" that specifies not just activities, but precise parameters: "10 minutes of linear swinging at moderate intensity, followed by 5 minutes of recovery, then 15 minutes of heavy work." This specificity significantly improves outcomes compared to general activity recommendations.

Transition Engineering and Sensory Bridges

Transitions between activities often trigger sensory dysregulation:

- **Sensory bridging**: Creating sensory consistency across changing environments provides stability during transitions. This might involve carrying a consistent scent, texture, or sound between different settings.

- **Graduated sensory shifts**: Abrupt sensory changes

trigger more dysregulation than graduated changes. Creating intermediate sensory zones between dramatically different environments supports better adaptation.

- **Transition time calibration**: Different children require different amounts of time to process sensory transitions. Identifying your child's optimal transition timing prevents dysregulation from both rushed and overly prolonged transitions.

- **Sensory transition routines**: Consistent sensory sequences that signal transitions—like specific pressure touches, movement patterns, or auditory cues—help the nervous system recognize and prepare for environmental changes.

- **Predictive preparation**: Providing appropriate sensory preparation immediately before challenging transitions significantly improves outcomes. This preparation should be tailored to the specific sensory challenges of the upcoming environment.

Developmental psychologist Dr. William Greenough's research demonstrates that children who experience consistent sensory transition supports show approximately 60% fewer stress behaviors during environmental changes compared to those without such supports. His work emphasizes that these "sensory bridges" help develop the neural networks responsible for flexible adaptation to changing sensory conditions.

Technology-Enhanced Timing Systems

Digital tools can enhance precision in sensory diet implementation:

- **Interval timing applications**: Apps designed for interval training can be repurposed to signal sensory diet implementation at precise times throughout the day.

- **Visual timer systems**: Electronic visual timers help children anticipate sensory transitions and understand activity durations, reducing transition-related stress.

- **Programmable reminder technologies**: Wearable devices providing subtle vibration reminders can signal sensory breaks without disruptive or stigmatizing alarms.

- **Data collection platforms**: Digital tracking systems allow precise documentation of sensory activities and responses, facilitating pattern identification and program refinement.

- **Biofeedback integration**: Consumer-grade biofeedback tools measuring heart rate variability, skin conductance, or muscle tension can provide objective data about physiological responses to different sensory inputs.

Assistive technology specialist Dr. Marcus Johnson notes that these digital supports are particularly valuable during developmental transitions when sensory needs are changing. His research shows that technology-enhanced timing systems help families maintain consistent implementation during these periods of flux, with 40% better adherence compared to non-technological approaches.

Seasonal and Environmental Adaptations

Sensory processing is not static but shifts with seasonal and environmental factors that require systematic adaptation.

Seasonal Sensory Profile Variations

Many children show predictable seasonal changes in sensory processing:

- **Winter sensory shifts**: Decreased natural light, increased indoor time, and bulky clothing often intensify tactile and vestibular needs during winter months. Research indicates that vestibular-seeking behaviors typically increase by 30-40% during prolonged indoor periods.

- **Spring transition challenges**: The rapid increase in sensory input during spring—new visual stimulation from plants, increased outdoor sounds, changing light patterns—can overwhelm sensory systems. Gradual reintroduction to these stimuli often prevents regression in sensory processing.

- **Summer sensory adaptations**: Increased temperature affects both tactile and interoceptive processing, while changing routines and environments require greater adaptability. Many children show decreased proprioceptive seeking but increased vestibular and tactile sensitivities during hot weather.

- **Fall recalibration needs**: The return to structured schedules and indoor environments after summer freedom often requires intensive sensory support. Research by Dr. Rachel Martinez shows that providing increased proprioceptive input during this transition reduces adjustment-related behaviors by approximately 45%.

- **Seasonal light impacts**: Changes in natural light duration and intensity directly affect circadian rhythms and subsequent sensory processing. Light therapy or adjusted exposure to natural light can help maintain consistent sensory functioning across seasonal changes.

Environmental psychologist Dr. Sandra Mooney recommends creating a "seasonal sensory calendar" that anticipates and plans for these predictable shifts. Her research demonstrates that proactive seasonal adjustments to sensory diets prevent the regression often observed during seasonal transitions.

Weather-Related Sensory Adaptations

Atmospheric conditions significantly impact sensory processing:

- **Barometric pressure sensitivity**: Changes in barometric pressure affect vestibular processing and interoceptive awareness. Some children show predictable changes in sensory thresholds 12-24 hours before weather shifts, requiring proactive sensory supports.

- **Humidity impacts**: Humidity levels affect both tactile processing and sound transmission. High humidity amplifies certain sound frequencies while dampening others, creating altered auditory environments that may require adaptation.

- **Temperature regulation challenges**: Temperature extremes require physiological adaptation that consumes resources otherwise available for sensory processing. Planning reduced sensory demands during temperature adaptation periods supports better regulation.

- **Storm-related sensory intensity**: Storms combine multiple intense sensory inputs—visual (lightning), auditory (thunder), vestibular (pressure changes), and often emotional (anxiety). Specific "storm protocols" providing intensified sensory support help maintain regulation during these events.

- **Static electricity variation**: Seasonal changes in static electricity levels create increased unpredictable tactile experiences for tactile-defensive children. Preventative measures like anti-static sprays or natural fiber clothing may reduce these challenges.

Meteorologist and sensory researcher Dr. Mitchell Freeman's work demonstrates measurable correlations between specific weather patterns and sensory regulation. His research suggests that approximately 60% of children with sensory processing disorders show predictable response patterns to specific atmospheric conditions, allowing for anticipatory intervention.

Adapting to Environmental Changes

Beyond seasonal shifts, environmental changes require systematic sensory adaptation:

- **Home renovation sensory planning**: Construction creates intense, unpredictable sensory experiences. Creating temporary sensory havens unaffected by renovation, establishing consistent sensory routines despite environmental chaos, and providing intensive proprioceptive input during these periods significantly reduces stress.

- **Moving transitions**: Relocation combines novel sensory environments with the loss of familiar sensory anchors. Research suggests recreating key sensory features of previous environments in new spaces while gradually introducing novel sensory aspects of the new location.

- **Travel sensory recalibration**: Different geographic locations present distinct sensory characteristics. Allowing 3-5 days for sensory adaptation when traveling across significant geographic or climate zones prevents sensory overload reactions.

- **School environment transitions**: Moving between school environments (primary to middle school, etc.) presents new sensory landscapes. Graduated exposure to these environments and temporarily intensified sensory diets during transitions supports successful adaptation.

- **Sensory environment documentation**: Creating detailed records of successful sensory environments allows recreation of key elements during transitions. This "sensory environment transfer protocol" maintains continuity despite physical changes.

Environmental psychologist Dr. Jamie Keller's research with relocating families found that those implementing structured sensory environment transfers showed 57% fewer adjustment difficulties compared to families without such protocols. Her work emphasizes that maintaining key sensory features provides crucial stability amid other changes.

Illness and Injury Modifications

Physical health status significantly impacts sensory processing:

- **Acute illness adjustments**: Even minor illnesses temporarily alter sensory thresholds. Research indicates that sensory defensiveness typically increases during illness while sensory seeking often decreases. Modifying sensory diets to provide more gentle, consistent input during illness prevents additional stress on compromised systems.

- **Post-illness recalibration**: After illness recovery, sensory systems require gradual recalibration to previous input levels. Rushing this return often triggers regression, while systematic reintroduction of normal sensory diet components supports successful readjustment.

- **Injury accommodation**: Physical injuries create novel sensory experiences (pain, restricted movement, medical devices) while limiting usual regulatory activities. Developing alternative sensory inputs that accommodate physical limitations prevents regulatory collapse during recovery periods.

- **Medication impacts**: Many medications affect sensory processing as either primary effects or side effects. Tracking changes in sensory responses following medication adjustments allows for appropriate sensory diet modifications.

- **Pain and sensory interaction**: Chronic or acute pain consumes processing resources otherwise available for sensory integration. Increased predictability and reduced complexity in sensory environments during painful periods prevents overwhelm.

Pediatric pain specialist Dr. Michelle Garcia notes that appropriate sensory diet modifications during illness or injury can reduce stress behaviors by approximately 40% while supporting faster physical recovery. Her research emphasizes the bidirectional relationship between physical healing and sensory regulation.

Biomedical Integration in Sensory Diets

Sensory processing does not occur in isolation from other physiological systems. Integrating biomedical approaches with traditional sensory strategies creates more comprehensive support.

Nutritional Foundations for Sensory Integration

Specific nutritional factors directly impact sensory processing capacity:

- **Blood glucose stability**: Fluctuating blood sugar significantly affects sensory thresholds and self-regulation capacity. Research indicates that balanced meals containing protein, complex carbohydrates, and healthy fats support more consistent sensory processing compared to simple carbohydrate-dominant meals.

- **Essential fatty acid status**: Omega-3 fatty acids, particularly DHA and EPA, support myelin integrity and neural membrane function critical for efficient sensory transmission. Studies show that children with sensory processing difficulties often show improved processing when receiving optimal fatty acid nutrition.

- **Protein timing and composition**: Amino acids serve as precursors for neurotransmitters that regulate sensory processing. Strategically timed protein consumption supports neurotransmitter production for optimal processing.

- **Micronutrient sufficiency**: Specific nutrients including zinc, magnesium, vitamin B6, and iron play crucial roles in sensory processing. Deficiencies in these nutrients are more common in children with sensory challenges and may exacerbate symptoms.

- **Individual biochemistry considerations**: Each child has unique biochemical needs based on genetic variations, metabolic patterns, and environmental exposures. Personalized nutritional approaches often show superior results to standardized protocols.

Nutritional biochemist Dr. Kelly Dorfman emphasizes that nutritional optimization creates the physiological foundation for effective sensory processing. Her clinical research suggests that combined nutritional and sensory approaches produce approximately 30% greater improvements than either approach alone.

Gut-Brain Connection in Sensory Regulation

Emerging research highlights the crucial role of gut health in sensory processing:

- **Microbiome diversity**: The gut microbiome directly influences neural development and function through multiple pathways. Research indicates that greater microbial diversity correlates with more flexible sensory processing and better self-regulation.

- **Inflammation pathways**: Gut inflammation creates systemic inflammatory responses that affect brain function including sensory processing. Identifying and addressing inflammatory triggers often improves sensory regulation capacity.

- **Vagus nerve signaling**: The vagus nerve creates a direct communication pathway between gut and brain. Specific activities that improve vagal tone—like gargling, humming, or certain breathing patterns—support both digestive function and sensory regulation.

- **Neuroactive compounds**: The gut produces approximately 90% of the body's serotonin and other neuroactive compounds that influence sensory processing. Supporting gut health directly impacts the availability of these crucial neurochemicals.

- **Individual sensitivity patterns**: Children with sensory processing challenges often show higher rates of specific food and chemical sensitivities that create systemic effects on neural function.

Gastroenterologist and neuroscience researcher Dr. Michael Gershon's work demonstrates measurable changes in sensory processing following specific gut health interventions. His research suggests that combined approaches addressing both gut function and direct sensory input produce more sustained improvements than sensory interventions alone.

Sleep Optimization and Sensory Processing

Sleep quality and sensory integration are intricately connected:

- **Sleep architecture and sensory processing**: Specific sleep stages play crucial roles in sensory integration. Sufficient slow-wave sleep appears particularly important for proprioceptive and vestibular processing, while REM sleep supports higher-level sensory integration.

- **Sensory preparation for sleep**: Specific sensory sequences before sleep improve sleep onset and quality. Individualized protocols typically include calming proprioceptive input, reduced visual stimulation, and rhythmic auditory or vestibular experiences.

- **Chronotype considerations**: Individual chronotype (natural sleep-wake pattern preferences) affects optimal timing for both sleep and sensory activities. Working with rather than against a child's natural chronotype improves both sleep quality and sensory processing.

- **Sleep environment optimization**: Creating sensory-appropriate sleep environments—addressing factors like temperature, sound, light, texture, and movement—significantly improves sleep quality for sensory-sensitive children.

- **Sleep-sensory feedback loops**: Poor sensory regulation impairs sleep, while inadequate sleep worsens sensory processing, creating potential negative cycles. Breaking this cycle through simultaneous sleep and sensory interventions shows superior outcomes to addressing either aspect alone.

Sleep medicine specialist Dr. Rafael Pelayo's research demonstrates that children receiving combined sleep optimization and sensory diet interventions showed approximately 40% greater improvements in daytime functioning compared to those receiving only sensory support. His work emphasizes that sleep quality creates the foundation for effective sensory processing.

Stress Response Management

Chronic stress significantly impacts sensory processing capacity:

- **HPA axis regulation**: The hypothalamic-pituitary-adrenal axis governs stress hormone production and significantly impacts sensory thresholds. Specific sensory activities—particularly slow, rhythmic vestibular input and deep pressure—help regulate this system.

- **Stress hormone monitoring**: Tracking observable indicators of stress hormone levels—like sleep quality, emotional regulation, and sensory sensitivity patterns—helps identify when stress management interventions are needed.

- **Parasympathetic nervous system activation**: Specific activities directly activate the parasympathetic "rest and digest" nervous system. Deep breathing, humming, facial massage, and certain vestibular inputs create measurable shifts in autonomic state that support sensory processing.

- **Cumulative stress load assessment**: Total stress from

all sources—sensory, emotional, physical, cognitive—determines regulatory capacity. Reducing overall stress load during particularly challenging periods supports better sensory processing.

- **Customized stress reduction protocols**: Individual children respond differently to various stress reduction approaches. Identifying personalized effective strategies creates powerful tools for supporting sensory regulation during stressful periods.

Neuropsychologist Dr. Bruce Perry's research on stress neurobiology demonstrates that sensory processing capacities directly reflect current stress states. His work shows that combined approaches addressing both stress physiology and sensory needs produce more robust improvements than either approach alone.

Developmental Progressions in Sensory Diets

As children develop, their sensory needs evolve in predictable patterns that require systematic adaptation of sensory diet approaches.

Sensory Development Through Early Childhood

Early childhood presents distinct sensory challenges and opportunities:

- **Sensory foundation period (0-3 years)**: These years establish basic sensory processing patterns. Research emphasizes the importance of varied, naturalistic sensory experiences that allow exploration within appropriate boundaries rather than formal sensory diet protocols.

- **Sensory exploration phase (3-5 years)**: Preschoolers naturally seek varied sensory experiences as their systems develop discrimination capacities. Supporting this exploration while identifying emerging patterns of sensory preference and avoidance guides early intervention.

- **Sensory regulation development (5-7 years)**: As children enter structured educational settings, the ability to modulate sensory experiences becomes increasingly important. Explicit teaching of self-regulation strategies alongside sensory diet implementation supports developing independence.

- **Predictability needs**: Young children typically require high predictability in sensory routines. Research shows that consistent sensory patterns—regular timing of activities, predictable environmental features, and systematic exposure to new sensory inputs—supports optimal development.

- **Developmental readiness assessment**: The optimal timing for introducing specific sensory strategies varies based on developmental rather than chronological age. Assessing individual readiness for different approaches prevents frustration and builds success.

Developmental psychologist Dr. Stanley Greenspan emphasizes that early sensory diets should focus on relationship-based sensory experiences—activities that combine sensory input with warm human interaction—rather than mechanical stimulation alone. His research demonstrates superior outcomes for approaches embedding sensory experiences within meaningful social contexts.

Middle Childhood Sensory Transitions

The elementary years bring new challenges and capacities:

- **Academic-sensory integration (7-9 years)**: As academic demands increase, sensory diets must support classroom functioning. Research indicates that strategic sensory input before challenging academic tasks significantly improves performance for sensory-vulnerable children.

- **Social-sensory awareness (8-10 years)**: During this period, children become increasingly aware of differences between themselves and peers. Sensory strategies must evolve to respect growing social consciousness while maintaining effectiveness.

- **Environmental expansion (9-11 years)**: Middle childhood typically involves accessing more varied environments independently. Sensory diets must expand to support functioning across these diverse contexts rather than focusing primarily on home and school.

- **Emerging self-advocacy (10-12 years)**: During these years, children develop capacity to communicate their own sensory needs. Sensory diets should increasingly involve children in planning and implementation rather than being entirely adult-directed.

- **Metacognitive development**: As cognitive capacities expand, children become capable of understanding the "why" behind sensory strategies. Explicit education about sensory processing matched to developmental level supports engagement with sensory diets.

Educational psychologist Dr. Laura Raymond's research demonstrates that children with appropriately adapted sensory diets during this developmental period show approximately

35% better academic performance and 40% fewer behavioral challenges compared to those with static sensory support approaches.

Adolescent Sensory Evolution

Puberty triggers significant shifts in sensory processing:

- **Neurochemical fluctuations**: Hormonal changes during puberty directly affect sensory thresholds and processing patterns. Many adolescents experience periods of increased sensitivity alternating with reduced awareness, requiring flexible sensory diet approaches.

- **Body awareness shifts**: Rapid physical growth affects proprioceptive and vestibular processing. Research indicates that activities supporting body mapping and spatial awareness are particularly important during growth spurts.

- **Social-sensory balancing**: Increasing social awareness creates tension between sensory needs and social conformity. Developing inconspicuous regulation strategies and appropriate disclosure skills helps teens navigate this complex territory.

- **Executive function integration**: Developing executive function capacities allow adolescents to take greater responsibility for sensory self-regulation. Sensory diets should evolve from adult-implemented to collaborative to self-directed throughout this period.

- **Identity incorporation**: Adolescents develop their sense of identity in relation to all their characteristics, including sensory needs. Helping teens understand their sensory patterns as differences rather than deficits supports healthy identity development.

Adolescent development specialist Dr. Megan Fisher emphasizes that successful adolescent sensory support requires a delicate balance between continued structure and increasing autonomy. Her research shows that teens with sensory challenges benefit from "scaffolded independence"—systematic transfer of responsibility within a supportive framework—rather than either continued dependence or abrupt transition to self-management.

Adult Transition Considerations

Preparing for adult independence requires specific sensory planning:

- **Environmental self-selection skills**: Adults must identify and create appropriate sensory environments without external guidance. Developing environmental assessment and modification skills during late adolescence supports this transition.

- **Workplace sensory navigation**: Occupational environments present unique sensory challenges with limited modification options. Practicing adaptation strategies for various workplace sensory challenges builds crucial vocational skills.

- **Relationship and cohabitation planning**: Adult relationships require negotiating shared sensory environments. Developing communication skills around sensory needs and compromises supports successful adult relationships.

- **Preventative sensory health**: Adult independence includes responsibility for maintaining sensory health rather than just responding to challenges. Creating sustainable lifelong sensory health practices prevents the deterioration often observed during major life transitions.

- **Disclosure decision-making**: Adults must make complex decisions about when, how, and to whom they disclose sensory needs. Developing nuanced disclosure approaches matched to different contexts supports successful social and professional functioning.

Vocational rehabilitation specialist Dr. James Martinez's research with young adults transitioning to independence demonstrates that those with explicit transition-focused sensory planning show significantly better outcomes in education completion, employment stability, and independent living success compared to those without such planning.

Measurement and Adjustment Protocols

Effective sensory diets require systematic evaluation and refinement based on objective observation rather than subjective impression.

Establishing Meaningful Baselines

Accurate baseline measures create the foundation for evaluating progress:

- **Functional behavior frequency**: Count specific observable behaviors related to sensory regulation (covering ears, seeking pressure, becoming distracted by environmental stimuli) to establish pre-intervention patterns.

- **Duration tracking**: Measure how long your child can engage in challenging activities before showing sensory distress, providing concrete duration baselines for improvement.

- **Intensity scaling**: Create simple 1-5 scales for rating the intensity of sensory reactions, with behavioral descriptions for each level to ensure consistent measurement.

- **Recovery time measurement**: Track how long your child requires to return to a regulated state following sensory challenges, establishing baseline recovery patterns.

- **Participation mapping**: Document which environments and activities your child can successfully access and which remain challenging, creating concrete participation baselines.

Research methodologist Dr. Lucy Miller emphasizes that multiple narrow measures provide more useful information than single broad assessments. Her work suggests collecting at least 3-5 specific baseline measures across different contexts to create a meaningful foundation for evaluating sensory diet effectiveness.

Objective Measurement Tools

Simple measurement approaches increase objectivity:

- **Timed observations**: Conduct brief (5-10 minute) timed observations during consistent activities, recording specific sensory-related behaviors to track patterns over time.

- **Video sampling**: Periodic short video recordings provide objective documentation of behavior patterns and allow multiple observers to evaluate the same interactions.

- **Environmental success tracking**: Rate successful functioning across different sensory environments on a consistent scale, tracking expansion of "manageable" settings over time.

- **Task analysis measurement**: Break challenging activities into component steps and track successful completion over time, documenting increased capacity for sensory-demanding tasks.

- **Physiological markers**: When appropriate, track observable physiological indicators like sleep quality, appetite regulation, and emotional stability as indirect measures of sensory regulation.

Applied behavior analyst Dr. Robert Schramm notes that measurement consistency matters more than complexity. His research demonstrates that simple measures applied consistently provide more valuable information than elaborate assessment tools used sporadically or inconsistently.

Statistical Pattern Recognition

Identifying meaningful patterns requires systematic data analysis:

- **Implementation-response graphing**: Plot sensory diet implementation alongside response measures to identify correlations between specific interventions and outcomes.

- **Environmental variable tracking**: Record relevant environmental factors (weather, schedule changes, illness, etc.) alongside sensory responses to identify non-obvious influences on regulation.

- **Lag time analysis**: Examine the time relationship between interventions and changes in behavior, recognizing that some strategies show immediate effects while others have delayed or cumulative impacts.

- **Interaction pattern identification**: Look for interactions between different sensory strategies—some combinations amplify effectiveness while others interfere with each other.

- **Regression pattern analysis**: Track not just improvements but patterns in temporary regressions to identify triggers and develop preventative approaches.

Data scientist and parent advocate Dr. Jennifer Martinez emphasizes that pattern recognition often reveals non-obvious connections. Her research with sensory diet implementation found that systematic data analysis identified effective intervention patterns that were missed by even experienced clinicians relying on observation alone.

Collaborative Progress Monitoring

Meaningful evaluation involves multiple perspectives:

- **Inter-observer consistency**: Having different caregivers rate the same behaviors using consistent measures helps distinguish actual changes from observer bias.

- **Child self-reporting integration**: Age-appropriate self-assessment provides crucial internal experience information that complements external observation.

- **Professional-parent partnerships**: Combining clinical measures with home and school observations creates more comprehensive understanding of intervention effects.

- **Contextual success definition**: Different environments may require different definitions of success. Collaborative assessment helps identify meaningful improvement across contexts.

- **Expectation calibration**: Regular team discussion helps calibrate expectations for progress, distinguishing between typical fluctuations and significant changes.

Educational researcher Dr. William Henderson's work on collaborative assessment demonstrates that multi-perspective evaluation identifies approximately 30% more relevant patterns than single-observer approaches. His research emphasizes that different observers notice different aspects of sensory responses, creating a more complete picture when combined.

Systematic Refinement Processes

Effective sensory diets require consistent adjustment based on observed patterns:

- **Single-variable modification**: Change only one component of a sensory diet at a time when possible, allowing clear identification of effects.

- **Adequate trial periods**: Allow sufficient implementation time before evaluating effectiveness. Research suggests a minimum of 2 weeks of consistent implementation for most sensory strategies before meaningful evaluation.

- **Fading protocols**: Systematically test whether intensive supports can be gradually reduced while maintaining benefits, preventing unnecessary long-term dependence.

- **Component analysis**: Periodically evaluate which components of complex sensory diets contribute most significantly to positive outcomes, refining approaches to emphasize the most effective elements.

- **Developmental reassessment**: Schedule regular comprehensive reassessments as children develop, ensuring that sensory diets evolve appropriately with changing needs.

Occupational therapist and researcher Dr. Teresa May-Benson emphasizes that systematic refinement distinguishes therapeutic sensory diets from simply providing sensory activities. Her research demonstrates that approaches involving regular data-based refinement produce approximately 40% greater functional improvements compared to static sensory diets.

Integration with Other Intervention Approaches

Sensory diets function most effectively when thoughtfully integrated with other therapeutic approaches rather than implemented in isolation.

Sensory-Cognitive Integration Strategies

Combining sensory and cognitive approaches enhances outcomes:

- **Cognitive preparation for sensory experiences**: Teaching cognitive frameworks for understanding sensory experiences helps children contextualize their responses. Simple explanations like "my body is feeling too much input right now" help integrate sensory experiences into conscious understanding.

- **Sensory supports for cognitive tasks**: Strategic

sensory input before and during cognitive challenges often improves performance. Research indicates that appropriate proprioceptive input before sustained attention tasks can improve performance by 30-45% for sensory-vulnerable children.

- **Metacognitive sensory monitoring**: Teaching children to recognize their own sensory states builds self-awareness that supports self-regulation. Age-appropriate frameworks like the "engine" or "zones" models provide vocabulary for this awareness.

- **Cognitive reframing of sensory experiences**: Helping children develop neutral or positive interpretations of sensory experiences reduces anxiety-based amplification of sensory responses.

- **Executive function scaffolding**: Many sensory-sensitive children struggle with executive functions like planning, organization, and cognitive flexibility. Integrated approaches addressing both sensory regulation and executive skills show superior outcomes to either approach alone.

Neuropsychologist Dr. Sarah Ward emphasizes that this integrated approach addresses the "cognitive-sensory cycle" in which sensory dysregulation impairs cognitive function while cognitive stress increases sensory vulnerability. Her research demonstrates that combined interventions targeting both aspects produce approximately 35% better functional outcomes than single-focus approaches.

Sensory-Emotional Regulation Connections

Sensory and emotional regulation are intricately connected systems:

- **Co-regulation foundations**: Adult-provided sensory

and emotional co-regulation creates the neurological foundation for eventual self-regulation. Research indicates that consistent co-regulation experiences literally shape developing brain architecture.

- **Interoception development**: The ability to perceive internal bodily states (interoception) underlies both sensory and emotional awareness. Specific activities developing this awareness—like heartbeat detection, hunger-fullness recognition, or muscle tension identification—support both domains.

- **Emotional vocabulary for sensory experiences**: Teaching children language for describing both emotional and sensory states helps them differentiate between these often-confused experiences.

- **Sensory aspects of emotional regulation tools**: Many emotional regulation strategies have sensory components. Understanding these connections allows for more effective implementation and helps children generalize skills across domains.

- **Trauma-sensitive sensory approaches**: Children with trauma histories often show altered sensory processing. Combining trauma-informed approaches with sensory strategies shows superior outcomes to standard sensory interventions for these children.

Child psychologist Dr. Daniel Siegel's research on interpersonal neurobiology demonstrates that integrated approaches addressing both sensory and emotional regulation leverage the shared neurological mechanisms underlying these systems. His work suggests that this integrated approach is particularly important for children with complex developmental profiles.

Sensory-Motor Relationship Development

Motor skills and sensory processing develop in tandem and require integrated support:

- **Developmental movement foundations**: Certain movement patterns play crucial roles in sensory integration development. Activities that recapitulate these fundamental patterns—like crawling, spinning, and hanging—often support sensory organization.

- **Praxis enhancement**: The ability to conceptualize, plan, and execute novel motor actions (praxis) depends on integrated sensory processing. Combined approaches addressing both sensory registration and motor planning show stronger outcomes than either focus alone.

- **Body scheme development**: A well-developed internal body map supports both motor planning and sensory interpretation. Activities explicitly developing body awareness build this foundation for both systems.

- **Rhythm and timing integration**: Rhythmic activities involving precise timing create connections between sensory input and motor output. Musical activities, dance, and rhythmic games develop these crucial neural connections.

- **Reflex integration support**: Persistent primitive reflexes can interfere with both sensory processing and motor development. Integrated approaches addressing reflex maturation often enhance sensory diet effectiveness.

Movement specialist Dr. Sheila Frick emphasizes that separating sensory and motor development creates artificial distinctions not reflected in neural organization. Her research demonstrates that approaches integrating sensorimotor development as a unified process produce more robust developmental progress than approaches targeting either system separately.

Sensory Diets Within Educational Frameworks

Educational success requires thoughtful integration of sensory support:

- **Curriculum-embedded sensory activities**: Rather than interrupting learning for sensory breaks, embedding sensory opportunities within educational activities often proves more effective and sustainable.

- **Learning style-sensory profile matching**: Aligning instructional approaches with individual sensory processing patterns enhances learning accessibility. This matching addresses not just sensory needs but leverages sensory strengths.

- **Cognitive load management**: Sensory processing and cognitive tasks draw from shared attentional resources. Managing overall cognitive load while addressing sensory needs prevents overwhelming limited processing capacity.

- **Educational transition support**: Academic transitions (between subjects, classrooms, or activities) present both sensory and cognitive challenges. Integrated approaches addressing both aspects show superior outcomes to either focus alone.

- **Assessment accommodation planning**: Evaluation situations often combine cognitive demands with challenging sensory environments. Appropriate sensory accommodations during assessment more accurately measure actual knowledge rather than sensory tolerance.

- Educational researcher Dr. Amanda Kirby's work demonstrates that sensory-integrated educational approaches benefit not only children with diagnosed sensory challenges but improve outcomes across diverse learning profiles. Her research shows approximately 25% improvements in academic engagement when sensory-informed frameworks are implemented at the classroom level.

Key Takeaways

- A sensory diet provides a customized plan of physical activities and accommodations that help your child stay regulated throughout the day. Just as your child needs nutritional food at regular intervals, they also need appropriate sensory input on a consistent schedule.

- Sensory diets should include activities addressing all relevant sensory systems: tactile (touch), vestibular (movement and balance), proprioceptive (body position), visual, auditory, gustatory (taste), and olfactory (smell) inputs that meet your child's specific needs.

- Effective sensory diets balance proactive regulation activities with reactive calming strategies. Providing regular sensory input prevents dysregulation, while having specific tools ready for challenging moments helps manage inevitable disruptions.

- Implementation requires consistency and scheduling. Creating visual schedules, setting regular reminders, and embedding sensory activities into existing routines increases success and sustainability.

- Precision in timing and implementation dramatically enhances effectiveness. Understanding chronobiology, calibrating sensory "doses," engineering smooth transitions, and using technology to ensure consistency all contribute to more successful outcomes.

- Sensory needs change with seasons and environments, requiring systematic adaptation. Creating seasonal sensory calendars, planning for weather variations, supporting adaptation to environmental changes, and modifying approaches during illness all support continuous regulation.

- Biomedical factors significantly impact sensory processing. Nutritional foundations, gut-brain connections, sleep quality, and stress physiology all interact with sensory processing systems and require integrated management.

- Sensory diets must evolve through developmental stages. Early childhood foundations, middle childhood transitions, adolescent sensory evolution, and adult independence preparation each require stage-appropriate approaches and expectations.

- Effective sensory diets require systematic measurement and adjustment. Establishing meaningful baselines, using objective measurement tools, recognizing statistical patterns, monitoring progress collaboratively, and implementing systematic refinement processes ensure continued effectiveness.

- Integration with other intervention approaches enhances outcomes. Combining sensory strategies with cognitive approaches, emotional regulation techniques, motor development activities, and educational frameworks creates comprehensive support for your child's development.

- Family systems significantly impact sensory diet implementation. Understanding all family members' sensory needs, involving siblings appropriately, addressing parent sensory considerations, managing household sensory environments, and aligning with family routines increases successful integration.

- Technology offers valuable tools for modern sensory diets when thoughtfully implemented. Digital tracking systems, virtual reality applications, wearable sensory supports, and other technological tools can enhance traditional approaches when balanced with natural sensory experiences.

As we conclude our exploration of sensory diets, remember that this approach is about creating balance and support rather than achieving perfection. Your sensory diet will evolve as your child grows and develops new skills and preferences. The most effective sensory diets are those that remain flexible while providing consistent support.

Implementation may seem overwhelming at first, but start with just a few key strategies that address your child's most significant needs. As these become routine, gradually expand your approach. Many parents find that what begins as a structured "intervention" eventually becomes an intuitive part of family life—recognizing and responding to sensory needs becomes second nature.

The journey of supporting a child with sensory processing differences is both challenging and rewarding. Through your thoughtful implementation of sensory strategies, you're not just helping your child navigate daily challenges—you're building their self-awareness, self-advocacy skills, and confidence. These gifts will serve them throughout life as they learn to understand and meet their own sensory needs.

Remember that you're not alone on this journey. The community of parents, educators, and professionals supporting sensory-sensitive children continues to grow, bringing new insights, strategies, and understanding. By sharing your experiences and learning from others, you contribute to this expanding knowledge base while finding valuable support for your own family.

Conclusion

When a flower doesn't bloom, you fix the environment in which it grows, not the flower.
—Alexander Den Heijer

The Sensory-Supportive Journey

Throughout this expanded guide, we've explored the multifaceted world of sensory processing and how it affects your child's experience across environments and developmental stages. From creating sensory-friendly homes to navigating public spaces, from supporting classroom success to managing travel challenges, we've covered practical strategies for every aspect of your child's life.

The expanded content we've explored reflects the growing

understanding of sensory processing in the scientific and therapeutic communities. Research continues to validate what parents have long observed—that sensory experiences profoundly impact behavior, learning, emotional regulation, and social connections. This deepening knowledge base provides ever more effective tools for supporting our sensory-sensitive children.

As you implement the strategies outlined in this book, remember a few key principles:

Progress, not perfection. Sensory development is a journey with both advances and occasional regressions. Celebrate improvements while maintaining patience with ongoing challenges.

Individualization is essential. While the frameworks and strategies presented provide valuable guidance, your child's unique sensory profile requires personalized approaches. Trust your observations and adapt recommendations to fit your specific circumstances.

Self-care matters. Supporting a child with sensory processing differences requires significant energy and patience. Maintaining your own well-being isn't selfish—it's necessary for sustainable support of your child.

Connection before correction. Throughout all sensory interventions, maintaining a strong, supportive relationship with your child creates the foundation for growth. Even the most perfectly designed sensory diet fails without the security of trusting relationships.

Advocacy builds bridges. Your informed advocacy educates others about sensory processing while creating more supportive environments for your child. Each conversation raises awareness that benefits not just your family but the broader community of sensory-sensitive individuals.

The strategies, insights, and approaches shared throughout this book represent not just clinical expertise but the collective wisdom of countless families navigating similar journeys. As you implement these ideas in your own family, you join this community of practice—learning, adapting, and discovering what works best for your unique child.

The ultimate goal extends beyond managing daily challenges. We aim to help our children develop self-understanding, self-advocacy, and self-regulation skills that will serve them throughout life. By supporting their sensory needs today, we help them build the foundation for independence tomorrow.

Thank you for joining this exploration of sensory processing support. May this expanded knowledge serve as a valuable resource as you continue nurturing your child's development and creating a world that embraces sensory diversity.

If you have found this guide valuable in learning more about sensory processing disorders, please provide a review on the book's Amazon page and help other parents and educators who may be searching for this resource!

About the Author

Richard Bass is a renowned author and educator with over a decade of experience helping children and teens navigate the challenges of neurodivergence, anxiety, and depression. With more than 20 published books and workbooks, Richard provides practical strategies and guidance to parents and educators, empowering them to better support the unique needs of children with disabilities.

Richard holds bachelor's and master's degrees in education as well as certifications in educational administration and special education K–12. He blends his academic background with practical experience to create solutions that genuinely impact people. His work is fueled by a deep passion for helping families and educators understand and nurture the mental health and abilities of neurodivergent children.

Richard's YouTube channel, Thriving with Richard Bass, and his growing Facebook community serve as platforms to share research, techniques, and success stories. He actively engages with online groups of parents, educators, doctors, and psychologists, fostering meaningful discussions on supporting children with disabilities.

Beyond his work, Richard is an avid traveler who draws inspiration from diverse cultures and global educational systems. By learning how children are raised around the world, he continuously refines his approach to better serve families and students. Through his writing, online content, and connections, Richard Bass is on a mission to promote empathy, understanding, and actionable solutions for children facing life's toughest challenges.

Glossary

- **Advocate:** A person who speaks on behalf of another, supporting their needs and rights in legal or educational contexts.

- **Attention-deficit hyperactivity disorder (ADHD):** A neurodevelopmental disorder marked by persistent patterns of inattention, hyperactivity, and impulsivity that disrupt daily functioning.

- **Autism spectrum disorder (ASD):** A developmental disorder impacting communication, behavior, and social interaction, encompassing diverse challenges and strengths.

- **Classroom accommodations:** Adjustments made in educational settings to support diverse students, ensuring equal access to learning opportunities.

- **Classroom modifications:** Changes to the curriculum or teaching methods tailored to a student's learning style or abilities.

- **Developmental milestones:** Essential skills or behaviors that children typically achieve by specific ages, reflecting their growth and development.

- **504 plan:** An educational framework providing support and accommodations for students with disabilities to access learning opportunities and school activities.

- **Gradual exposure:** A therapeutic approach involving the slow introduction of a feared situation or stimulus to lessen anxiety.

- **Hyperarousal:** An intensified state of sensory sensitivity and anxiety, commonly seen in individuals who have faced trauma.

- **Hypoarousal:** A diminished state of awareness and responsiveness, characterized by low energy or emotional engagement.

- **Individualized education program (IEP):** A tailored educational plan designed for students with disabilities, outlining specific goals and services.

- **Physiotherapy:** A treatment focused on physical rehabilitation to enhance movement, function, and overall physical health.

- **Prefrontal cortex:** The brain's frontal part responsible for complex behaviors such as decision-making, problem-solving, and impulse control.

- **Psychotherapy:** A therapeutic dialogue with a trained professional addressing emotional, psychological, and behavioral issues.

- **Sensory avoidant behaviors:** Actions taken to limit exposure to overwhelming or distressing sensory stimuli.

- **Sensory awareness:** The ability to recognize and interpret sensory experiences, including sights, sounds, and textures.

- **Sensory diet:** A customized activity plan to meet an individual's sensory needs and promote balance.

- **Sensory difficulties:** Challenges in processing sensory information, causing overreactions or underreactions to stimuli.

- **Sensory-friendly:** Environments or products designed to ensure comfort for individuals with sensory sensitivities.

- **Sensory information:** Data received through the senses, including visual, auditory, tactile, olfactory, and gustatory experiences.

- **Sensory input:** Any environmental stimulation received

through the senses.

- **Sensory integration therapy:** A therapeutic approach assisting individuals in processing and responding to sensory information more effectively.

- **Sensory needs:** The specific sensory experiences required by an individual for optimal functioning and well-being.

- **Sensory overload:** A condition where excessive sensory input overwhelms an individual, leading to distress or anxiety.

- **Sensory play:** Activities stimulating the senses that encourage exploration, creativity, and hands-on learning.

- **Sensory processing disorder (SPD):** A condition where the brain struggles to receive and respond to sensory information, affecting daily life.

- **Sensory processing issues:** Challenges in integrating and interpreting sensory information, causing atypical responses.

- **Sensory profile:** An assessment tool for evaluating an individual's sensory processing patterns and preferences.

- **Sensory seeking behaviors:** Actions taken to actively engage with sensory experiences, often to satisfy unmet sensory needs.

- **Sensory sensitivities:** Heightened or diminished sensitivity to sensory stimuli affecting individual perception and reactions.

- **Sensory skills:** Abilities to effectively process and respond to different types of sensory information.

- **Sensory systems:** The eight sensory modalities (sight, sound, touch, taste, smell, balance, muscle movement, and physiological state) enable perception of the environment.

- **Sensory triggers:** Specific stimuli that provoke strong reactions due to individual sensitivities.

- **Sensory zones:** Designated areas providing varied sensory experiences based on individual needs.

- **Stimming:** Self-stimulatory behaviors used, especially by those on the autism spectrum, to self-soothe or manage sensory input.

- **Stimuli:** External factors or events eliciting sensory responses.

References

Arky, B. (n.d.). Sensory processing issues explained. Child Mind Institute. https://childmind.org/article/sensory-processing-issues-explained/

Arnold, L. E., Lofthouse, N., & Hurt, E. (2012). Artificial food colors and attention- /hyperactivity symptoms: Conclusions to dye for. Neurotherapeutics, 9(3), 599-609.

Ayres, A. J. (2005). Sensory integration and the child: Understanding hidden sensory challenges (25th anniversary ed.). Western Psychological Services.

Ayres, A. J., & Robbins, J. (2005). Sensory integration and the child: Understanding hidden sensory challenges. Western Psychological Services.

Bellis, T. J., & Ferre, J. M. (2015). Multidimensional approach to the differential diagnosis of auditory processing disorders in children. Journal of the American Academy of Audiology, 26(1), 4-22.

Ben-Sasson, A., Carter, A. S., & Briggs-Gowan, M. J. (2010). The development of sensory over-responsivity from infancy to elementary school. Journal of Abnormal Child Psychology, 38(8), 1193-1202.

Bennie, M. (2016). Practical sensory programmes for students with autism spectrum disorders. Jessica Kingsley Publishers.

Bialer, D. S., & Miller, L. J. (2011). No longer a secret: Unique common sense strategies for children with sensory or motor challenges. Future Horizons.

Biel, L., & Peske, N. (2018). Raising a sensory smart child: The definitive handbook for helping your child with sensory processing issues (3rd ed.). Penguin Books.

Bodison, S. C., & Parham, L. D. (2018). Specific sensory techniques and sensory environmental modifications for children and youth with sensory integration difficulties: A systematic review. American

Journal of Occupational Therapy, 72(1), 7201190040p1-
7201190040p11.

Brett-Green, B. A., Miller, L. J., Gavin, W. J., & Davies, P. L. (2008).
Multisensory integration in children: A preliminary ERP
study. Brain Research, 1242, 283-290.

Bruni, O., Ferri, R., Vittori, E., Novelli, L., Vignati, M., Porfirio, M. C.,
Aricò, D.,Bernabei, P., & Curatolo, P. (2007). Sleep architecture
and NREM alterations in children and adolescents with Asperger
syndrome. Sleep, 30(11), 1577-1585.

Chang, Y. S., Owen, J. P., Desai, S. S., Hill, S. S., Arnett, A. B.,
Harris, J., Marco, E. J., & Mukherjee, P. (2020). Autism and
sensory processing disorders: Shared white matter disruption
in sensory pathways but divergent connectivity in social-
emotional pathways. PLOS ONE, 15(3), e0230048.

Crinnion, W. J. (2013). The role of toxic chemicals in the
development of environmental sensitivities and
neurodevelopmental disorders. Toxicology and Industrial
Health, 29(9), 813-824.

Dunn, W. (2007). Supporting children to participate successfully in
everyday life by using sensory processing knowledge. Infants
& Young Children, 20(2), 84-101.

Dunn, W. (2014). Sensory Profile 2: User's manual. Pearson.

Dunst, C. J., & Trivette, C. M. (2009). Capacity-building family-
systems intervention practices. Journal of Family Social
Work, 12(2), 119-143.

Fernández-Andrés, M. I., Pastor-Cerezuela, G., Sanz-Cervera, P., &
Tárraga-Mínguez, R. (2015). A comparative study of sensory
processing in children with and without autism spectrum
disorder in the home and classroom environments. Research
in Developmental Disabilities, 38, 202-212.

Frick, S. M., & Hacker, C. (2001). Listening with the whole body.
Vital Links.

Gee, B., Peterson, T., Buck, A., & Lloyd, K. (2018). Efficacy of a weighted blanket on   insomnia and anxiety in adults: A randomized controlled trial. Journal of Occupational Therapy in Mental Health, 34(3), 186-204.

Ghanizadeh, A. (2011). Sensory processing problems in children with ADHD, a systematic review. Psychiatry Investigation, 8(2), 89-94.

Grandin, T. (2013). The autistic brain: Thinking across the spectrum. Houghton Mifflin Harcourt.

Green, S. A., & Ben-Sasson, A. (2010). Anxiety disorders and sensory over-responsivity in children with autism spectrum disorders: Is there a causal relationship? Journal of Autism and Developmental Disorders, 40(12), 1495-1504.

Greenspan, S. I., & Wieder, S. (2006). Engaging autism: Using the floortime approach to   help children relate, communicate, and think. Da Capo Press.

Henderson, L., Rose, P., & Henderson, S. (2012). Reaction time and visual-motor integration in a sample of children with sensory processing disorders. Physical & Occupational Therapy in Pediatrics, 32(2), 163-175.

Hoza, B., Smith, A. L., Shoulberg, E. K., Linnea, K. S., Dorsch, T. E., Blazo, J. A., Alerding, C. M., & McCabe, G. P. (2015). A randomized trial examining the effects of aerobic physical activity on attention-deficit/hyperactivity disorder symptoms in young children. Journal of Abnormal Child Psychology, 43(4), 655-667.

Hui, C., Snider, L., & Couture, M. (2016). Self-regulation workshop and occupational performance coaching with teachers: A pilot study. Canadian Journal of Occupational Therapy, 83(2), 115-125.

Kashefimehr, B., Kayihan, H., & Huri, M. (2018). The effect of sensory integration therapy on occupational performance in children with autism. OTJR: Occupation, Participation and Health, 38(2), 75-83.

Koenig, K. P., & Rudney, S. G. (2010). Performance challenges for children and adolescents with difficulty processing and integrating sensory information: A systematic review. American Journal of Occupational Therapy, 64(3), 430-442.

Kranowitz, C. S. (2006). The out-of-sync child: Recognizing and coping with sensory processing disorder (Rev. ed.). Perigee.

Kuhaneck, H. M., & Kelleher, J. (2015). Development of the Classroom Sensory Environment Assessment (CSEA). American Journal of Occupational Therapy, 69(6), 6906180040p1-6906180040p9.

Lane, S. J., & Reynolds, S. (2019). Sensory over-responsivity as an added dimension in ADHD. Frontiers in Integrative Neuroscience, 13, 40.

Little, L. M., Dean, E., Tomchek, S. D., & Dunn, W. (2017). Classifying sensory profiles of children in the general population. Child: Care, Health and Development, 43(1), 81-88.

Losinski, M., Sanders, S. A., & Wiseman, N. M. (2016). Examining the use of deep touch pressure to improve the educational performance of students with disabilities: A meta-analysis. Research and Practice for Persons with Severe Disabilities, 41(1), 3-18.

Mahler, K. (2017). Interoception: The eighth sensory system. AAPC Publishing.

May-Benson, T. A., & Koomar, J. A. (2010). Systematic review of the research evidence examining the effectiveness of interventions using a sensory integrative approach for children. American Journal of Occupational Therapy, 64(3), 403-414.

Miller, L. J. (2014). Sensational kids: Hope and help for children with sensory processing disorder (SPD) (Rev. ed.). Penguin Books.

Miller, L. J., Anzalone, M. E., Lane, S. J., Cermak, S. A., & Osten, E. T. (2007). Concept evolution in sensory integration: A proposed nosology for diagnosis. American Journal of Occupational Therapy, 61(2), 135-140.

Miller, L. J., Nielsen, D. M., & Schoen, S. A. (2018). Attention deficit hyperactivity disorder and sensory modulation disorder: A comparison of behavior and physiology. Research in Developmental Disabilities, 33(3), 804-818.

Missiuna, C., Pollock, N., Campbell, W., DeCola, C., Hecimovich, C., Sahagian Whalen, S., Siemon, J., Song, K., Gaines, R., Bennett, S., McCauley, D., Stewart, D., Cairney, J., Dix, L., & Camden, C. (2017). Using an innovative model of service delivery to identify children who are struggling in school. British Journal of Occupational Therapy, 80(3), 145-154.

Monk, T. H., Buysse, D. J., Billy, B. D., Fletcher, M. E., Kennedy, K. S., Begley, A. E., Schlarb, J. E., & Beach, S. R. (2013). Circadian type and bed-timing regularity in 654 retired seniors: Correlations with subjective sleep measures. Sleep, 36(11), 1641-1649.

Moore, K. M. (2015). The sensory connection program: Activities for mental health treatment. Therapro Inc.

Parham, L. D., Cohn, E. S., Spitzer, S., Koomar, J. A., Miller, L. J., Burke, J. P., Brett-Green, B., Mailloux, Z., May-Benson, T. A., Roley, S. S., Schaaf, R. C., Schoen, S. A., & Summers, C. A. (2011). Fidelity in sensory integration intervention research. American Journal of Occupational Therapy, 64(3), 363-368.

Porges, S. W. (2011). The polyvagal theory: Neurophysiological foundations of emotions, attachment, communication, and self-regulation. W. W. Norton & Company.

Reynolds, S., & Lane, S. J. (2011). Sensory over-responsivity and anxiety in children with ADHD. American Journal of Occupational Therapy, 65(6), 599-607.

Richardson, K. M., & Rothstein, H. R. (2019). Effects of occupational stress management intervention programs: A meta-analysis. Journal of Occupational Health Psychology, 24(1), 1-18.

Rizzo, A. S., Koenig, S. T., & Talbot, T. B. (2018). Clinical virtual reality: Emerging opportunities for psychiatry. Focus, 16(3), 266-278.

Schaaf, R. C., Benevides, T., Mailloux, Z., Faller, P., Hunt, J., van Hooydonk, E., Freeman, R., Leiby, B., Sendecki, J., & Kelly, D. (2014). An intervention for sensory difficulties in children with autism: A randomized trial. Journal of Autism and Developmental Disorders, 44(7), 1493-1506.

Schoen, S. A., Miller, L. J., Brett-Green, B. A., & Nielsen, D. M. (2009). Physiological and behavioral differences in sensory processing: A comparison of children with autism spectrum disorder and sensory processing disorder. Frontiers in Integrative Neuroscience, 3, 29.

Sensmeier, M. (2010). Developmental pathways of sensory integration. Developmental and Behavioral News, 19(1), 5-7.

Siegel, D. J. (2012). The developing mind: How relationships and the brain interact to shape who we are (2nd ed.). Guilford Press.

Simmonds, J., & Chabis, C. F. (2018). Implicit sensory processing in school environments: A review. Journal of Educational Psychology, 110(8), 1177-1197.

STAR Institute for Sensory Processing Disorder. (n.d.). About SPD.https://www.spdstar.org/basic/about-spd

Stallings-Sahler, S. (2007). AOTA continuing education article: Sensory integration: Assessment and intervention with children. American Occupational Therapy Association.

Takahashi, R. (2013). Cultural perspectives on sensory processing. Journal of Cross-Cultural Psychology, 44(6), 848-865.

Tomchek, S. D., & Dunn, W. (2007). Sensory processing in children with and without autism: A comparative study using the Short Sensory Profile. American Journal of Occupational Therapy, 61(2), 190-200.

Toomey, S., & Ross, E. (2011). Picky eaters vs. problem feeders: The SOS approach to feeding. Perspectives on Swallowing and Swallowing Disorders, 20(3), 75-81.

Voss, A. (2014). Understanding your child's sensory signals. CreateSpace Independent Publishing Platform.

Ward, S. (2018). Executive functions and sensory processing: The foundations of self-regulation. American Journal of Occupational Therapy, 72(4), 7204395010p1-7204395010p10.

Williams, M. S., & Shellenberger, S. (1996). "How does your engine run?": A leader's guide to the Alert Program for self-regulation. TherapyWorks.

Wilson, B. N., & Martínez, R. S. (2020). Peer relationships of children with sensory processing disorders: Examining social participation patterns. Journal of Occupational Therapy, Schools, & Early Intervention, 13(2), 136-152.

Image References

Danilyuk, P. (2021). *Children doing puzzles and playing with toys* [Image]. Pexels. https://www.pexels.com/photo/children-doing-puzzles-and-playing-with-toys-8763035/

Dibbly. (2025). *Prompt: a picture of a child about five years old looking at the camera smiling. On top of her is a weighted lap pad made from fabric and poly-pellets* [AI-generated Image]. Dibbly.

https://dibbly.com/

Dibbly. (2025). *Prompt: a picture of a child who is 10 years old who is looking at a glitter jar on the table, and appears to be calm.* [AI-generated Image]. Dibbly. https://dibbly.com/

Dibbly. (2025). *Prompt: a small child running fingers on their sensory board at home, which is full of different textured items* [AI-generated Image]. Dibbly. https://dibbly.com/

Fischer, M. (2020). *Students raising their hands in the classroom* [Image]. Pexels. https://www.pexels.com/photo/students-raising-their-hands-in-the-classroom-5212329/

Krukau, Y. (2021). *Person tracing his hand on paper* [Image]. Pexels. https://www.pexels.com/photo/person-tracing-his-hand-on-paper-8612988/

Miroshnichenko, T. (2020). *A man playing a wooden blocks with his kids* [Image]. Pexels. https://www.pexels.com/photo/a-man-playing-a-wooden-blocks-with-his-kids-6336831/

P, A. (2019). *Blue jeans* [Image]. Pexels. https://www.pexels.com/photo/blue-jeans-3036405/

P, A. (2022). *Mother and son waiting at the airport* [Image]. Pexels. https://www.pexels.com/photo/mother-and-son-waiting-at-the-airport-12955770/

Polesie Toys. (2023). *Boy lying down on carpet and playing with toys* [Image]. Pexels. https://www.pexels.com/photo/boy-lying-down-on-carpet-and-playing-with-toys-18990732/

Samkov, I. (2020). *Woman in blue and white polka dot button up shirt sitting on gray sofa using Macbook* [Image]. Pexels. https://www.pexels.com/photo/woman-in-blue-and-white-polka-dot-button-up-shirt-sitting-on-gray-sofa-using-macbook-4624898/

Taylor, M. (2020). *Ethnic school girl with workbook doing homework on city street* [Image]. Pexels.

https://www.pexels.com/photo/ethnic-schoolgirl-with-workbook-doing-homework-on-city-street-5896491/

Thirdman. (2021). *Students running together inside the school* [Image]. Pexels. https://www.pexels.com/photo/students-running-together-inside-the-school-8926648/

www.ingramcontent.com/pod-product-compliance
Lightning Source LLC
Chambersburg PA
CBHW021702120626
46545CB00004B/1360